The Complete Idiot's Reference Card

The Intuition Checklist

The following questions will help you determine whether you're intuitively ready to make a decision and take positive action. As you read each question to yourself, be aware of your immediate reaction of yes or no. If any part of you feels uncomfortable, blocked, resistant, or closed in any way, consider it a no and come back to the question later (see the box below).

This list is intended to stimulate your intuitive response to any important decision you are making and firmly fix your attention internally. The more yes responses you give, the greater your readiness to move forward with your decision.

Yes No

- ☐ ☐ I know what I need to do.
- ☐ ☐ I see the "open door."
- ☐ ☐ This decision has "cooked" and feels done.
- ☐ ☐ I can see myself completing this.
- ☐ ☐ I know how I really feel about this.
- ☐ ☐ I know my other choices, and this one still feels right.
- ☐ ☐ I have a plan for responding to the objections of others.
- ☐ ☐ This decision fits with my long-term goals.
- ☐ ☐ The time to act is right now.
- ☐ ☐ I will feel relieved, grateful, or energized when this action is complete.

If You Answered "No" to a Checklist Item

If you answered "no" to any of the above checklist items, re-examine your reasons for doing so by answering the following questions about each one:

- ➤ Is it just part of the situation that feels uncomfortable, or the whole thing?
- ➤ If it's a part of the situation, which part or parts?
- ➤ Can the uncomfortable part(s) be modified or clarified?
- ➤ What would make this situation feel right?
- ➤ Is there anyone or anything applying pressure?
- ➤ Is there a push to make something happen that may not be what you really want?
- ➤ How can more time be allowed to make this decision?

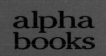
alpha
books

tear here

Validate Your Intuition

When you think you know what your intuition is telling you to do, check it out by doing the following:

1. Write down or articulate clearly in your mind the action steps you are considering.
2. Ask yourself: How does it taste?
3. Imagine trying the decision on like a new pair of pants and ask yourself: How does it fit?
4. Check your "joy meter": On a scale from 1 to 10, how much joy does it bring?

10 Power Pointers for Intuitive Investing

1. Never bet on someone else's strategy.
2. Stay in flow with the market.
3. If it seems obvious to you, it's a gift.
4. Know how to "let go" without giving up.
5. Deserts are part of the intuitive terrain. When you're off, don't take the blame—just take a break.
6. Tension needs to be managed not avoided.
7. Prayer doesn't work—"God is not a market manipulator."
8. Keep learning, keep growing.
9. Live your life and your investments will follow.
10. When you start looking for others to validate your moves, get out—or at least rethink your position.

What To Do When You Just Can't Get to What Your Intuition Is Telling You

1. Articulate the question you would like answered by your intuition and write it down.
2. Pick three things from your desk, room or wherever you find yourself—and line them up in a row.
3. Let the first thing represent what you need to do more of in this situation.
4. Let the second thing represent what you need to do less of in this situation.
5. Let the third thing represent what you need to be open to.

5 Questions To Stimulate Intuitive Thinking in Your Workplace

1. "Now that I've looked at the data, what do I really feel?"
2. "Which options have the most juice, the most vitality? The most negative juice?"
3. "What am I ready to do to move this along right now?"
4. "What opportunities, people, and events are emerging in relationship to this project?"
5. "What is happening at the edges? What does that tell me about the viability of this project?"

THE COMPLETE IDIOT'S GUIDE® TO

Making Money Through Intuition

by Nancy Rosanoff

alpha books

A Division of Macmillan General Reference
A Pearson Education Macmillan Company
1633 Broadway, New York, NY 10019-6785

Contents at a Glance

Contents

Foreword

Hunch is a word not often found in the manager's lexicon. Yet the biggest roadblock to creative decision-making is not having the guts to heed a gut feeling. Nancy Rosanoff provides ample fodder for trusting your intuition and following those faint, but often unmistakable signals that seem to come from some distant echo chamber deep in your subconscious.

It takes courage to rely on those interior messages because they usually defy explanation. By helping you to understand the scientific basis of intuition, *The Complete Idiot's Guide to Making Money Through Intuition* will arm you with the courage that it takes to trust your intuition and turn it into a valuable tool.

Intuition is a slippery subject all right. Just writing about it first requires coming up with a solid structure—in other words the strong skeleton outline on which to hang the meat. As is clear from the table of contents, Rosanoff has very skillfully provided a sequence of meaty chapters that will show you step-by-step how to hone your intuition and put it to practical use when making a career change, investing your money, overcoming a personal or business obstacle, or even in developing your spiritual self.

I have always considered that mystical, magical facility called intuition, our guardian angel. Allowed to function and listened to, it can take care of us and protect us in the most surprising ways. But since it comes from some stratum of awareness just below the conscious level, it is elusive to say the least. Nevertheless, those subconsciously perceived factors are sorted out and integrated into retained impressions that guide our future actions. However, as this book makes clear, you must not be afraid to let your subliminal powers work for you.

Few business leaders would dare admit to being guided by intuition. They like to consider themselves logical and analytical creatures, number-crunchers who take pride in their ability to keep emotions from creeping into their planning. Evenhandedness and consistency are considered key attributes. Yet, pinned down about a particular choice, how for instance, they happened to pick one subordinate over another for promotion, they may even confess, "I had this gut feeling."

In today's fast-changing world, management studies have shown that a chief executive who strives for consistency, instead of intuitively bending, often becomes a "cropper." But then as philosopher Ralph Waldo Emerson wrote: "A foolish consistency is the hobgoblin of little minds."

Scientists, too, have credited the "Eureka Factor"—that sudden, illuminating, "I've found it" flash—as the key element in their discovery process. Most are quick to admit that scientific breakthroughs do not seem to evolve slowly from a series of deductions.

Still, you might wonder, why all the fuss about intuition? Do I have to read a book about it? Isn't it something instinctive that comes naturally and automatically to all of us?

Not so. Like body-building, developing your intuition and making it more powerful, takes disciplined training. As Rosanoff proves so convincingly in *The Complete Idiot's Guide to Making Money Through Intuition,* you need to learn how to build that intuitive muscle. And what is even more remarkable about her book, she actually shows you how to do it.

—Roy Rowan
    Author of *The Intuitive Manager*

Introduction

I once presented a seminar on intuition to a group of successful entrepreneurs. (And, I do mean successful: Everyone there had become a millionaire before the age of 35.) During the program, one gentleman continually interrupted, slapping his hands together and saying, "No way!"

After the program I walked over to meet him, and he apologized for his behavior. "I'm sorry for giving you such a hard time," he said, "but I just don't believe anything you said."

"That's okay," I replied, "but tell me: What is it that has made you so successful?"

"Funny you should ask," he said. "I go into these states of mind where I know what's going to happen *before* it happens. That's when I make my best decisions."

My jaw dropped. Here was someone who clearly used his intuition successfully, but didn't believe in it. I was able to pull myself together enough to ask, "Well, what do you call that?"

"I call it a psychotic break due to stress."

Sound strange? Think again. This culture we live in is anti-intuitive. It encourages entrepreneurial spirit and applauds those who find a way through the system to succeed—but it doesn't accept anything that can't be proved, documented, or statistically validated. No wonder our friend chose to be "psychotic" rather than intuitive: It was safer and easier to explain.

It's time to bring intuition out of the shadows and into the real world. If ever there was a time that innovation, insight, and foresight were needed, it is now. And you, dear reader, have an opportunity to let your life be an example of how intuition helps build wealth. I imagine you as fitting one or more of the following categories:

➤ Interested in making money and having a fulfilling life at the same time

➤ Drawn to things of a "spiritual" nature, yet wanting to keep your feet firmly on the ground

➤ Always interested in practical tools that can help you be more successful, as long as they work

➤ Ready for a transition in your life to something that has more meaning and value to you, without giving up some of the "treats" you've been able to afford

This book delivers what you need. It takes the abstract subject of intuition and brings it right down to the everyday, concrete world where decisions are tough and competition fierce. It will connect you to a source of information, power, and confidence that you can take anywhere, and it will provide the guidance to get you to the right place at the right time.

Part 1, "Intuition 101," begins with the basics, defining the concept from a variety of different viewpoints. It shows you how you're already using your intuition (are women really more intuitive than men?), how to find out what you're best at, and where your intuition is "located" in your body. You'll get started right away in developing your intuitive "muscle" and putting it to work in your life.

Part 2, "Get a Life—and a Career," takes you immediately into the real world of work, giving you practical tools for planning your life and a career that fits it. You'll take intuition right into the workplace as you build better teams, communicate your bright ideas effectively, take advantage of golden opportunities (including other careers), and head for the lifestyle of your dreams.

Part 3, "Growing Your Money Tree," removes any mental blocks you may have to making money and helps you build a plan to meet your specific needs. No one gets wealthy alone, and this section helps you build your financial dream team. Then you'll use your intuition to make successful investments and build an entrepreneurial business. Whew! Then you take a power break.

Part 4, "Getting Over Fear, Greed, and Self-Doubt," shows you how to do just that. As with any serious endeavor, playing the wealth-building game at this level is a mental game. You'll learn how to get out of your own way, stop making excuses, and allow yourself to succeed.

Part 5, "Enjoying Your Intuition's Fruition," solidifies your success by showing you how to stay the course for fun and profit—without losing sight of your values. You'll learn to avoid self-sabotage, make selfless sharing pay off big-time, and be grateful for how far you've come. The big finish "shows you the money" by bringing it all together in one package.

Extras

Each chapter contains "intuition workouts," exercises that will help you apply your newfound knowledge right away. Don't skip them! Get a personal intuition journal to go with this book, and take notes as you do each workout. Some of the workouts require a blank sheet of paper, and colored markers or pencils will make it more fun.

This book is designed to help you create a personal wealth-building plan. I suggest that you skim through it, then dip deep into each chapter, keeping track of the workouts and assignments. Then use the book as a handy reference for particular workouts when you need them.

Finally, much as your intuition works in real life, the following boxed nuggets of information will appear throughout the book just in time to inform, guide, and inspire:

Tried & True

Bits of intuition history, amazing anecdotes, and inspirational quotes provide an ample supply of models for success.

Practical Wisdom

Tasty tidbits of advice on bringing your intuitive skill into the real world.

Yellow Light

Warnings on the misuse of, or misunderstandings about, intuition help keep you on track and in the flow.

Sixth Sense

Words are defined which may be unfamiliar to you, and words and phrases which may be familiar are specifically defined for how they are being used in the context of building intuitive skill.

Acknowledgements

Nothing is accomplished alone, and this book is no exception. Many people provided help, insight, guidance, and support. First I want to thank Divine Order and the Intuitive Web for providing this wonderful opportunity to share my work, and for all of the guidance and support throughout the writing of this book and throughout my whole life. Many parts of my life have come together to enable me to write this book from deep, personal experience.

Next I want to thank all of those who have studied with me, explored new intuitive territory with me, and entrusted their teams, their projects, and their futures to working in a different and unusual way.

Thank you, Chris Marquardt, for fine editing and for helping me to be a better writer. Thank you, Nancy Mikhail, for discovering me over the Internet and giving me the chance to write this book. Thank you, Jessica Faust, for keeping the project moving all the way to the end. And thanks to Ted Goff for his contribution of comics.

Thank you, Bill and Judy Joyce, for your quick reading and wonderfully helpful comments all along the way. Also, thank you for your continuing belief in me and my work through the years. You have truly seen it all and know that it works.

Thank you, Jessie and Tamar, for providing endless inspiration and for always asking tough questions. You are the true wealth of my life. Finally, thank you, John Krysko, for being the loving life partner that you are, for continuing to learn new dance steps, and for being a source of constant support and love.

Part 1
Intuition 101

"The most important trait of a good leader is knowing who you are. You have to do all your homework, but then you have to go with your intuition without letting your mind get in the way."

Edward McCracken, CEO of Silicon Graphics, makes it sound so easy. But what is intuition, anyway? How does it work, and how can you keep your busybody mind from butting in?

This part lays out the basics of the what, why, how, and—gosh, even the where of intuition. A healthy dose of exercises, or "intuition workouts," will help you solve the problems facing you now and prepare you to walk your intuitive road to riches. You'll be on your way to using your intuition as easily as Ed McCracken.

The Basics

Conrad Hilton relayed the following story of his first hotel bid. "My first bid, hastily made, was $165,000. Then, somehow, that didn't feel right to me. Another figure kept coming: $180,000. It satisfied me. It seemed fair. It felt right! I changed my bid to the larger figure on that hunch. When they were opened, the closest bid to mine was $179,800. I got the Stevens Corporation by a narrow margin of $200. Eventually the assets returned me $2 million."

Have you ever watched in amazement as someone took a huge risk and landed not only on her feet but in ruby slippers? Some people seem to have a "golden gut" that tells them when to act and when to wait. They may not always be right, but they're right often enough to be highly successful. The times they miss don't seem to inhibit their ability to take the next opportunity that comes along and do well. Wouldn't you love to clone the "gene" that gives them that ability and create a little for yourself?

The truth is that you already have the intuition gene. It's standard issue. But although everyone is born with intuitive ability, it's often overlooked or even stifled in the educational process. There's no doubt the intuition factor makes the difference between someone who just gets by in life and someone who thrives with success and personal fulfillment. It is never, never too late to discover your intuitive muscle, build its strength, and gain confidence in using it to live your dream.

This chapter discusses the building blocks of intuition. What the heck is it? How does it compare to other ways we gather information? Are women more intuitive than men? The end of the chapter contains our very first series of intuition "workouts" to help you begin to build your intuitive muscles right away.

The Many Faces of Intuition

So what is this intuition stuff? *Webster's* defines it as "immediate apprehension or cognition; direct or immediate knowing, whether mystical, perceptual, intellectual, or moral."

That's pretty heavy! Let's try again. Weston Agor, author of *Intuitive Management,* defines intuition as "the human ability to make decisions with inadequate information."

Okay, my turn. My definition of intuition is "knowing something without knowing how you know it."

While the definitions are numerous and diverse, they seem to revolve around a few principles—mainly, that intuition is a deeply *personal* resource, a way of knowing something *directly* without thinking about it. I would bet that you already have a "sense" of what intuition is for you and how it has shown itself in your life and in the lives of those around you.

Tried & True

Barry B., owner of an electrical contracting company, told me his father encouraged him to discover his intuition by always asking him: "How do you feel about this?" That simple question, asked over and over again throughout his youth, encouraged Barry to trust his own internal sense of things.

The Intuition Watchdog

One of the attributes of intuition that I happen to love is that it's very firmly based in reality. Many people consider intuition a bit too "touchy-feely," but it's actually very practical: It's always there to help.

Intuition is like a sleeping watchdog that remains perfectly dormant and uninvolved until something triggers it. All of a sudden it's completely alert and ready for action. After the fun is over, it goes right back into its doghouse. The trick is to look for it and use its power. Examples are the best teachers of what intuition is; maybe the following stories will trigger memories of your own run-ins with intuition.

Peyton Budinger was waiting at a corner for the traffic light to turn green. It turned green—but her foot wouldn't push the accelerator pedal. Her whole body froze for a few moments. Then it happened: Out of nowhere, a car on the cross street ran the red light, going right across her path. If Peyton had proceeded as normal, there would have been a terrible accident. Peyton listened to her inner voice, her watchdog.

Richard Haupt, former executive vice president of the Electric Hydracon Company, told this story: "Five major steel companies advised me to use harder materials for the containers, dies, tooling, and so forth. Instead, I decided that softer tooling was the better answer. Our president directed me to abide by the decision of the major steel mills. Nevertheless, I followed my own intuition and spent two-and-a-half times more money for the softer material. The result was an outstanding success with the softer tooling. It lasts six times as long as harder steels. The entire industry has now followed this procedure."

A woman in one of my seminars related: "My husband and I had been trying to get pregnant for six years. We had tried everything and spent many thousands of dollars. Finally, our doctors sat us down and said that we needed to give up and begin adoption proceedings if we wanted to have children. I had a deep feeling that it was important to see one more doctor. My well-meaning family, friends, and doctors thought that I was delusional, that I was living in a fantasy world where somehow I could get pregnant. I followed my intuition and found one more doctor. He discovered a rare but easy-to-treat vaginal infection. Within three months we were pregnant."

Another seminar veteran had this story: "When I proudly showed my engagement ring to my mother, I suddenly burst into tears and sobbed for several minutes. When I was through sobbing, we looked at each other and hastily decided it must be 'nerves.' Six months into the marriage it was clearly a disaster and had to be annulled. The visceral memory of bursting into tears is etched into my heart."

Ann shared this story 15 years after it had happened. "I had just finished a complete physical exam with all tests coming back negative. A nagging, internal voice kept telling me to go back to the doctor. I was working full time and didn't have the leisure to continue making doctor appointments and missing work. Still, the voice persisted. Finally, to shut up the voice, I returned to my doctor. She repeated most of her exam and found nothing. I told her about my nagging

Practical Wisdom

Intuition emerges like memory—a memory of something we never learned yet know to be true. And like memory, intuition has to be *allowed*; it can't be forced.

intuition. She decided to trust my inner voice and repeat the mammogram way before the usual time period. To both of our amazement, the beginning of breast cancer showed up. It was quickly removed, and since that time there has been no recurrence. Oh, and the voice stopped nagging me after I had the test."

At first these stories seem astounding. How can these people know this stuff? From an ordinary perspective it seems fantastic and miraculous that such inventions and interventions can occur. Yet, from an intuitive point of view, it seems amazing that they don't happen more often. After all, we are the ones living in our bodies. Who else would know when something is amiss? How else can something new be created except through some intuitive flash of insight? History tells us that the human mind is the most inventive, creative source of new ideas, solutions to problems, and fantastic leaps of discovery. Intuitive people have these insights frequently. The question is really, why don't we all have experiences like these, all the time? The answer is that we all can—*if* we listen to our intuition.

Perhaps you've had experiences that parallel one or more of these stories. But because you haven't been trained to use your intuition, the intuition watchdog only emerges sporadically, usually when the stakes are high. Like creative ability, intuition is largely trained out of us, or at least relegated to the basement of acceptable information, by the time six or seven years of age rolls around. Each of us is born intuitive and then learns to dismiss and ignore it.

Practical Wisdom

Belief is no adequate substitute for inner experience.

—Carl G. Jung

Sixth Sense

Analytic thinking is the skill of evaluating situations by gathering key data, plugging it in to a formula and coming up with an answer that applies equally to similar situations. For example, you can "analytically" evaluate the prices of different kinds of cereal to compare the price per ounce, and thus buy the least expensive cereal.

Ain't No Box Can Hold Intuition

Analytic thinking is a skill we've been taught since the beginning of school. It's a useful tool. Analytic thinking developed out of the need to find some way of simplifying decisions. For example, consider a bank loan officer trying to determine whether someone is credit-worthy enough to purchase a home. Instead of spending huge amounts of time researching each applicant, she considers a few significant factors—job longevity, salary, debt load, and credit history—and puts the picture together.

Thus, the value of analytic thinking. We have been trained to do this in all parts of our lives. When making a career decision, we look at factors such as salary, location, status, and company reputation. We think that if we look at enough factors, both pro and con, a good decision can be made.

Certainly this works some of the time, but often it doesn't. Maybe a job applicant who looks good on paper doesn't fit. People with immaculate credit histories run into hard times, or prove dishonest, and default on their loans. On the flip side, there are those whose credit history is sketchy but who, given half a chance, would become credit-worthy. And there are potential job applicants who don't fit the criteria, but who might ultimately turn out to be valuable assets to the company.

Intuition deals with the two ends of the decision-making spectrum: the part that looks good on paper but doesn't pass the "sniff test," and the part that looks doubtful on paper, yet feels good. In this era of quick decision-making, slick marketing, and information overload, these ends are quickly growing and taking up most of the analytic middle ground. More and more situations require a deeper, intuitive feel to come out on top.

Barry, the owner of the electrical contracting company mentioned before, used to decide which contracting jobs to take based solely on the analytic approach. If it looked like he could make money, he did it; if not, he let it pass. This approach worked most of the time, but he knew he could do better. He began applying simple intuitive decision-making. After looking at the numbers, he would sit back and ask himself how he really *felt* about this job.

Practical Wisdom

Before acting on any decision, ask yourself: "How do I really feel about this?"

An amazing thing began to happen. He actually got very clear emotional and physical sensations associated with each job. (We'll talk about these sensations later on.) Some jobs that looked great on paper would elicit a bad feeling. He started passing on those jobs and noticed that whoever took them on ran into problems that, while unforesee-able, were serious enough to turn the job into a nightmare. Other jobs that looked like losers on paper felt good intuitively. When he took on these jobs, they turned into gold mines. His hit rate skyrocketed.

Think of it as internal and external evidence. Someone presents an opportunity and he paints it well. It looks good. The *external* evidence is in. But when it sinks in, it doesn't feel so great. The *internal* evidence is in. Because there is a conflict between the two, more information is necessary from both the internal and external sources. When they match—*bingo*—it's time to take action.

Experience vs. Intuition

Some of you may be thinking: "Isn't intuition just based on experience? What made the electrical contractor so good was all of his years of experience." Indeed, it sometimes looks like intuition is a form of wisdom attained through experience.

There are two problems with this. First, often it is the young and inexperienced folks who come up with the answer to a problem based on their fresh perspectives. And second, we've all come into contact with those whose 20 years of experience only serves to put them to sleep. They've used their experience to learn to do the same thing over and over again, rather than to continue to learn and grow.

Experience does help develop intuition, but only if you're paying intuitive attention! With experience, you can

➤ Learn which intuitive signals work best for you

➤ Recognize and eliminate emotional signals that interfere

➤ Learn to use analytic skills to complement your intuitive skills

Look at how some television producers fail to learn from experience. Someone innovative gets a great show on the air and the next season there are 16 copycats. Experience says: "If it worked once, it'll work a thousand times." Too bad they don't talk to their audiences!

On the other hand, if you're lucky, you've found an intuitive car mechanic with a real *feel* for what's going on with your car. This guy will have used his experience to build his intuitive muscle—and will use both to pinpoint the problem.

If you're really lucky, you'll come across the octogenarian—life-long learner with both experience *and* intuitive wisdom. Such a person is a gem and a joy to listen to for hours. Tell us another story, Gramps!

Sixth Sense

Evidence is information which confirms or denies a theory or hunch. It also is information which points to a theory or hunch. *External evidence* is data occurring outside yourself and *internal evidence* is data occurring inside yourself.

Yellow Light

Here are two pearls of ignorance from famous folks who let their experience outweigh their intuition:

"I think there's a world market for about five computers."

—Thomas J. Watson, founder and Chairman, IBM, in the era of typewriters

"This fellow Charles Lindbergh will never make it. He's doomed."

—Harry Guggenheim, millionaire aviation enthusiast

Hold the Scalpel!

Look out! Just because you might be able to use your analytic half alongside your intuitive half doesn't mean they'll ever understand each other. They might respect each other and work together, but intuition will never be "provable" to the analytic mind. Similarly, analysis will never "get to the core of the issue" enough for intuition!

Trying to dissect intuition like a classroom frog is like expecting poetry to fit the rules of prose. They are two different ways of communicating—both valid, both with their own set of rules, yet completely different from each other. To the prose mind, a poem does not give enough information; to the poet, a piece of prose may lack depth or simplicity.

Become a Cosmic Couch Potato

Don't kill your television just yet; it's a good metaphor for how intuition works. Imagine that your intuition is a television, receiving electrical signals from many sources and translating the airwaves into one channel at a time. (Talk about too many channels!) When we know what channel we want, we get usable information and even wisdom.

Let's get a little metaphysical. The amount of available information your intuition TV has access to is virtually infinite. No one really knows where it comes from or what the ultimate possibilities are. What we do know from experience is that intuition taps into a source that combines past, present, and future. It transcends the experience of individual lives and links us to what I call *collective wisdom*.

If your cosmic *remote control* is working and you know what channel you want, you can use your intuition TV effectively, receiving the intuitive information you want, when you need it. You can become a cosmic couch potato!

Yellow Light

When your *internal* evidence conflicts with the *external* evidence, don't push ahead. Get more information and ask more questions before taking any action.

Practical Wisdom

The courage to make the decisional leap is found in that lonely place where no additional input can be either added or detracted. Only action can be taken. This is the place that separates those who succeed from those who maintain.

—Ron Schulz, *Unconventional Wisdom*

Practical Wisdom

Most of us are living at the periphery of consciousness while intuition invites us into the center.

—Willis Harmon

> ### Tried & True
>
> When I was asked to discuss 10 future work skills for a Nightingale-Conant audio tape series, I agreed immediately—without knowing what I would talk about on the tape! Several days later, on a cross-country plane ride home, the 10 skills flowed out of my brain onto a piece of paper. It was as if all I had to do was ask for the information and wait to receive it.
>
> —Jeff Zakaryan, President, Global Strategies

Fortunately, your intuition TV is also proactive. It'll frequently pull your attention away from your regularly scheduled programming and—you guessed it—bring you an important message. Staying open to these bulletins is a skill in itself, and we'll talk more about it in Chapter 2, "Nuts and Bolts: Your Intuition Computer."

The Gender Bender

The most frequently asked question about intuition is whether women are more intuitive than men. The answer is quite simple, and given what's been covered so far in this book I'll bet you can answer it yourself. Everyone has intuition, and is born with an equal amount. Most of us have been trained to ignore it, or pretend that we don't use it. A few lucky ones have been encouraged to listen to their intuitive voices. Still others have been so challenged by circumstances that following their intuition was the *only* way to get ahead.

Man vs. Nature

Traditionally, men have not been encouraged to listen to their intuition. However, men who don't fit the cultural "norm" in some way have developed and used their intuition more than those who fit the cultural norm. Entrepreneurs, artists, actors, inventors, and others who listen to the beats of different drummers are more likely to have found another path through their life using their intuition.

Similarly, men who are successful in this culture have learned to use their intuition, whether they talk about it or not. Often they have developed an uncanny skill to know intuitively what to do, then back up their intuition with analysis.

A note about sports. Many professional sports players have incredible intuitive skill, which supports their success. Devotion to their sport puts them into the category of someone who does not fit the cultural "norm." Sports fans admire and are devoted to sports figures who, with great skill, transcend the limits of the analytic mind to make powerful choices and take heroic action. The fans are appreciating and applauding intuition at work.

Women and the Horse They Rode In On

Traditionally, women have been encouraged to be sensitive to the needs of others, to nurture, and to be nonconfrontational. Women have been encouraged to use their intuition to anticipate the needs of others. Like men, women who have not fit the cultural mode, either by choice or by chance, have had to rely on their intuition to pioneer a new life.

Also, women have generally been more encouraged to listen to their intuition in a variety of circumstances where men have not. Many men have confessed to me that they would never make a business deal or go into a new venture without having the potential partner meet their wife. They relied on their wives to tell them whether this person was trustworthy or not.

Practical Wisdom

Men are more comfortable having a "gut feel" or a "hunch" while women are perfectly comfortable having an "intuition." It all comes from the same source!

Practical Wisdom

Before making a major business decision, invite a trusted friend, lover, or spouse to meet the person or people you are considering doing business with. Ask the third party what their "gut feeling" tells them about your venture.

I can't let this subject go by without a little politicizing. Often intuition has been referred to as "women's intuition," categorizing it as flaky, soft, and irrational. Relegating intuition to something that "women do"—when "women" is code for second-class citizens—dismisses the value of knowing something, even when the logical reasons and analytic data are not apparent or cannot be articulated.

On the other hand, this characterization has given women more of an opportunity to develop and use their intuition effectively, which often is highly valued by the men in their lives.

This is all changing very rapidly as gender stereotypes break down and opportunities broaden. In my experience, men and women are equally intuitive yet express it in different ways. Intuition is now an essential ingredient for success for everyone.

Time To Flex Your Intuitive Muscles!

Why wait for intuition to come to you when you can build a strong relationship with it that will enable you to use it when you need it? The following *intuition workouts* will begin to build your intuitive muscles. We'll start with a few simple exercises to familiarize you with how intuition works. Throughout the book these "workouts" will become more demanding, building on the skills you'll soon be developing.

For now, write down three current issues or problems in your life that could benefit from some intuitive insight:

➤ Write the first issue as a yes-or-no question.

➤ For the second issue, use a new relationship or situation you're thinking about getting more involved in.

➤ For the third issue, pick a situation in which the next step is unknown or undecided.

Set these aside for just a moment and review the following guidelines, which will "warm you up" for the workouts.

➤ Intuitive information is *effortless*. If you're thinking too hard, go on to the next part of the exercise and come back later. Allow space for intuition to work without forcing it.

➤ Intuition is *subjective*. Go with whatever you feel is right. These exercises are a way to make the intuitive connection. Look for an internal "light" to switch on, or a sense of "rightness" to accompany any images or thoughts.

➤ Intuition is *practical*. If the information you receive isn't useful now, let it go.

➤ *Write down* your results. Keep track of what works and what doesn't.

Give yourself about 15 minutes of uninterrupted time for each exercise. Take a couple of deep breaths, releasing some of the tension and pressures of the day.

Practical Wisdom

In you, as in all men, are natural powers. You have a will, learn to use it. Make it work for you. Sharpen your senses as you sharpen your knife. We can give you nothing. You already possess everything necessary to become great.

—Legendary Dwarf Chief of the Crow Nation, quoted in Cheewa James's *Catch the Whisper of the Wind*

Practical Wisdom

When you've lost your keys, does it help to get angry and tight? No. It takes relaxing, allowing the image or feeling to emerge of where you left the keys. Intuition works the same way.

The Taste Test

Many decisions come down to a yes or no answer. At any moment, you can choose either to take action—or not. The following basic workout will help you get comfortable with intuitively sensing whether a situation or decision is a go or no-go.

1. Consider Issue #1, your yes-or-no question. Imagine that you are handing over the decision to your intuition.

2. Now, imagine that you are holding the word yes in one hand and the word no in the other. Imagine how they look and feel. Do they have any weight? Are they different from each other in any way?

3. Repeat your question to yourself. Focus on the word *no*. Note any sensations, impressions, or images that come to mind. Hold the word up to your ear and hear it spoken. Note how your body responds to the sound.

4. Bring the word around to your nose and smell it. Does it have a scent? Now, take a bite out of the word—chew it, taste it, and swallow it. How does your body respond to eating this word?

5. Take a few moments to "digest" all the sensations and responses to the word *no*.

6. Repeat your question to yourself and focus on the word *yes*. Repeat steps 5–7 using *yes*.

7. Write down your impressions and note whether you know more about how to proceed with this situation.

If the Shoe Fits...

This workout triggers *body intuition*. With a little practice, it becomes an instantaneous way to assess new opportunities and relationships.

1. Take Issue #2 and imagine that this opportunity or relationship is something you can *wear*.

2. Try it on and see how it fits. You may have a specific image of clothing or not. You may sense the whole situation as something you can "try on" to determine fit.

3. Write down any feelings, impressions, thoughts, or sensations you have while "trying on" this situation.

Yellow Light

If you find yourself thinking, "It could mean this, or it could mean that," stop. You're in your analytic mind, not your intuitive mind. Let go of having to make a choice and start paying attention to what you are feeling both emotionally and physically.

Objects of Your Desire

This workout uses your immediate environment to stimulate intuitive knowing. Use it to help you determine your next step in a specific situation.

1. Move on to Issue #3, where your next step is unknown or undecided.

2. Close your eyes and count to five. While counting, pass the decision-making responsibility for this situation over to your intuition.

3. When you open your eyes, look around the room and focus on something that attracts your attention—something you like and find attractive. Write it down as Item #1.

4. Now look around the room and focus on something that you don't like, something that disturbs you for any reason. Write it down as Item #2.

5. Item #1 represents positive action that, if taken, will lead to a successful outcome. Look at the item metaphorically. What does it represent to you? If you were inside this item, how would it feel? If this item could take action, what would it be? Use these questions and others to stimulate your intuitive knowing.

6. Item #2 represents what makes it difficult to take positive action. If there is something blocking the success, this is it. This item has a message for you about what makes it difficult for you to take action. What does this item represent to you? What does it make you feel? If this item could speak to you, what would it say?

7. Write down all your results, let it sink in, and keep paying attention to how you feel. Notice how you feel about taking the suggested action.

These workouts are easy to practice every day. They only take a few moments and, once you know the steps involved, can be done anytime and anyplace. I use them all the time. They help me get unstuck and see situations in new ways, to notice choices I hadn't considered, and to become aware of artificial limits that don't really need to be there.

The Least You Need to Know

➤ Intuition is a practical and natural human ability to solve problems and take positive action.

➤ Intuition is the alertness behind experience that helps you apply what you've learned in the future.

➤ Intuition connects individual need with collective wisdom.

➤ Men and women are equally intuitive, although they've been culturally trained to use it in different ways.

➤ The basic practice of intuition is asking "How do I really feel about this?" before proceeding.

Nuts and Bolts: Your Intuition Computer

The James Bond movie *Tomorrow Never Dies* opens with Agent 007 having three minutes to disarm or kill several terrorists and take off on a jet armed with nuclear warheads before a missile hits. He accomplishes the impossible with style and grace, averting World War III (again). He has no apparent plan, a few tools, and lots of guts. Of course, Hollywood ingenuity helps, but for now let's look at 007 as an intuitive archetype. He is the ultimate intuitive.

Some of the attributes that have made James Bond an enduring character for more than 30 years are the ease with which he handles stressful situations; his willingness to walk into extremely dangerous situations; his lack of fear; his confidence in finding a solution when all else has failed. All of these are skills that are part of intuitive development. You may not become as bold and fearless as James Bond, but developing intuitive skill will increase your self-confidence in all situations and your ability to create solutions to seemingly impossible problems—before the missile hits.

In the last chapter, you learned about the "what" of intuition. Now you'll learn about the "how." In this chapter, you will discover your intuitive "computer." Thank goodness, it comes fully assembled. However, you'll have to plug it in and install some software to fully use it. Once the hardware and software are in place, the next step is to understand what intuition can do for you and what it cannot.

Remember that intuition, like life, is not linear, but rather is circular and interdependent. Although each chapter in this book builds on what has come before, there is also a ripple effect. You might not notice something as it pops into your mind, but through intuition it may well surface later when needed or when bounced off some life experience.

Sixth Sense

Perception is the taking in and understanding of information. Aldous Huxley's phrase "Doors of Perception" refers to the ability to take in information from many organs of perception such as your skin, your ears, your feelings and your "gut."

Sixth Sense

A *magnetic field* is a naturally occurring force of attraction or repulsion. Gravity is an example of an attracting magnetic field, as is static electricity (what happens when your hair stands straight up during super dry weather).

Your Intuitive Hardware

If you are alive, you have a head, a heart, and a body. These constitute your intuitive hardware. With this equipment, you can access intuitive information. It is through these three doors of perception (to borrow Aldous Huxley's phrase) that intuition flows.

Where the body is concerned, scientific evidence is mounting that validates the physical experience of intuition. For example, there is actually a large nexus of nerves in the stomach that responds to external situations with a "gut feel." Other common expressions reveal how intuition can speak through other parts of our bodies. For example, consider the phrases "I smell a rat," "That gives me the chills," "It makes my knees weak," "It leaves a bad taste in my mouth," and "My ears were burning!" Research done on human biochemistry and immunology indicates that the body responds to stimuli before the brain has a chance to realize what's going on.

The heart has its own way of making itself felt. It has a strong electrical pulse that generates a magnetic field around our bodies. Like your body chemistry, this field interacts with the environment, responding to external signals as "safe" or "dangerous" before the mind can analyze the situation.

Similarly, the mind is much more than the physical brain. Science is just beginning to uncover the incredible ability we all have to find meaning and detect patterns and function while being constantly bombarded with new data.

To learn more about how science has validated the existence and usefulness of intuition, I list several books and articles in Appendix A, "Further Reading."

If one of the three pieces of intuitive hardware is not fully functional, the other two will make up for it. For instance, a friend of mine spends most of his time in a wheelchair due to having multiple sclerosis. He is deeply intuitive and teaches workshops of his own. He was asked whether being "physically fit" was essential to intuitive development. The idea was a new one to him as he could barely remember being physically fit, and his intuition worked perfectly well.

Your Intuitive Software

All this hardware is useless, however, without the right software to run it. You need to program your computer to access and apply intuitive skill.

Your intuitive software has three components: attitude, awareness, and approach. Although each of these elements will be discussed separately, they all work together interdependently.

Attitude

Attitude is the style with which you live your life. On the street, the term "attitude" can be a rough, "here I am—take it or leave it" message conveyed through body language and clothes, or it can describe people who succeed "their way," with their own, personal style. Your attitude can be open or closed. Whatever it is, it sets the tone of what can happen next.

Did you ever share a great idea with other people who immediately said, "That'll never work"? Are they right or wrong? Both. In a certain sense they're "right" because their own negative attitude will prevent them from giving the new idea a shot—so it's dead at the beginning, at least as far as they are concerned. Of course, they're also wrong because the idea might have merit if given a chance. The initial attitude you take toward a new idea or intuition will either allow it to grow or kill it. I'd say that's pretty powerful medicine. Equally powerful is the experience of being completely sure you're right about something only to discover that you were dead wrong. The problem with an attitude that designates things as either "right" or "wrong" is that you only have two categories in which to put things.

Yellow Light

Be vigilant in discovering your own bias. Intuition has been criticized as an excuse for prejudicial treatment. "I just don't feel right about that person," can be used to justify unjust action. Notice when you always feel the same way about something (or someone) and grow beyond it.

Let's start linking the hardware you've got with the software you need. For your head, the required attitude software is "open mind." With an open mind, intuitive information is allowed in and things are neither right nor wrong. Instead, you evaluate the incoming stream of data on the basis of whether it is relevant or not, or useful or not, in each moment. A closed mind ignores millions of intuitive flashes, not to mention other types of opportunities.

Keeping an open mind doesn't mean you eliminate skepticism. An inquiring, questioning, investigative attitude is a powerful tool—as long as outright cynicism doesn't click that mind shut. In fact, skepticism supports discernment and tempers impulsiveness.

Like an open mind, the heart's attitude software is an open heart. Try saying the phrase, "Let me be open to the possibilities." Just be open—there is no commitment to action. Be open to opportunities and information in all forms; you can decide what to do with them later. Saying this phrase to yourself a few times a day opens your heart to intuitive feelings.

Your body needs attitude software, too. Aim for relaxed alertness. Careful, though—if you're too relaxed you'll just get sleepy; too alert, and you may become tense. Awake yet relaxed leaves you most open to intuitive impressions.

The following table reviews the connection we've been talking about between your intuition hardware and your attitude software.

Hardware	Attitude Software
Head	Open Mind
Heart	Open Heart "open to possibilities"
Body	Relaxed alertness

Tried & True

In 1906, Ole Evinrude was boating with his girlfriend, Bess Emily Cary. She wanted a lakeside picnic complete with ice cream. He boated over to shore to get the ice cream, but by the time he returned the ice cream had melted. Turning desperation to inspiration, he thought of motorizing the boat—and invented the outboard motor in 1909.

Awareness

Awareness also functions differently through your head, heart, and body. Where your head is concerned, awareness programs your mind to pay attention to the incredible diversity of information available to you at any given moment. Take a moment right now to notice the sounds going on around you. Now, without looking, describe to yourself what is behind you in the room or place you are in. Can you do it? How much were you aware of, and how much did you miss? Often we can work or live in a room for years and still not be able to describe it when not looking at it directly. We also hear only what we've been trained to listen for. A naturalist might hear a grasshopper chirp on a busy street, whereas most of us would hear a coin drop on the same street.

Being aware supports the intuitive process because intuitive information often comes in subtle cues or changes in the environment. If we are aware, we notice and note it. When we have enough non-analytic data, appropriate action can be taken.

A salesman shared this story with me: "I began my usual pitch to a team of decision-makers. Within 2 or 3 minutes I knew I'd lost them. They were looking at me, nodding their heads, but something was missing. I stopped my pitch, took a deep breath and changed the conversation immediately, starting to talk about something from left field—something I'd done over the weekend. It flashed through my head that I'd completely lost my mind and was blowing this sales call. But my body felt relaxed, my heart was open, and I could sense that they were now paying attention. I asked them some questions about their business and we began to flow. Within 15 minutes, I knew I'd made the deal."

Someone less aware than this salesman might have stuck doggedly to the script and left the meeting without a clue as to why the deal hadn't panned out.

Awareness is developed by asking the question, "What do I notice?" Stop a few times each day and notice the things that you haven't noticed, the things you wouldn't normally pay attention to.

Tried & True

Elmer Ambrose Sperry began to use his intuition early in life. At the age of six he presented his aunt with his first invention—a horseradish grater. His entire life was punctuated with moments of sudden, inspired inventive flashes in which a new idea seemed almost to hang in the air before his eyes, waiting for him to see it. He founded the Sperry Electric Company in 1880 and patented 350 inventions.

Similarly, the heart level of awareness is developed by asking yourself, "What are my choices?" You know you're blocking your intuition when you think you can't see any alternatives. If it feels like the only choice available, one that you're being forced to take, look again. There's always another choice.

Finally, at the body level the question, "What am I feeling?" expands awareness to encompass physical sensations. For example, if you meet someone likable or trustworthy, your whole body smiles—you relax and feel comfortable and open.

Tried & True

I shook his hand and he looked at me and said, "Hi." And I said to myself, "I don't like him. I don't trust him. There's something about him."

—Roberta Williams, founder of Sierra On-Line,
speaking of the first meeting of a new business
relationship that almost destroyed her company

Let's review the awareness software you need:

Hardware	Awareness Software
Head	What do I notice?
Heart	What are my choices?
Body	What am I feeling?

Approach

Okay, so far we've got attitude software and awareness software. Our intuition computer is almost operational. The last bit of programming we need is approach software.

Just the other day I was setting up some new files (the paper kind) and was faced with a snap-on tab that was different from the tabs already inserted into the file folder. At first I was frustrated, and you can imagine my thoughts: "Why do they have to constantly change everything? As soon as I get comfortable with how something works, it changes and I have to learn a new thing. This doesn't even work that well." I struggled for a few minutes with no luck getting this tab to snap.

"Wait a minute," I said to myself. "Let me approach this differently. This is a puzzle. Let me see if I can be creative here." As soon as I changed my approach, the tab snapped into place. I couldn't believe how easy it was. It was actually easier than the old tabs, once I approached it openly.

How you approach a situation can make the difference between success and failure. A curious approach to new situations helps unlock the secrets it holds. A tight, forced approach only strengthens the barrier to understanding. The intuitive mind approaches new situations with curiosity; the intuitive heart feels how to proceed from moment to moment; and the intuitive body responds to the flow of the situation.

The following table recaps how our intuitive hardware and software work together:

Intuition Hardware and Software

Hardware	Software		
	Attitude	Awareness	Approach
Head	Open mind	What do I notice?	Curiosity
Heart	Open heart	What are my choices?	Moment by moment
Body	Relaxed alertness	What am I feeling?	Respond to flow

Get comfortable with these three intuitive software programs—attitude, awareness, and approach—and your intuition will expand tremendously. Even if you do nothing else from this book, you will have accomplished a great deal.

Tried & True

Melitta Bentz, a housewife in Dresden, Germany, in 1908, became annoyed with the usual time-consuming method of brewing coffee, which involved wrapping the loose grounds in a cloth bag and boiling water around it. Worse, coffee made that way was both bitter and grainy. She ripped a piece of blotting paper from her son's school book, cut out a circle, stuck it into the bottom of a brass pot she had poked full of holes, put coffee grounds into the pot, and poured boiling water over it. She and her husband Hugo had a tinsmith build a commercial version—and the Melitta drip coffee-maker was born!

What This Sucker Can Do

For any given problem I tend to analyze all the options over and over again, and it's true that sometimes I seem to come to a solution without using my intuition. The major difference for me is that getting to the solution intuitively hits me at such a deep, interior place that I actually have the energy and motivation to do some of the challenging things I know are the right thing to do.

The power of intuition comes not just from the information that it provides but also from the unity of mind, heart, and body that occurs when an intuitive answer emerges. The more you are involved in the answer, the more energy you have to follow through. An action taken just from the head, or solely as a response to heart and body feelings, has less power than something done from all three in harmony.

Now that you understand how intuition works, it's time to discover what your intuition "computer" can do for you. You'll soon be ready to install your intuitive software and take it for a test run.

There are three things that intuition can do for you: guide you, inform and inspire you, and enhance your timing. It may not seem like much at first, but take a few moments to reflect on how your life might change if you had the ability regularly to do things like:

➤ Anticipate problems before they grow and be guided toward success

➤ Receive information when you need to know it

➤ Act with impeccable timing and be inspired with new ideas

Without training, these intuitive moments happen irregularly. It seems magical and mysterious when they do. With a little practice, however, these skills can be part of your everyday repertoire. Read on to discover how to recognize and develop these skills in your life.

Warning Lights

When a traffic light moves from green to yellow, it's anticipating the red, warning you to slow down (some people think it means "speed up," but we'll just ignore them).

Like the "Yellow Light" sidebar in this book, intuition works in much the same way. Intuitive warning lights come in many forms. They're often subtle signals that can easily be ignored or overlooked unless you're keeping an eye out. What they're doing is guiding you out of potentially bad situations or directions and keeping you "in the flow."

Remember a time in your life when you experienced a complete disaster—perhaps an unfortunate relationship, a wasted trip, or a personal or business failure. Although there are disasters that you honestly had no way of averting, often there were intuitive warnings all along the way.

If you look back on what preceded the disaster, you'll notice that the intuitive yellow lights were brightly lit. You drove right through them at the time, yet there they were: clear signals in hindsight that if heeded—if you'd slowed down just a little bit—might have helped avert the disaster.

Tried & True

Jos Sanchez, a New York City taxi driver, has developed a philosophy for driving in the city. "Cultivate regular clients, so you know the person staring at the back of your head. Be nice to the police, but don't expect them to protect you. And most importantly, listen to your instincts. If a situation feels funny, drive on past."

Here's a good example. Mike owns an airport transportation business with locations in several airports all over the country. Because he can't visit each one on a constant basis, he relies on on-site management to handle day-to-day operations. During one routine check-in phone call with a site-manager he began to feel uncomfortable. Without hesitation, he contacted his assistant on another phone and instructed the assistant to make a site visit the next day. When the assistant asked what to look for, Mike could only say, "I don't know, but something isn't right."

When the assistant arrived, everything looked normal and the manager was cordial. Just before they looked over the accounts, however, the manager excused himself from the room—never to return. The assistant discovered an embezzlement plan in progress.

The lesson is clear: Mike's intuition was picking up signals over the phone that something was very wrong. The details weren't obvious, and there was no reason to think that there was a problem, the business was going fine according to all the usual indicators. In business, it is extremely important to check out all uncomfortable feelings—and Mike, being a good businessman, followed his hunch even without knowing where to have the assistant look for the problem.

Often it takes a failure or two before we begin to listen to our intuitive guidance system. You might even say that those who don't experience failure at a young age are handicapped! If we don't learn that failure is part of the process—something that will be lived through—it becomes something to be avoided at all costs, and the warnings go unheeded.

Sixth Sense

A *signal* is a universally recognized symbolic sign telling you what action to take. A blinking yellow light is signaling you to slow down, a stop sign signals you to stop. There are also intuitive signals which convey the similarly immediate, simple and direct instructions.

Bonnie W. was successful. Her meeting-planning business was booming. The work kept pouring in and she worked more late nights. Not wanting to decline new business, she took on more and started missing important family events. Finally her health took a dive—and gave her an opportunity to rethink everything. Her health crisis became her wake-up call to realize that she was unhappy, over-extended, and burned out.

Bonnie's story isn't unusual. She "felt" something had to be done, but she ignored the warning signs. Like a rubber band that is slowly stretched, it's easy to miss the signals that tension is mounting and life is becoming increasingly uncomfortable. Finally, something snaps and the jolt forces a life "rethink," often under difficult circumstances.

As in Bonnie's case, our intuition sometimes uses physical stress symptoms, aches, and pains to tell us that the direction we're going in is either not in our best long-term interests, or needs to be adjusted to stay on track with our long-term goals. Of course, that's no guarantee that we won't prefer pain-killers to listening to our intuition.

Your warning lights keep you on track, in the flow, following the current of your intuition. Like a river, our intuitive life flows downstream; there are different speeds and different terrains, yet the direction is constant. We know we're "in the flow" when there is harmonious, positive movement. We know we're going against it when those warning lights starting popping up. We'll talk more about flow in Chapter 5, "Into Wishin': Life and Career Planning."

Here's a simple table to help you notice and respond to your intuitive yellow lights.

Practical Wisdom

Stress is what happens when your gut says "NO!" and your mouth says "Sure, I'd love to."

Receiving Intuitive Guidance

Signal	Action
Uncomfortable feeling	Check it out! Get more information! Slow down! How are you feeling?
Project breakdown/lots of annoying delays	Review the situation from the beginning. Are you going in the right direction? Are you missing something? What are you feeling? Is there something nagging at you that needs to be said or done?
Recurring physical pain	Take care of the pain and ask yourself: "What am I doing that I really don't like to do?" Your intuition is telling you that something you are doing is way off track.
Mental and emotional stress	Ask yourself: "Where am I over-extending myself and receiving little or no compensation?" Your intuition is telling you that you are not paying enough attention to your real needs.
Unhappiness	Get creative and find a way to be happy doing what you are doing. If that doesn't work, look around for something new. Your intuition wants you to get your creative energies in gear and start using them.

Somehow You Just Know

Remember Conrad Hilton's closed-bidding story at the beginning of Chapter 1? Somehow he just knew what figure to submit, and won the bid by the slimmest of margins. His intuition was feeding him a useful bit of inspired information.

Joyce Gioia gives us another great illustration of intuitive information arriving just in time.

When Joyce walked into her first meeting with a potential client, she saw that she was clearly interrupting his search for something. He was looking through drawers and going through papers on his filing cabinets, and virtually ignored her entrance. Without thinking, and without ever having stepped into this office before, she said, "Look in your lower right drawer." Staring at her in disbelief, he looked in the drawer—and found the folder he was looking for. Well, as you can imagine, that got his attention.

Joyce's experience was uncanny, but many people have this kind of experience—knowing exactly what to do or say without knowing how they knew it. When the timing is right, intuitive information seems to flow.

Tried & True

Margaret Knight, born in 1838, is perhaps best known for inventing machinery that made the flat-bottomed paper sack possible. But she had other insights as well. At 12 years of age, she visited her brother, who was working at the local textile mill. While she was visiting, she saw a worker injured when a shuttle slid out of its loom, piercing the man with its steel tip. On the spot, she designed a stop-motion device that would prevent further accidents. As soon as she saw the problem, she knew the answer without having to stop and think about it.

Intuition can provide important information, right when it's needed—not a moment before or after. I can't explain it, but through this book I can share with you how to encourage it. It seems to work when the stakes are high, the need is great, and the mind is open. Another factor for success, as in Joyce's story earlier, is the willingness to risk looking foolish. Many of us in her situation might have had the intuitive insight to look in the lower right drawer, but how many of us would have said anything? The fear of being wrong and looking foolish would have stopped the flow of information. The need for the information has to be stronger than the fear of the risk.

To practice this skill is easy; to hear and act on the information requires courage. The trick is simply to ask. When you feel stuck, when you need an answer to something, stop what you're doing and ask yourself: "What can I do now?" or "What more do I know about this?" Ask and allow some room for intuition. Create a mental space for the answer to emerge. Either it will or it won't. It won't be forced. If there is no answer, just do what is in front of you to do. The answer or information may emerge as you move forward.

The following table lists a few ways to open the channel to intuitive information and inspiration.

Accessing Intuitive Information and Inspiration

Signal	Action
Your mind feels blocked	Take yourself out of your current environment and ask your intuition for help.
You need a new idea	Stop thinking and go with what is in front of you. Intuition works best when things are moving.
You want something unattainable	Delegate one part of your mind to research ideas and bring you opportunities for this desire. Imagine an open room in one part of your mind that really wants this thing.

Right Time, Right Place

When something is done is at least as important as *what* is done. Timing is everything, as the old saying goes. In matters of personal and financial success, it is deeply true. Knowing when to act and when to wait can make the difference between success and failure, or at least the difference between a big success and a small success.

Intuitive timing is experienced as an inner motivating moment. It can be a thought that floats through saying "Do this now." Sometimes it is completely unconscious mentally and acted upon physically. For example, you might cross the street just in time to run into someone you know, or to avoid danger. Although mentally there was no signal or clue, your body physically responded to some sense of timing.

Practical Wisdom

To practice intuitive timing is difficult. It's an extremely sensitive and delicate sense. If you think too much about it, it's gone. But stick with it. As your intuitive skill develops in other areas, your sense of timing will, too. You can practice by following up on the thoughts that float through your mind. If you think of someone, call him or her; if a task comes into your mind, do something about it. Stop hesitating and reduce the time between when you think of something or someone and when you respond.

It also works in reverse. There are times when, although you know a certain task is important, you wait. It doesn't get done, and every time you think about doing it something gets in your way. Then one day, it happens. You do what you need to do and the timing is perfect. This is no excuse for being lazy or procrastinating! You're just giving your intuition computer some time to crunch the numbers and download helpful files for you.

Accessing Intuitive Timing

Signal	Action
You're unsure of the next step	Take a deep breath. Imagine going one way. Then imagine going the other way. How does each feel? If you still feel unclear, try consulting an oracle (see Chapter 22).
Events moving too fast; you're feeling overwhelmed	Take a deep breath and slow down. There may be something happening that you aren't comfortable with; perhaps you were talked into something or are feeling pressured to act. Review the situation thoroughly.

Three Final Plug-Ins

In the computer world, "plug-ins" are little programs that plug into bigger ones to help with specific tasks. Let's round out this chapter with three plug-ins that will help our intuition computer run even faster: purpose, movement, and confidence.

Practical Wisdom

Procrastination is the thief of time, unless it is really your intuition. Then it may be saving you from yourself.

—Edward Young, *Night Thoughts*

Purpose

As I've already said, intuition works on a need-to-know basis. An idea needs to have a purpose for being created. For example, the idea for Velcro would not have happened without the need for sticking things together in a quick new way. Once the idea is born, it can be used in many different ways, but the original idea needs a home to go to. Intuition works like gravity—it flows toward something. Create the something for it to flow to and it will happen.

Movement

Intuition works best when there is movement. If you are stuck on a project, don't give up and don't stop. Even when you have no more ideas and everything seems to have shut down, keep doodling and fiddling. Slow down, but keep going. Read something, talk to someone, take a physical exercise break—but keep moving.

Confidence

Finally, you need confidence that there is always a solution. If you thought of the question, it has an answer. It may not occur to you right away, and you may need some help, but it is there. Whatever you do, don't sink into hopelessness. Keep the door open in your mind that there is a solution, a new idea out there somewhere, and that you just haven't run across it yet. Nothing closes that door more quickly than giving up. Even though you can't buy any of the ????? at Macy's or on the Internet, you can find them very easily just by looking in the back of your mind.

The Least You Need to Know

➤ Your intuitive "hardware" consists of your head, heart, and body.

➤ Install the intuitive "software" of attitude, approach, and awareness.

➤ Use the software to stay curious, focused, and in the flow.

➤ Jump-start your intuition with purpose, movement, and confidence.

➤ Enjoy the way intuition guides, informs, and puts you in the right place at the right time.

Chapter 3

The Lost City of Intuition

> ## In This Chapter
>
> ➤ Discover the important role intuition has already played in your life
>
> ➤ Distinguish four types of intuition
>
> ➤ Take the intuition quiz to determine your "type"
>
> ➤ Learn to make room for intuition to grow in your life
>
> ➤ Test-drive your intuitive abilities

Two of my husband's consistent intuitive experiences have become part of our family mythology. When we're traveling by car to a new location, we always know when we're about a minute away. John, my husband, becomes extremely anxious and agitated and is sure that we have missed the turn and have gone too far. Within one minute after he shares that feeling, we come to the correct turnoff. It's become a family joke. Even John has to laugh when it happens because it's so consistent.

Another intuitive skill of my husband's drove me nuts during the first few years of our relationship, although I've since learned to respect and enjoy it. When traveling, I tend to want to just get to where we are going without stopping. John has an ability to stop in the middle of what appears to be nowhere, only to discover some gem that I surely would have overlooked. He has pulled over to what appears to be the diviest of dives only to discover a fabulous antique store or local museum with wonderful people and experiences that have become the most remembered part of the trip.

In this chapter, we're going to search for your Lost City of Intuition. That is, I'll encourage you to explore the personal role intuition plays in your life and become more familiar with the signs and signals guiding and directing you. You'll also learn to expand your repertoire of intuitive skill and learn to make room for intuition on a daily basis. More intuition workouts at the end of the chapter will further build your intuitive tool kit, leaving you with more ways to connect with your inner wisdom.

The Best Things in Life Are Intuitive

How have you gotten to where you are in your life right now? Take a moment to think back on the turning points in your life: where you went to college, whom and when you married, when or if you had children, the milestones of your career. How did they happen? Whether you methodically planned your path, or whether you stumbled into something that worked or moved by trial and error to where you are now, there are a few things we all have in common:

1. What happened after you made a choice was different from how you expected it to be.

2. You had feelings, reactions, or responses to the situation that determined whether you were happy or not, pleased or displeased.

3. These responses led you to stay or go.

Practical Wisdom

Life can only be understood backward; but it must be lived forward.

—Soren Kierkegaard, *Life*

Pain Before Beauty

Most of the time decisions are made, we adapt and grow from the experience, and continue to move forward in life. Sometimes events are not only different from what was expected, but are downright painful. Here's where you have to watch out. Pain can either enhance intuitive development or stunt it, depending on the type of pain and how you respond to it.

There is no value judgment here, no right or wrong. Sometimes staying through the initial pain of a situation pays off, and you undergo what might be called growing pain. At other times pain is part of a destructive pattern. The difference between the two is identifiable.

Growing Pain

Growing pain is like stretching a muscle. There is a place where pain is felt, yet it feels opening, relaxing, stretching. The pain may continue for a few days as the stretched muscle loosens up. Growing pains are associated with learning something new. The learning can be either technical or emotional.

The pain will pass and something new will grow in place of the pain: understanding, insight, empathy. The intuitive message of growing pain is to stay with it and keep learning. There's gold there if you can be patient.

Destructive Pain

Another kind of pain is destructive pain. Destructive pain has no end. Its purpose seems to be to demean you and deplete your vitality. Even though the alternative may be frightening and unknown, destructive pain will never go away. It is associated with fear, control, and limitation. The intuitive message of destructive pain is to change, move, get out of the space, or to allow the mind-set to shift.

Your intuition is constantly gathering data from collective wisdom as well as from the events and experiences of your life. It then relays messages to you about how to proceed. You will respond to that information in your own unique way. Your facility with using your intuitive software discussed in the last chapter, plus the basic circumstances of your life and your current state of mind, will determine how you use the intuitive information coming in.

For example, someone might choose a college and feel miserable there. Their intuition is communicating that this is not the right place. Some personalities will feel "stuck" with the decision, whereas others will pick up and leave right away. Still others will adapt and find a way to work it through.

It's useful to reflect on how you've responded to those moments in your life up to now. Use the following table to help you reflect on how intuition has informed and guided you through some of the important events of your life. The heading of "What did you know" refers to intuitive knowing. It means, "What did you know about the situation that no one had to tell you—that you knew internally?"

	What Did You Know?	What Did You Feel?	What Did You Do?
College	_____	_____	_____
Job/Career	_____	_____	_____
Marriage	_____	_____	_____
Children	_____	_____	_____

When my older daughter was deciding which college to attend, we visited campus after campus, but none of them felt right. While visiting my sister, we decided on a whim to visit a college nearby that was not at the top of my daughter's list. The moment we stepped foot on the campus, we all knew it was the right place for her.

She was quite happy there for two years, after which she started to feel uncomfortable. The college no longer fit her needs, and she was ready to move on to a larger school with an expanded department for her major.

Pop Quiz!

We experience intuition in four main ways: physically, emotionally, mentally, and spiritually. You most likely have one or two modes in which you're naturally gifted, and others that could use a little work. In each of the following four sections, check off the questions to which you can answer "yes."

Lemme Hear Your Body Talk

The following questions have to do with your physical intuition:

1. Do you have "gut feelings" about situations?
2. Have you ever found yourself moving physically out of the way of danger before it happens without thinking about it first?
3. Do you ever slow down while driving, just before passing a police officer?
4. Have you ever heard some news and had an immediate physical reaction, either positive or negative, and later on you discover your initial response was accurate?
5. Do you have a good sense of direction?

I Second That Emotion

These questions explore your emotional intuition:

1. Do you sometimes have strong initial feelings about people upon first meeting them—feelings that prove accurate over time?
2. Do you think of people you haven't seen for a while just before you have some kind of contact with them?
3. Are you good at "reading" people?
4. Do you experience feelings or physical sensations of friends and relatives, no matter how far away they are, whether or not you are consciously aware of what they are going through?
5. Do you have a good rapport with animals?

It's All in Your Mind

These questions cast an eye on your mental intuition:

1. Can you sense positive energy? In other words, do you smell success?
2. Do you hear words, guidance, or instruction about which action to take?
3. Have you ever had a full-blown vision of something you later created or experienced?
4. Have you ever communicated with plants—for instance, walked by and known (or mentally heard) that a plant needed water or fertilizer?
5. Have you ever just known something that you have no way of knowing in the usual way?

High Spirits

These questions will help reveal your spiritual intuition:

1. Do you feel guided by some higher force?
2. Have coincidences and synchronicities played an important role in your life?
3. Have you ever known something was going to happen before it did?
4. Do you sometimes say the right thing, without even knowing or thinking about what you are saying?
5. Have you ever sensed the moment of someone's death from a distance?

Let's take a look at each of these intuitive styles—physical, emotional, mental, and spiritual—in turn.

The Body Knows

You know you're a physical, or kinesthetic, intuitive when your body is the main source of your intuitive wisdom. This is when your "gut" or stomach really speaks to you about people and situations, or you act automatically to avoid danger and have a good sense of direction.

While hiking in the Sierra Nevadas many years ago, my kinesthetic intuition played a major role in getting me out safely. My friend and I were novice hikers. (Unfortunately, *The Complete Idiot's Guide to Hiking, Camping, and the Great Outdoors* didn't exist yet!) We began a seven-day trek with no maps and no compass. We were just going to follow the trail to Evolution Valley.

A few days into the hike we met someone who told us about a really neat trail. If we hiked down a dried-out river bed and took the deer trail at the bottom, in a couple of days we would find ourselves at a beautiful waterfall. If we kept hiking after that, in two days we'd be at our car. It sounded like a great adventure to us, so we decided to do it. We actually discovered something that looked like a dried riverbed, followed it down the mountain, and stumbled onto something that seemed like a deer trail.

Then a funny thing happened: after a few steps I could go no further. My body just stopped. It then occurred to me that perhaps we were going the wrong way on the trail. I told my friend that we had to turn around. Since he was as clueless as I was, we did, and it felt much more comfortable to me. Sure enough, after two days, we came upon a magnificent waterfall and then went on to find our car. That was kinesthetic intuition at work—although I don't recommend that you try this for yourselves!

There are a lot of common terms for this kind of intuition: the "sniff test," a "pain in the neck (or any other body part)," "weak knees," "a lump in the throat," "someone walked on my grave." A stockbroker I know gets "chills up the spine" telling him when it's time to move on a stock.

Sixth Sense

Kinesthetic refers to the ability of your physical body to learn and respond. It is the physical feeling and physical understanding that is different from mental understanding. Your body knows how to climb a tree or learns to ride a bicycle and if you were asked to explain it to someone who had never done it, it would be quite challenging, if not impossible—because your kinesthetic understanding is physically based, not mentally based.

Your Mother Really Did Know

Did your mother ever say "I don't feel good about this," and turn out to have been right? Did she have an uncanny ability to know what you were doing, even when you thought you had hidden the truth well? She was probably an emotional intuitive. Emotional intuitives have strong feelings about things, people, and situations.

Tried & True

Here is a perfect example of emotional intuition from Alexandra Stoddard, an interior designer:

I went wading in a country brook with my daughter, Alexandra. As we held hands in the clear, sparkling water, I felt great joy. We had struggled with names for the new baby. Now, in a flash, one choice became clear: We would name her "Brooke." And we did.

Emotional intuition is experienced in the metaphorical heart. Information concerned with feelings, emotional connections, relationships, and resonance are all part of emotional intuition. Love at first sight is emotional intuition. Feeling comfortable or uncomfortable about a situation is, too.

A woman in one of my seminars shared the following story:

I went for an interview for a job I didn't initially think was for me. They were offering neither the salary nor the work opportunities I wanted. But while I was sitting in the waiting room, I got such a feeling of comfort and rightness that I knew that this was the job for me. Even though they didn't offer me what I wanted in salary, I took the job on that intuition and spent the next 23 years there, learning new skills and growing professionally with the company."

The Dream of the Flying Hunches

Buck Charleson grew up during the Depression and was unable to go to college. His love of engineering and mechanics led him to the library to study on his own. He had an idea of something that could be invented, something that had never been done before and that experts said was impossible. He spent a little time every day meditating and visualizing the purpose of his invention, waiting for a solution to the engineering problem.

One day it happened! In 3-D, a vision of the mechanism he was looking for came into his mind. He could see the whole thing, top, bottom, and sides. All he had to do was go into the lab and build it. The hydraulic lift was born and the patent has needed no improvements for more than 40 years.

Many inventors have their "Eureka!" moments in dreams or meditative states. Mental intuition is usually involved.

Tried & True

Here's another of Alexandra Stoddard's stories:

"I became fascinated by the shiny, lettuce-green seaweed forming a wavy pattern in the ripples of the wet, golden sand. The sight inspired my design for a soft, green velvet bedspread quilted in wavy ridges."

Hunches, insights, dreams, and visions are the ways of mental intuition. There may be emotion attached to the image once it occurs, but the initial intuitive information is mental.

Celestine Dreamin'

If you resonated deeply with James Redfield's book *The Celestine Prophesy* you under-stand spiritual intuition. It is spiritual intuition when you feel that something has a larger purpose, that you are guided, and that coinci-dences occur often and significantly.

A few years ago, I presented a workshop and keynote speech on intuition to a conference of Adult Protective Service (APS) providers. I arrived at the conference early to get a sense of the people and their concerns. While attending a workshop, I sat next to an ex-police officer from Chicago who was now working with APS. We started a conversation, and I asked him about intuitive experiences that he had had as a police officer. After a great conversation, he admitted to me that when he'd first seen my topic listed in the program he'd thought, "Who gets away with speaking on a flaky subject like intuition, and what idiot hired her?" He subsequently went to my workshop and intuitively solved a deep problem that had been bothering him for more than five years.

If he hadn't met me before the workshop, he never would have attended. I see this as something that was meant to be. Some force guided us together and we took the opportunity. That is spiritual intuition.

Sixth Sense

A *coincidence* is when two or more events occur which by their timing or relationship stand out. For example, you may think of an old friend you have not seen in years and then within a few days receive a postcard from them, or hear about them from a mutual friend. A *synchronicity* is a meaningful coincidence, such as the above example, rather than a random occurrence of non-related events. In the world of intuition, most coincidences are seen as meaningful.

Tried & True

In *Superman*, the comic book series, the superhero goes to his Fortress of Solitude, a crystal palace, when he is in trouble and needs counsel from his parents and ancestors. The crystals in the palace are encoded with all the wisdom from his relatives. A young reader from New Mexico sent a letter to the series editor saying that he had imagined his own Fortress of Solitude and received guidance on how to speak with his father about some difficulties they were having. He spoke with his father, his father was moved to tears, and they began to change some family patterns because of this discussion.

Memory Lane

It's time to take your intuition on another test drive. Taking it through different types of terrain will help you see how your intuition maneuvers in different settings. This test drive is going to be pulled from your memory. By remembering how you maneuvered in different experiences, you will highlight and sharpen your intuitive skills.

As you record how your intuition has intervened in certain past events, you may notice that you tend to combine some or all of the intuitive styles or that one particular style seems to dominate. Keep in mind that intuition is fluid, and there are no hard distinctions between the different styles.

That First Meeting

Think of someone who has been deeply important to your life. Perhaps a lover, but not necessarily. Perhaps a mentor or important teacher, a good friend or business partner. Remember the time and the circumstances under which you first met. Reflect on what occurred during that first meeting. How were you brought together? What was your first response to them? Theirs to you? What thoughts and feelings did you have after your first meeting?

A Complete Disaster

Think of a catastrophe, a complete disaster in your life that you might have averted if different steps had been taken at crucial times. Remember when you first sensed that something was not right. How did you experience that? Did you notice something? Feel something? React to something? Hear something? Remember all the warning signals you ignored at the time and ask the same questions. Write down your reflections. This is not an exercise in personal guilt or responsibility, but in recognizing how your own intuition works.

A Great Idea

Remember a time when you came up with a fantastic idea. What were the circumstances surrounding this idea? Was there something or someone that stimulated it? Was it "out of the blue" or linked to a particular project? How did the idea come to you? In a vision? While exercising or walking? Dreaming? Sitting at your desk? Talking to someone? How did it feel?

> **Practical Wisdom**
>
> Whenever you meet someone new, take a moment to look in their eyes, connecting with the deepest part of who they are. Take a breath, and let them meet you in an equally deep place.

A Moment of Joy

Reflect on one moment of joy. Think of a time in your life when you were completely joyful. If you can't think of any particular moment of joy, make it up. What would it feel like if you could? Imagine that your body and mind are hooked up to a "joy faucet." Turn on the faucet and imagine yourself filling up with joy. What happens when you feel joyful?

Share Your Seat with Intuition

Developing your intuition requires a slight adjustment in perception. Intuition is always there, but it's not always at center stage. All it requires is remembering that you have an inner resource that can be useful in many situations if you allow it to be part of the process.

I know that at some point you've heard yourself say: "I knew that was going to happen. Why didn't I do something about it?" Like the folks in the commercials for V-8 juice, everyone occasionally feels that instead of doing the ordinary, expected thing, they could have used their intuition and changed the course of their lives.

It really is as simple—and as difficult—as remembering to ask, then listening to the answer. Let's finish up with a few weekday-style workouts to trigger your memory and allow room for intuition in your life.

Yellow Light

The more we work, the more tired we get, the less creative or open-minded we are, and the less we accomplish. We get further behind and then think we have no time for play.

—Ann McGee Cooper,
*Time Management for
Unmanageable People*

Intuition on the Run

The following workout takes about five minutes on your commute to work:

1. Have pen and paper ready.

2. Hand over the thinking to your intuition by taking a few deep breaths and imagining a transfer of power from your "get going to work" mind to your intuitive mind. Silently ask your intuition to be present.

3. Just start writing. Whatever occurs and whatever flows is perfect. Without editing or censuring, let your intuition speak to you through writing.

4. Look at what you wrote and "hear" what your intuition is telling you.

5. Now review your agenda for the day and notice how you feel about each item.

6. Write down any hunches, images, or feelings you have about each item.

Unload the Day

Take five minutes on your commute home from work for the following workout:

1. Reflect on your day in writing from the perspective of your intuition.

2. Listen quietly to what your intuition has to tell you about the day.

3. Review your day, noting what worked, what didn't, and what you could pay more attention to next time.

Practical Wisdom

Here's an idea for an intuition "trigger." On your desk, place something that reminds you to pause and listen to your intuitive voice a few times a day. Some students of intuition have used a stone from the beach. You could just as easily use a baseball, a toy boat, or a beanbag.

The Least You Need to Know

➤ Intuition takes many forms—yours is unique to you.

➤ Physical intuition is best known as a "gut feeling."

➤ Mental intuition takes the form of hunches and visions.

➤ Emotional intuition has to do with issues of the heart.

➤ Spiritual intuition lends a sense of purpose and meaning to events.

➤ Remembering how your intuition has worked in the past will reinforce it now.

Chapter 4

Care and Feeding

In This Chapter

➤ Identify specific issues and solve them intuitively

➤ Become comfortable with the language of intuition

➤ Learn several quick intuitive exercises

➤ Develop a tracking system for your intuition

➤ Use the Intuition Checklist

There comes a time when the chicks need to hatch; the faucet gets turned on; the elevator doors close and you start to move. This is the chapter where you learn how to take care of your fledgling intuition and how to start translating it into practical action. If intuition can't help you make better decisions faster, use more opportunities, and avoid costly mistakes, what use is it?

For those readers who've never exposed their analytic minds to the wisdom of their intuition, it may be a little uncomfortable at first. Stick with it and repeat it a few times. Treat this as you would the learning of any new skill, and give yourself time to make mistakes. Give yourself permission to *not* get it right!

The last three chapters provided theoretical and practical background on the "what" and "how" of intuition. This chapter shows you how to apply what you've learned to the situations facing you in your life today. A section on tracking and maintaining your intuition will help you build a daily program to strengthen your intuitive skill. Do the intuition workouts in this chapter and you'll begin to see results right away, plus you'll be ready to tackle the advanced intuitive work of wealth building and career planning.

The Call of the Wild

There's a terrific scene in the movie *Men in Black* where Tommy Lee Jones's character reveals to Will Smith's character that huge numbers of extraterrestrials are living in New York City. He does this by showing him weapons and capabilities never seen by the vast majority of humans. They're sitting on a park bench and Will is readjusting his thinking to this new reality when Tommy Lee says: "Yesterday you 'knew' that we were alone on this planet and that there was no such thing as an extraterrestrial. Think of what you'll know tomorrow!"

Your intuition has a problem similar to Tommy Lee's problem: how to reveal new information to you when your mind has a tendency to lock on to one way of thinking and never let go. It's like a child who has seen something that she knows the adults will never believe.

Your intuition sneaks around this communication problem by using methods that aren't based in the rational mind. Instead, it uses physical sensations, emotions, dreams, synchronistic events, symbols, and metaphors. Intuition jolts us into awareness by highlighting, underlining, and starring information. If you have a hunch—a random thought about something, accompanied by a strong emotional feeling, and followed up with a coincidence—you're likely to pay attention.

A meeting planner I know was managing a huge event. The day after she'd spoken to the printer and straightened out all the details, she had a persistent feeling that she should call the printer again. She tried to ignore it, but the nagging feeling returned to the pit of her stomach. When she called the printer, convinced in her mind that she was wasting her time, the printer told her that the client had just called to change some of the times and events in the program. The new information changed everything else the meeting planner was working on. If she hadn't found out when she did, much of her work would have been wasted.

This kind of intuitive communication happens all the time. Anyone who works in a field where things change rapidly knows the experience of having a feeling or a hunch about something that is *supposed* to be settled and done. Responding to intuitive information makes life easier because problems and changes are anticipated.

Practical Wisdom

We must always change, renew, rejuvenate ourselves; otherwise we harden.

—Johann W. Goethe

Parlez–Vous Intuition?

Recognizing the language of intuition can take a little practice. Here is a list of the main elements of intuitive language and how they often present themselves:

➤ Hunch: A stray, persistent thought

➤ Gut feeling: An uncomfortable sensation in the stomach area

➤ Coincidence or synchronicity: One or more events that stand out because of their juxtaposition to other events

➤ Symbol: A particular event or thing that recurs frequently, perhaps in dreams, reading material, or conversations

➤ Metaphor: Like a symbol, but representing some larger intuitive communication, such as losing things

➤ Dream: Images and feelings dreamt that show up in real life

➤ Emotion: Positive and negative feelings about situations, people, or places

➤ Desire: The specific emotion of wanting something

➤ Fear: The specific feeling of discomfort and an urge to move away from a situation or person

By contrast, intuition is not any of the following:

➤ Anxiety: Fearful anticipation of possible future events

➤ Rigidity: A fixed focus on a particular outcome

➤ Magic or fantasy: A manifestation of a large dream with no personal effort

The Drama Channel

Even an undeveloped intuition often shows up dramatically. During emergency situations and powerful personal events, intuition somehow breaks through the normal walls around the mind. We need help and we get it—from within ourselves.

For instance, many people have experienced some communication or intuitive knowing of the death of a close friend or relative. The experience is so dramatic and powerful that it scares many people, and they build a stronger mental wall against any other intuitive knowing.

A woman recently shared with me that while relaxing and watching television, she got up for no particular reason and walked into the room where her baby was sleeping—only to discover him silently choking on something. If she hadn't walked in, he would have died.

In cases like this, many people associate intuition with such fear and negativity that they close down their intuitive mechanism.

Other people keep their intuition tuned only to positive information. In describing a bad thing that has happened to them, many people have said to me: "I never saw that coming." One very successful business woman said to me: "I'm not good at hiring. I always see the best potential in everyone and completely miss their shortcomings, so I let someone who is more discerning do the hiring." She understood where her intuitive gifts would bring the most results, and she let others handle the situations where her intuition did not work as well.

Take a moment to think about what channel your intuition is tuned to. Is it weighted to the disaster and trauma side or on the side of overly positive images? Experiment with the idea that your intuition can change channels. You can access lots more information of various kinds if you begin to broaden your receptivity. Remember the intuition TV from Chapter 1? Your intuitive link-up is connected to a vast amount of information, so why limit it? Play with the image of changing intuitive channels from disaster to stock market quotes to positive news.

Yellow Light

When you are anxious or afraid, it's difficult to distinguish intuitive messages from thoughts generated by your fear or anxiety. When you are in a frightened state, you often expect the worst—a feeling usually founded in your imagination, not your intuition.

—Richard Contino, *Trust Your Gut*

Get Intuit!

The following four workouts are quick ways to connect with your intuition on a daily basis. After a little practice, you'll be able to do them quickly, when you need them most.

Practical Wisdom

It's more productive to spend five minutes every day listening to your intuition than to spend an hour once a week.

Over the course of this book, these workouts will be used again in many different ways. As in Chapter 3, the workouts stimulate a range of intuitive preferences, so you may find that one or two of the exercises work better for you than others. Stick with the ones that work best.

Before we begin, list four current issues in your life for which you'd like new insights or answers:

Yes or No

At a very basic level, any situation can be reduced to a yes-or-no answer. If neither yes nor no seems right, maybe takes over, meaning that you're either not ready or don't have enough information to decide.

As discussed in Chapter 3, in each moment of decision there is either a yes or no intuitive sense of how to proceed. This "in the moment" sense is very different from approaching situations with a set or standard answer before you get there.

For this workout, start with the first issue written above and phrase it as a yes-or-no question. Take the following steps, closing your eyes after reading each instruction (you can do it with your eyes open if you prefer). Pause after each instruction.

1. Imagine that you're holding the word no in one hand and yes in the other.
2. Sense as many details about the words as possible: weight, size, color, shape.
3. Repeat your question mentally.
4. Focus on the word "no." How does it respond to your question?
5. Lift the word up to your ear and hear the word no spoken. Notice how your body responds.
6. Bring the word to your nose and smell it. How does it smell?
7. Take a bite out of the word. Chew it, taste it, swallow it. How does your body respond to eating the word no?
8. Now focus on the word "yes."
9. Repeat your question mentally and notice how you respond.
10. Lift the word to your ear and hear the word yes spoken. Notice how your body responds.
11. Bring the word to your nose and smell it. How does it smell?
12. Take a bite out of the word. Chew it, taste it, swallow it. How does your body respond to eating the word yes?
13. Repeat your question mentally one more time. Reflect on what your intuition is communicating to you about this question.
14. Write down your results so you can track your success.

If, after completing this workout, you don't have a clear sense of whether your answer is yes or no, remember maybe. For all of us action-oriented, workaholic doers, the most difficult thing to do in any situation is to wait. Sometimes, though, it's the most powerful thing we can do. To postpone a decision and to take no action may be what is called for if intuitively you feel unclear or uncertain.

Tried & True

The long and short of it is when I returned home to California, following my intuition, I quit my lucrative but demanding job. To the amazement of my friends, I sold most of my furniture, and shipped the rest of my belongings to New Mexico. I packed myself and the kids into my old blue Volkswagen square-back and drove the three of us to Santa Fe.

—Carol Adrienne, *The Purpose of Your Life*

Try It On for Size

Review the second issue you wrote down. Take a deep breath and let your imagination lead you through the following workout:

1. Imagine that this situation is an article of clothing. Go with the first image that comes to mind, whether it is something you like or not.

2. Now, try on the situation as if it were the article of clothing. Put it on and notice how it fits.

3. Let the feeling of the fit provide information on how to proceed with the situation. After a few practice runs, this will be all you need to get an intuitive overview of any situation.

4. If you want to go further, ask yourself the following questions as a way to stimulate more information: How does wearing this make me feel? Do I like the way I look? Is this a new look or an old look? What activities happen in this outfit?

5. Allow the connections between the answers to these questions and the situation to happen naturally. Let the intuitive information sink in before jumping to conclusions. Live with the physical sensations and feelings that go with "trying on" the situation.

6. Write down your results.

The Applause Meter

In the golden age of the TV quiz show there was a machine called an applause meter. (If you watch Nickelodeon, you may still see one occasionally.) They were used to determine which contestant or dance couple had received the most applause from the audience. The host would raise his hand above the person or group and ask the audience to applaud. The meter would register the level of applause on a scale of say, 1 to 10. The person or group who received the most applause won!

Let's use the applause meter as an intuitive tool. Here's how it works. When something is intuitively right for us, it's accompanied by a feeling of support. When you get on track intuitively, you won't feel alone; rather, you'll feel a wave of universal support behind you. There may be many people in your life who think you're nuts, but internally you will feel at peace. There may be chaos, change, or turbulence, but joy will be there, too, indicating that this is the right track to be on.

Tried & True

The day I left the firm, I crossed the threshold. From that point on, what happened to me had the most mysterious quality about it. Things began falling into place almost effortlessly—unforeseen incidents and meetings with the most remarkable people who were to provide crucial assistance to me.

—Joe Jaworski, *Synchronicity*

Look at the third issue you wrote down at the beginning of this section. What is it asking of you? What involvements and commitments does this issue imply? Are there a few alternative ways to approach this situation? Do you have options? If so, identify the different options you have and write them down. Now you're ready for the applause-meter workout.

1. Imagine a chorus of supporters behind you—a group of people rooting for your success in life. Sometimes I imagine a crowd of guardian angels encouraging me, being my audience as I play through my life. Perhaps you imagine yourself playing a sport with a full stadium of people watching and wanting you to win. Use whatever image works best for you.

2. Let the audience decide whether this situation, Issue #3, is something you need to get involved in or not. Phrase a question to the audience in a way that they can let you know through their applause how they feel about your situation. Is this the way to go? Or is there something else?

3. Imagine that applause meter letting you know which option received the most energy from the audience.

4. Take a moment to enjoy the crowd of support, cheering you on as you do the right thing.

5. Write down your results.

Objects of My Direction

This workout is based on the intuitive principle that every situation, every problem has an answer and you can find it if you know where and how to look. With this method, the answer pops up or floats to you metaphorically. The confidence necessary to keep intuition flowing described in Chapter 2 is key here. Be confident that there is an answer. You aren't making it up or pretending—it's true. If you don't quite believe it, believe me and give it a try! Soon your own experience will confirm the truth.

Practical Wisdom

"Maybe this is an omen," said the Englishman, half aloud.

"Who told you about omens?" The boy's interest was increasing by the moment.

"Everything in life is an omen," said the Englishman, now closing the journal he was reading. "There is a universal language understood by everybody, but already forgotten."

—Paulo Coelho, *The Alchemist*

Focus on your fourth issue. Phrase an open question to yourself and write it down. It doesn't have to be a yes or no question; it can begin with "how" or "what."

1. Begin by taking a deep full breath and completely exhaling. Do it again, releasing tension as you exhale. Take one more deep breath, imagining that you're handing your intuition the responsibility for answering this question. As you do this, close your eyes and count to five.

2. When you open your eyes, look around your desk or your room for three things that attract your attention. Don't spend much time thinking about it, just pick three things and place them in front of you.

3. Arrange the three things in a row. The criteria you use in placing them in order is purely aesthetic. Line them up in a way that feels right to you.

I guided Deborah, a journalist, though this exercise when she was considering looking for a new job. The three objects were her watch, a picture of her girlfriends, and a bottle of water, lined up in that order. Follow along for yourself as I repeat here the conversation we had about discovering her intuitive message.

These three things, in their order, have the answer to your fourth issue. Below is the key to help you discover what message your intuition has for you. What you're looking for is a feeling of rightness with each object. If the answer is not clear to you, don't dwell on it. Instead, move on to the next object and come back to the one that you don't understand later.

4. The first object represents the overview of your situation. It symbolizes what you really want out of this situation, what you are looking for—what it means to you, personally.

   As you look at the first object, the answer may emerge immediately. If not, or for more information, try asking the following questions. Remember that the intuitive answer will be underscored by an accompanying feeling of rightness or recognition. You will recognize the answer as right for you. Otherwise, this becomes a mental exercise in creative thinking.

   Ask yourself the following:

   ➤ If this object could communicate with me, what would it say?

   ➤ What about this object attracts me? What about it do I like?

   ➤ If I were this object, how would I see my situation?

   I asked Deborah, "How is your watch symbolic of what you need to start doing? What is it telling you?"

   "It's telling me that it is the right time," she said.

5. The second object represents what is blocking or in the way of solving your issue.

   Ask yourself the following:

   ➤ If this object could communicate, what would it say?

   ➤ If I were this object, how would I feel?

   ➤ Is there anything about this object that makes me uncomfortable?"

   I asked Deborah, "What is getting in the way of looking for and moving on to a new job?"

   "Maybe I need to stop putting so much energy into my friends and start concentrating on myself," came the reply.

   Deborah reflected that her friends are not a bad influence, but that perhaps she pays just a little too much attention to them and their needs, rather than taking care of herself and her own needs. She realized that "paying more attention out there, rather than in here" is a common pattern in her life.

6. The third object represents the solution or a new approach to take to this situation.

   Ask yourself the following:

   ➤ How would this object approach my situation?

   ➤ If this object could communicate, what would it say?

   ➤ If I acted like this object, what would I do?

   Deborah knew immediately that the water bottle represented taking care of her physical self—drinking and eating healthily and staying fit.

Remember to take an open, creative approach to this exercise. Your intuition has an answer for you and you have the opportunity to discover what that answer is. If you get too serious, your intuition won't work. Intuition works with an open mind. At the same time, you are looking for the feeling of recognition. You know what is right for you and only you can recognize it. Use the open heart and open mind hardware–software combo we developed in Chapter 2.

Live with the images for a full day. Record your results in your journal.

Practice, Practice, Practice

Intuition, like everything else in life, thrives when it gets attention. As my friend and colleague Sharon Franquemont says, "Intuition follows the energy of love." What she means is that intuition flows when you are engaged with something you love. If you're doing something you don't love, intuition is less likely to flow. This is just common sense.

Tried & True

Here's what Ron Schulz, author of *Unconventional Wisdom*, says about Robert Pittman, creator of the MTV music channel and now CEO of America Online:

> As a leader, he believes he has to find a way to stop that executive from saying, "It'll never work." For Pittman, the creative process and the analytical process are two completely separate systems that shouldn't be mixed. "Let's consider how it might work before we say it won't work."

In this chapter, you will develop an ongoing maintenance and tracking system for your intuition so that you can watch and enjoy your progress.

When designing your daily maintenance program, keep in mind which exercises you enjoy doing. Make it fun. Think about how wonderful it will feel when you are more comfortable with and trusting of your inner voice. Visualize yourself in a successful position, living a life that is extremely comfortable for you, with your dreams coming true. Imagine living a full life where the contribution you make to the world is one you are proud of.

Basic Maintenance

To reach a base level of intuitive competence and to get the most from the rest of this book, a simple and consistent system for expanding the use of intuition needs to be implemented. As little as five minutes a day is enough to seed the process. Once intuitive thinking is firmly rooted in your daily awareness it will grow on its own.

Basic maintenance requires three elements:

➤ Consistency

➤ Enjoyment

➤ Tracking

Consistency

Practical Wisdom

How does your intuitive garden grow? Like every other living thing: with attention, care, and patience.

Consistency is as simple as remembering that intuition is available to you once or several times a day. Whenever faced with a decision or dilemma, remember to seek intuitive wisdom as well as any other information important to the decision.

Begin your day with a simple affirmation that will keep the door open to intuitive wisdom. Here are a few affirmations you can use or modify:

➤ Today intuitive wisdom will be available to me.

➤ Today, and every day, intuitive wisdom will be a part of every decision I make.

➤ The door to my intuitive wisdom is open.

➤ Intuitive wisdom is guiding me to success and fulfillment.

During the day, make it a habit to use one or more of the workouts outlined in this chapter. Insert the question, "How do I really feel about this?" before any important decision.

These simple steps require 5 or 10 minutes each day. Some of it can be done while commuting to work, some can be done during a quick break from work, and some can be done while working. The key is really remembering that there is a stream of information and advice available to you if you just shift your attention and awareness slightly.

Enjoyment

Joy is overlooked as a tool in most learning programs. The truth is that we learn and retain much more when we are having fun. As children we knew this, but through school it was all but forgotten. Education becomes serious and formal, even though every teacher knows that engaging the students' attention and interest will help them learn.

If intuition training seems like a chore to you, forget it! Find another path to success and personal fulfillment.

Tracking

If you use your muscles to get work done during the day, that is called hard work. If you track how you use your muscles and methodically use more of them, that is called muscle-building.

Tracking your intuitive process will build intuitive muscle. You use your intuition already, but may not be aware of it. Making yourself aware, practicing, tracking progress, and exercising all parts of your intuition will increase intuitive competency.

Tracking involves writing down your intuitive impressions and then returning to those impressions to find out how accurate they were. By paying attention in this way, your intuitive process will strengthen automatically. Once you let your mind know what you are looking for, it will highlight that information for you.

Remember our intuition TV metaphor from Chapter 1? Once you know what information is contained on the different channels, you can get what you need more effectively than surfing through all the possibilities (and become a more efficient cosmic couch potato).

It's like creating a bookmark on your computer for an Internet site you visit frequently. The site is always there, and noting it allows you to get to that information easily. Tracking your intuition creates a bookmark for intuitive information. Then, when you need it, you can get there easily.

Intuition takes it one step further and can contact you when important information is coming through. When strengthened, it behaves more like a clipping service, providing relevant information when and where you want it.

Tracking is extremely useful in work situations. When your group is wrestling with a decision and you have an intuition, how do you convince the rest of the group to listen to you? If you have built a track record over time of having valuable intuitive information, the team will be more likely to listen to you.

Step-by-Step: Three Daily Regimens

Here are three sample intuitive tracking regimens you can use or adapt. Try them each for one week and then put together your own program based on what works best for you.

Here's the Bare-Bones Basic regimen:

➤ Within the first hour of waking up, look at one of the previous affirmations that you wrote out and tacked to your refrigerator or other place you look every day.

➤ During the day, as you take breaks ask yourself: "How do I feel about what is going on today? Are there other choices I could make?" Then write down on a small notepad any thoughts you have.

➤ At the end of the day, ask yourself: "What happened today? What details stand out to me?" Write a few notes.

Ready for a step up to Moderate Motivation? Here we go:

➤ Repeat one of your affirmations a few times to yourself during your morning shower.

➤ Sometime during the morning, perhaps while commuting, review some of the events scheduled for your day, ask how important each event is, and give each the "applause meter test."

➤ Take five minutes to use one of the other intuition workouts during the day. Be sure to record your results.

➤ Review your day, writing down what you noticed intuitively.

Here's the regimen for the Ambitious:

➤ Sing one of your affirmations during your morning shower.

➤ Do Workout #4 with the question: "What is important for me to pay attention to day?" Record your results.

➤ Several times during the day, stop to take a breath and ask yourself how you feel about what is going on.

➤ Before making any big decisions, phrase the question as a yes or no and do Workout #1. Record your results.

➤ Review your day every evening. Look at your notes and reflect on the role your intuition played in your life that day.

Tried & True

I always urge people to take time from their busy days for reflection. After one workshop, a senior executive came to my office. Mild anger showed on his face. He said, "Mike, have you been telling people to take time to meditate during the day?" I said, "Sure I have. They need the time. They need to find new ways to solve the problems around here." He didn't understand. He came back with, "We can't have people doing this. What if an auditor came by their desks? What could they point to on their time cards? What could they say they're charging to for this?"

I tried to tell him this made them more productive. They saved time. They found more clever ways to do their work. It really was part of the job. But what I said didn't matter. The illusion of business had trapped him well. According to him, people who weren't active and busy must not be working!

—Michael Munn, Ph.D., TQM Trainer and Chief Scientist, Lockheed

The Intuition Checklist

The following questions will help you determine whether you're intuitively ready to make a decision and take positive action. As you read each question to yourself, be aware of your immediate reaction of yes or no. If any part of you feels uncomfortable, blocked, resistant, or closed in any way, consider it a no and come back to the question later. This list is intended to stimulate your intuitive response to any important decision you are making and to firmly fix your attention internally. The more yes responses you have, the greater your readiness to move forward with your decision; the more no responses, the less ready.

Yes	No	
❑	❑	I know what I need to do.
❑	❑	I see the "open door."
❑	❑	This decision has "cooked" and feels done.
❑	❑	I can see myself completing this.
❑	❑	I know how I really feel about this.
❑	❑	I know my other choices and this one still feels right.
❑	❑	I have a plan for responding to others' objections.
❑	❑	This decision fits with my long-term goals.
❑	❑	The time to act is right now.
❑	❑	I will feel relieved, grateful, or energized when this action is complete.

To follow up on a no response, by going back to it to answer the following questions:

➤ Is it a part of the situation or the whole thing that feels uncomfortable?

➤ If it is a part of the situation, which part or parts?

➤ Can the uncomfortable part be modified or clarified?

➤ What would make this situation feel right?

➤ Is there anyone or anything applying pressure?

➤ How can more time be allowed to make this decision?

➤ Is there a push to make something happen that may not be what I really want?

Just a reminder! The Intuition Checklist is on the tear-out card in the front of the book for easy reference. (By the way, the checklist is also on my Web site at www.intuitionatwork.com.)

The Least You Need to Know

➤ Intuition talks to you via physical sensations, emotions, synchronicities, and dreams.

➤ Intuition often first shows up during traumatic events—but don't let this scare you.

➤ Practice, practice, and more practice is the key to developing a strong intuition.

➤ Tracking your intuitive progress will build your competency and credibility.

➤ Enjoying the intuitive process is key to using it successfully.

➤ Do something to use your intuition every day.

Part 2
Get a Life—and a Career

*How do I know the ways of
all things at the beginning?
By what is within me.*

—Lao-Tzu

This part focuses your new and improved intuitive skills toward finding a life and a career (in that order) that work for you. You'll learn to make your dreams reality and develop the intuitive power to make good choices along the way.

You'll also invade the workplace, flexing your intuitive muscles to bring creativity, innovation, and just plain good decision-making to the teams you work with, whether you're the boss or the boss-to-be. And if you're thinking of switching careers, don't do it until you've read the chapter on taking intuitive career leaps: It's filled with powerful intuition workouts designed just for the occasion.

Chapter 5

Into Wishin':
Life and Career
Planning

In This Chapter

➤ Learn how intuition can help new and unusual things happen in your life

➤ Listen to the messages your life is sending you

➤ Set a powerful intention in motion

➤ Let your career support your life, rather than the other way around

➤ Learn to believe in magic

The joy of living intuitively makes each day an adventure: you never know what opportunities and experiences will show up. The challenge is to sneak your intuition into that highly structured life of yours, in an environment filled with strict deadlines, expectations, and huge amounts of rules to follow.

In this chapter you will learn four principles and one law you can live by. This chapter will help you use intuition to plan your life, including a career that will support your life and challenge you to continually create and learn. I'll show you how to expand your intuition until it becomes less a skill than a philosophy and tool for guidance, helping you to discern and manage the multitude of opportunities that come your way.

Four Principles, a Law, and a Party in Balamah

Harrison Owen, the author of *Expanding Our Now*, has developed what he called "open space technology," a method of bringing groups of people together to solve a common problem with a minimum of structure and interference. In this he was inspired by the residents of Balamah, a very small village he visited in the bush of West Africa.

The principles he observed and articulated in his book correspond to many of the intuitive success tools discussed in this chapter. He writes:

"One of the high experiences for all residents and visitors to the village was the rite of passage for the boys and a similar celebration for the girls. I was fortunate to participate, as much as a Westerner can participate, in both. These celebrations occurred on a seven-year cycle and were replete with complex ritual, pageantry, dance, and just plain fun. Profoundly moving, the renewal of the village was celebrated as its young people were welcomed to adulthood and acknowledged as the first fruits of the future.

"My natural curiosity, to say nothing of a perceived need to be at the right place at the right time, led me to ask what the starting time might be. Blamah, the chief, would just smile and say, 'When it's time.'

"And Blamah was right. The events always started when it was time. But how, I wondered, did anybody know? There were few calendars, and such clocks as there were rarely ticked. Even worse, there was no planning committee, and yet the events came off right on schedule, without a hitch. Every time."

Harrison gleaned four principles and one law from what he observed in Balamah, later applying them to corporate problem-solving sessions. The four principles are as follows:

1. Whoever comes is the right people.
2. Whatever happens is the only thing that could have.
3. Whenever it starts is the right time.
4. When it's over, it's over.

The law he formulated is the Law of Two Feet: If, at any point during the time together, anyone finds that they are neither contributing nor learning, they should use their two feet and move.

Practical Wisdom

As we began to fly over the field where we were supposed to drop the bombs, I felt a wave of incredible danger and told the pilot of the plane behind me to pull out, as I was doing. He kept going and was immediately hit by sniper fire.

—John D., Air Force pilot in the Vietnam War

These principles describe very colorfully how intuition helps things happen in our lives. In the same way that groups of people focused on a similar problem can discover new and creative ways to solve their problems using these principles, individuals who adapt and adopt these principles into their life and career planning also achieve dramatic results.

The striking difference between Western culture and the culture in Balamah is that in the West we strive to control and dominate time and events in our lives while in Balamah they work with a sense of natural timing.

Harrison's principles now can be adapted to speak specifically to how you can live your life more intuitively.

Practical Wisdom

There is an important humility associated with trying to direct our activities by setting goals or measures. Every act of observation loses more information than it gains. Whatever we decide to notice blinds us to other possibilities. In directing our attention to certain things, we lose awareness of everything else. We collapse the world of possibilities into a narrow band of observation.

—Margaret J. Wheatley and Myron Kellner-Rogers, *A Simpler Way*

Whoever Comes Is the Right People

We've all heard the adage, "It's who you know that counts." A lot of people don't think they have the connections necessary to succeed. But you do—you just don't realize it. Chances are you already know people who can help you get to your next step. It's a negative loop to hold on to the idea that if only you knew the right people, your dream would happen. The people in your life right now know much more than you give them credit for. Begin talking openly about what you want and what you are looking for and listen to how much they may know.

Whatever Happens Is the Only Thing That Could Have

Instead of complaining about something bad that happens to you, accept it as the way it is and move on. Stop blaming yourself or regretting what has happened and keep going. It's okay to have strong feelings, but don't let them stop you from exploiting the opportunities currently before you. The sun has set and is getting ready for a new day, while you may be hoping yesterday returns.

My father-in-law, who played the horses, was a master at accepting what happened to him. One day he started with a $20 bet that grew with each race. By the fifth race he had won about $8,000. He lost it all on the next race and when asked about it, he said, "I only lost $20." He was ready to bet again with a clean slate.

Whenever It Starts Is the Right Time

Do what is in front of you to do, right now, and let the future take care of itself. Trust that you'll know when to act and when to wait. There is a more precise timing at work that factors in all the events and people in your life. If you let it, it takes all of the information and guides you to the right place at the right time. If God is the ultimate, universal air traffic controller, intuition is His radio!

When you feel the urge to move, to research something, to begin something—do it. If I hadn't followed my intuition to study and create a career using intuition 20 years ago, I never would have been ready when the world caught up with me. Things in fashion now were on the fringe 20 years ago.

When It's Over, It's Over

Recognize when something is over and let it be over. When a situation no longer has any real juice, move on. You can keep dancing after the music has stopped, but it just doesn't have the same feeling. The same is true with business deals, jobs, relationships, and creative endeavors. Recognize and accept what has happened and move on.

The Law of Two Feet

The Law of Two Feet dictates that each person involved in any activity is responsible for their involvement. If at any time you're no longer learning from or contributing to the situation, it's your job to walk away. Don't rehash what has already been done. Time moves in one direction and it is pointless to think about "what is…" and "why didn't…" Take all those regrets, all that you would have done differently if you had the chance, and put them into your present and your future. Instead of mentally beating yourself or someone else up for what was done, decide to do it differently next time and move on. In other words, you no longer have the luxury of feeling victimized by any situation.

In the world of intuition, this is a cornerstone of all success. As discussed in Part 1, intuition is as simple as moving toward what feels nourishing and creative and away from what feels restrictive and depleting. The key here is that each individual is responsible for that determination. This is where intuition plays an important role.

A great time to practice this is at parties. Pay attention as you walk up and join conversations, and leave when there is no longer any stimulation. (Just don't do this with the host!) Conversely, notice what keeps you lingering when there is no more energy.

Another way to incorporate the four principles and one law into your life is to identify and encourage the following mental skills.

The Magnificent Seven Skills

Here's a little exercise to help you gauge where your intuitive strengths lie. The following is a list of seven skills that, although rarely taught in school, are essential for managing your life. Rate yourself on a scale from one to five, with *one* representing little or no use and *five* representing a skill you rely on frequently. Use your intuition to determine your place on the scale. Read the description of the skill, then ask yourself where you fit. Allow the number to come to you without effort. Circle the number, then look at it and consider whether it accurately describes your skill and experience level.

1. *Absorption of new information:* The ability to open yourself to new information, allow it to replace old information, and use it within a relatively short amount of time.

   1 2 3 4 5

2. *Acceptance of uncertainty:* The ability to live with the tension of not knowing the answer to something and to hold off making a decision until the time really feels right.

   1 2 3 4 5

3. *Awareness of paradox:* The ability to see and articulate conflicting views without having to deny one in order to support the other.

   1 2 3 4 5

4. *Anticipation of events/awareness of surroundings:* The ability to anticipate the movements of people and events before they happen—for example, driving a car and anticipating the actions of the drivers around you.

   1 2 3 4 5

5. *Sensitivity to flow:* The ability to keep moving with a view to the larger picture; also, the ability to recognize when a situation has no more vitality and to move on.

   1 2 3 4 5

6. *Timing:* The ability to be at the right place at the right time or to wait for the right moment to take action.

   1 2 3 4 5

7. *Self-reflection:* The habit of taking private time, on a regular basis, to reflect on events, experiences, feelings, and your life situation.

   1 2 3 4 5

Practical Wisdom

A *heuristic* is an incomplete guideline or rule of thumb that can lead to learning or discovery. An *algorithm* is a complete mechanical rule for solving a problem or dealing with a situation. If a task is algorithmic, it imposes its own tried-and-true solution. If a task is heuristic, it offers no such clear path. You must create one.

—Theresa Amabile, *The Social Psychology of Creativity*

Practical Wisdom

Don't put off for tomorrow what you can do today, because if you enjoy it today, you can do it again tomorrow.

—James A. Michener

All done? Evaluate yourself and think about which areas could use a little more attention and which areas you do well in. Remember, these skills are rarely taught formally, but they really can mean the difference between success and failure. They are simple to learn, yet challenging to apply consistently.

Take My Life—Please

You've learned the importance of being in the present moment from Blamah, now, take a snapshot of your "present moment" and let's see what it says about what will come in your future.

We're going to make two lists. For the first one, take a piece of paper and draw a line down the center. Title the left column "What Gives Me Joy in My Life Right Now." Under this title, list the activities in your life that fit the bill. You know you enjoy something when it does the following for you:

➤ You look forward to doing it

➤ While you are doing it you get involved and stay focused

➤ You feel challenged to keep finding new and better ways to accomplish what you need to

➤ You want to talk about what you are doing with your friends

In the right column, translate each of the things you listed in the left column into things you value and qualities you admire.

When I do this I end up with something like the following:

What Gives Me Joy	Personal Values or Admired Qualities
Work	Creativity, Productivity, Independence
Husband	Love, Loyalty, Intimacy, Partnership
Home	Stability, Comfort, Beauty, Nature
Children	Involvement, New Ideas, Deep Relationships

Articulating the good stuff in my life gives me a chance to appreciate more deeply the life I lead and to see that what I love about it really describes who I am. If, for any reason, I decided to look for another job or career, it would have to have many of these qualities in order to work for me.

Okay, now on to the second list. On another piece of paper, draw a line down the middle and title the left column "Things I Don't Like About My Life." Underneath, list the things and activities of your life that cause you distress and pain. We know we don't like something when we do one or more of the following:

➤ Avoid dealing directly with it

➤ Complain about it to others

➤ Do the bare minimum to get by

➤ Wait until the last minute to complete it

➤ Wish that we could pay someone else to do this for us

On the right column, translate each of these activities into the underlying contradiction, or paradox, that this represents in your life.

Here's what I wrote down:

Things I Don't Like About My Life	Underlying Contradictions
Clutter on the kitchen table	Clean space vs. need to browse
Insecurity of work schedule	I love working for myself vs. variable income
Working alone most of the time	Relying on myself vs. relying on others

I really don't like the clutter of mail, catalogs, and bills that accumulates on our kitchen table. I love a clean, open space. However—and here's the contradiction—I also like to look things over before making decisions on them, and the kitchen table is the perfect place for it. If I file something away, I forget about it. In order for me to stay on top of things that need to be dealt with, I need to see it in front of me and review it a few times before taking action.

Acknowledging these contradictions in our lives allows us to make different choices and come up with creative solutions.

X Marks the Spot

You might be wondering what this has to do with intuition. The answer is: plenty. The positive list marks the places in your life where intuitive information flows easily. With no contradictions there is no resistance and new thoughts and creative insights readily occur. Identifying points of conflict puts an X on the spots where intuitive informa- tion has a difficult time flowing. Remember that the things we dislike are the things we avoid, neglect, or don't want to get involved with.

Let's say that someone's conflict was that his job was no longer satisfying or enjoyable, yet his family obligations and responsibilities demanded the income that the job provided. The underlying conflicting values are (1) wanting satisfying work and (2) wanting to be responsible to the financial needs of the family. Both of these are admirable and appropriate values.

Many people in this situation tend to shut down and assume that there is no solution except to work through to retirement and then collapse. Intuition has a hard time getting through all that resistance. If both values can be brought to the table, new solutions and new choices can be allowed.

There's Something About Daniel

Daniel works for a large British bank. He and I met at a conference where he shared the following story.

He recently realized that he was bored with his job and that he wanted to do some- thing a little different, something involving facilitating teams of people. A few weeks later, he was contacted by a small consulting firm asking if he would be interested in working for them, doing facilitation! Although he really wanted to do it, he was the sole financial provider for his wife and five children, and the small company couldn't offer him the salary he needed.

At this point, many others would have given up, assuming that the dream was just that—a dream and not something that could be real.

Not Daniel. He went to his boss at the bank and told him about the offer. He asked if he could work a few days a month for the consulting group and continue to spend the rest of his time at his job at the bank. To the shock of everyone, including Daniel, his boss said, "Sure."

Daniel's story illustrates well how using intuitive principles allows for new and unusual events in our lives. Daniel was clear about what he valued and was open to working through the conflicts that arose. As he opened to the truth about his situation, includ- ing the inherent conflict, his life force opened to new possibilities and creative solu- tions. His intuition could work to guide him to success. Sometimes it takes more time to get to the resolution, and sometimes it happens just that quickly.

Setting Your Intention

Setting a life intention is like decorating your rental the way you want it, even though you don't own it yet. It is living "as if" your life were complete, while at the same time you are taking the actions which will complete it.

Setting your intention is the single most powerful thing you can do to put yourself on the road to success and personal fulfillment. It sets specific future goals and activates the forces at your disposal toward attaining it. It creates a tension between the present moment and a desired state.

When you intend something, you actually step into a desired state and decide that it's yours. Like making a big purchase, you first decide what you want, then you take it home, and the rest is making payments.

For example, if you're searching for a new home, there's a moment when you walk into a new house or apartment and realize that it is "yours." Not one sort of like it; *this one* is yours. In reality, maybe you haven't paid for it and you don't have the cash, yet emotionally, mentally, and spiritually it has become yours.

Intention works the same way. When you intend, you're choosing a specific future path and deciding that it is not only what you want, but that it's already yours. All that is left is making the payments. In this case, that means doing what's necessary to earn the money to pay for what you've chosen.

Bring your intention into clear focus by taking yourself through the following steps:

Practical Wisdom

Intention is that activity of the mind, energized by the passion of the heart, that wills something to happen. It is the wish or purpose behind the initiation of an action.

—Carol Adrienne, *The Purpose of Your Life*

Practical Wisdom

We earn what we want by connecting our gifts to the concerns of others. In this sense, the mission is a path of service, for nothing in this life comes free except the air.

—Julian Gresser, *Piloting Through Chaos*

See It

Setting the intention for your whole life isn't possible for most people; the endpoint is just too far away. It's best to look to the horizon of your life right now. Look as far forward as you can (for some of you that may be next week!) and determine what you'd like your life to be like. Give yourself some time, write it out. Give it a test drive in your imagination.

Feel It

How would it feel? If it feels right to you, set your intention. Say yes to what you want and feel yourself stepping into that new life just like you'd step into a new car, or some other large purchase. Feel some tension about how you are going to afford it. You may wonder how this particular future could ever happen to you. Don't worry—you're just beginning to feel the heat of commitment. It's a natural feeling and indicates that you've successfully set your intention.

Buy It

What would have to change in you to sustain this new life? Are you willing to buy it—to pay the price? When we want to accomplish something and have something new in our lives we have to earn it. Yes, there will be help from those universal sources of intuitive wisdom, but there is a price to pay, and the payment currency will be emotional, mental, and physical.

For example, you may intend to run a marathon. Great! The price is physical, mental, and emotional training. It won't happen without those things. Are you willing to commit the time and focused energy needed to run the marathon? *Intending* it will help focus attention on the goal and will attract to you coaches, support, and information that will help you. Still, it's up to you to decide to earn it.

Live It

Imagine that the forces of your life, instead of being scattered in different directions, are all focusing on achieving what you have just intended. Write your intention in a short phrase and place it where you'll see it every day.

Practical Wisdom

The journey begins in a place in which we have been taught to have very little faith—the black, contemplative splendors of self-doubt, something else they don't teach at Harvard Business School and something we would rather do without. But wanting soul life without the dark, warming intelligence of personal doubt is like expecting an egg without the brooding heat of the mother hen.

—David Whyte, *The Heart Aroused*

Put Your Career Goals on Cruise Control

If setting your life intention is like buying a home, setting your *career intention* is like buying a new car that will take you to your new home. It can be equally important, yet more flexible.

Your career is the vehicle through which you express your deeper values, achieve your goals, structure your day. It's the environment within which you grow and learn.

I'm using the word *career* very broadly. Your career may be raising children, taking care of an elderly or disabled parent, or taking care of yourself during a health crisis. Your career is whatever situation requires your focused attention and involvement for the majority of your time. You may be retired from traditional work, and your new career is traveling, playing golf, and taking care of your garden and your home. You may or may not receive money directly for it, but it's what you organize your time around. It's what occupies you.

When determining your career intention, you aren't necessarily going to choose a specific career. Right now you are determining the *qualities* you want in what you do. Ask yourself the following and write your answers down:

➤ What do I want to accomplish?

➤ What do I want to receive?

➤ How can I support or serve others?

Once you have a few lines describing what you want to do, how you want to do it, what you will get out of it, and how it will serve others, you're ready to set your intention.

See It

See yourself doing what you want to do. Visualize several possible situations to see which one fits you.

Feel It

Imagine what it would feel like to actually do what you wanted to do, to serve in the ways you'd like to serve, and to accomplish what you'd like to accomplish. In addition to a sense of personal satisfaction, your feelings may include your reaction to the challenges that go with any career choice.

Buy It

What is it going to take for you to earn what you intend? Maybe you'll need to go back to school, or get some other form of help. Perhaps you need to release some negative attitudes or bad habits that stand in your way. Maybe you need to speak up about what you want (as Daniel did earlier in this chapter) in your present situation. If what you intend won't unfold for some time, you need to develop patience. Look at the full price tag on attaining this goal, breaking it down into financial, emotional, physical, mental, and spiritual factors. Commit to paying the price and determine a "payment plan" that will work for you.

Live It and Let the Magic Begin

Setting your intention is like dropping a boulder in a calm pond of water. Many ripples are created that keep the water moving. The more focused you are on what you have intended, the more the ripples reach out and bring stuff back to you. Your job is to do what you need to do to *earn* what you have intended and watch for the opportunities, gifts, and support that you will encounter.

If you decide to take a trip, you first determine your destination. On your way there, you look for signs to tell you which way to go. The closer you get, the more signs there will be telling you how close you are and where the exact turnoff is.

Intuition works the same way. Once you determine where you want to go in your life and career, you can begin the journey. The signs along the way will tell you what to do and where to go. The closer you get to a turning point, the more signs you will see. When the time for a change is near, the signs become unmistakable. What many see as magic is really basic traffic control.

The Least You Need to Know

➤ Intuition works with natural timing as opposed to trying to control time.

➤ Only you can determine what is working for you in your life and what is not.

➤ If you are feeling uncertain and overwhelmed with new information, get used to it. It's part of building intuitive skill.

➤ Setting your intention is like buying a new home. You can live there before you own it as long as you make your payments.

➤ To set your intention, see, feel, buy, and live what you want in your future, today.

Chapter 6

Allowing Your Dream To Happen

In This Chapter

➤ Learn to take powerful action

➤ Allow miracles to be part of your life

➤ Learn to recognize the abundance of opportunities around you

➤ Adopt intuitive success strategies

➤ Use continuous intuitive planning

If you think it's tough to live your dream, think of Madame C. J. Walker. Born to former slaves on a Louisiana cotton plantation, she spent 20 years as a laundress. At the age of 37, however, she invented a hair-care product that made her the wealthiest black woman in the United States.

While delivering laundry Madame Walker often walked across the Eads Bridge, which spanned the Mississippi River and led to East St. Louis, Illinois. As she walked, she often marveled at the skill of the engineers who'd built this great brick-and-steel structure. There must be a way, she thought, to build a bridge to prosperity for herself and her daughter Lelia. This simple, daily prayer and intention, plus hard work, resulted in an actualized dream for her under incredibly difficult—many would say impossible—circumstances.

Everyone encounters points in their lives where they need to choose which direction to take. One direction promises something new, uncertain, exciting, with lots of positive energy. The other provides something known, seemingly secure and stable. There are no right or wrong choices, just the choice that is made. The best choices are made when you have a vision for a positive future, like Madame Walker did. Because of her vision, she recognized the opportunity when it came and made the choice to follow it. If she hadn't had a dream to begin with, the idea for her hair care products might have come and gone, without being recognized as part of her bridge to prosperity.

In the last chapter, you solidified your dream by establishing an *intention*. This chapter provides the tools you need to completely actualize your dream. The only ingredient you provide is the will to do it. That's the one thing no one can give you.

Practical Wisdom

Measure every choice as a step toward your dream.

Practical Wisdom

The moment one definitely commits oneself, then providence moves too. All sorts of things occur to help that never otherwise would have occurred. A whole stream of events issues from the decision raising in one's favor all manner of unforeseen incidents and meetings and material assistance which no man could have dreamed would come his way.

—W. H. Murray

Energize, Scotty!

Powerful action is doing what will further your goals without depleting your vitality. There's a secret all successful people have discovered: You actually *gain* energy when doing activity that brings you closer to your dream. When doing activity that takes you away from your dream, you lose energy.

Remember playing a game called "hot" and "cold"? You look for something while someone else directs you by letting you know how close you are using images of heat and cold ("getting warmer"). Intuition uses the same technique. Instead of heat, intuition uses energy. When you do something that propels you toward your goal, you feel great and gain energy. When your action takes you away from your dream, you feel tired and depleted by what you do.

Look for signs of vitality and depletion in how you spend your time by asking the following questions about your activities. To begin think of something you spend a fair amount of time doing right now in your life.

1. Is it hot or cold?
2. Does it feed you or deplete you?
3. Can you grow with it or does it stop you from growing?

You've probably had the experience of being revived by doing something wonderful and fun after a long, tiring, and perhaps frustrating day. I once saw a great refrigerator magnet that read something like: "If you want to see the dead rise, stick around until 5 PM."

The key here is to stop buying into the belief that work has to be tiring. You get tired when bored, unstimulated, unchallenged, and off your path.

Tried & True

Viktor Frankl, during his four-year imprisonment in a Nazi concentration camp, discovered that of the prisoners who escaped the gas chambers, those who had a life purpose (or dream) were far more likely to survive. Those who didn't, died. Bernie Siegel, a surgeon and teacher at Yale Medical School, and oncologist Carl Simonton also report that having a meaningful purpose is a primary factor for patients who successfully recover from cancer. In a new field of study called psychoneuroimmunology, we are learning that just thinking vividly about an exciting dream or goal, and imaging it as complete with all its benefits, can cause our body to create chemicals and hormones (such as endorphins) that balance our immune system, counter stress, and seem to create new energy.

—Ann McGee Cooper, *You Don't Have To Go Home Exhausted*

Take your boredom as an intuitive signal that you've lost contact with your dream. Get back in touch with where you're going and ask yourself: How can what I'm doing now help me realize my intention? Once you see that, you have instant energy.

Brooke Martis is a fashion designer. From the time she was two years old she knew that designing beautiful clothes for women was her talent and her life. After working for a well-known knit designer quite successfully, she decided to leave when they wouldn't meet her demands for her own label.

The next job that came along felt uncomfortable from the minute she met the owner of the firm. At the same time, she knew that the experience she would gain from the position would serve her well in achieving her ultimate dream, so she took it.

Sixth Sense

Boredom is being completely disinterested and uninvolved with something or everything going on in your life. I highlight it here because it is an important intuitive signal which is being ignored. To be so uninvolved and disinterested and to keep doing it, or to stay in the situation is self-sabotaging.

Brooke described her intuitive sense of timing as an "internal engine" that provided the information, motivation, and energy to take action on what she knew.

After fulfilling her initial contract, she knew it was time to leave and moved on without any prospects, knowing intuitively that the time was now. Within two days of leaving, she had a couple of consulting jobs and an opportunity to begin work on her own label.

Brooke's story is a good example of going ahead with something that doesn't feel right in the short-term but does provide a stepping stone to fulfilling the long-term dream. The negative intuition allowed her to prepare herself for the fact that the job would not be comfortable or long-lasting.

When working intuitively, your focus should stay on two points: the present moment and your intention. Energy spent trying to make something happen loses power. Working on and in the present moment creates power. Let's take a look at a few things you can do that will create more power in the present moment:

➤ Take pride in where you are

➤ Whatever you're doing, do it well

➤ Do your homework

➤ Set limits

Take Pride

Wherever you are on your life path has dignity and power. Whether it's at the nadir of a failed project or at the acme of a realized dream, each moment deserves respect. Each moment has something to teach and something to be proud of.

While having a manicure, I listened to the story of the manicurist, who had been born in Brazil to a farming family. She had always dreamed of living in another country. This was something that no one in her family had ever done. What gave her the dream? Her intuition was preparing her to live her dream. When the chance came to move, she took it. In her own words: "Some people may look down on what I do and say, 'it's not much,' but I know what it took to get here and I know where I'm going."

Excel

During the 20 years Madame Walker was a laundress, raising a child by herself, and living with the demeaning burden of racism, she maintained pride in what she did. She took care to do a good job of washing out stains, adding just the right amount of starch, ironing, folding, and then delivering. Even though she only made $1.50 per week at a time when the average white unskilled worker made $11.00, she kept going. For her own sanity and for the sake of her dream, she wanted to do a good job.

Focusing on doing her job well actually gave her the energy to keep going. Imagine if she had "let go" to the boredom and hopelessness of the job. What if she began to believe the negative messages she was getting about what she could do and what people considered impossible for a black woman in 1890? Her energy would have quickly dissipated and her dream would never have come true.

Doing what is in front of you to do and doing it well, regardless of whether it's your dream or not, will increase your energy and actually catapult you to the next phase of actualizing your dream.

Tried & True

To make a living, I took a variety of odd jobs. I cleaned houses, baby-sat, or did temporary office work.... The sheer boredom of the mundane tasks forced me to turn my attention inward. In quiet afternoons dusting a client's collection of precious glass objects or cleaning toilets, I had time to think...I enjoyed spending a little time with some of the old people I worked for who were homebound. For example, with one family I took care of their two children and their grandmother, Connie, who was in the beginning stages of Alzheimer's disease. Sometimes I would write down the things Connie said because they were full of poetry. I can see now how even that job was preparing me for my career as a writer.

—Carol Adrienne, *The Purpose of Your Life*

Do Your Homework

There are two types of homework that will build power for actualizing your dream. The first is to spend time *imagining* that you're already living your dream. Get in to how it would feel and what kinds of situations you will deal with.

By imagining what you want in full detail, a bridge is established between your intention and reality. Since your intention isn't limited by time and space, as is reality, it can pull together needed materials from the future to build your dream in the present. Here are a few ways to spark your imagination:

➤ Write stories about living your dream

➤ Draw pictures and sketches of your dream life

➤ Cut out magazine photos and paste together a collage of images that reflect the life you want to lead

The other power homework is to *research* your dream. Research also supports the intuitive process. Intuition thrives on an abundance of information. While the everyday mind can feel overloaded and shut down after receiving a certain amount of stimulation and new information, the intuitive mind can always absorb more. Research will also support your imagination to make the bridge discussed above stronger. Here are some simple guidelines for approaching research:

➤ Read about others who have done similar things

➤ Learn the skills that will be necessary for your dream to materialize

➤ Talk to people who are doing what you want to do

➤ Build a team of mentors, information providers, and role models

Take positive action toward the fulfillment of your dream and there's no way you can fail.

Just Say No

The limit that needs to be set in order to take powerful action is to limit activities that drain or lose power. Begin to notice which activities result in feeling tired and drained. You may be able to limit or stop completely some of those activities. Begin to do it. Say no to things that drain you and yes to activities that inspire and create energy. Some activities may be required, at least for the moment. In that case, limit the drain and

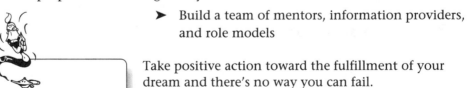

Practical Wisdom

The most important trait of a good leader is knowing who you are. You have to do all your homework, but then you have to go with your intuition without letting your mind get in the way.

—Edward McCracken, CEO, Silicon Graphics

exhaustion. Find something in the activity or job that you can learn from and something that you can contribute value to in the activity or job. Giving yourself a positive focus, even when there's not much to focus on, will create more personal power that you can use to actualize your dream.

Let Miracles Happen

Miracles happen when we experience the resolution of a problem, conflict, or painful situation without personal effort. When things come together in a way our conscious selves could never orchestrate, we experience a miracle.

The truth may be that our original intention is powerful enough to attract that miracle, yet the experience is one of effortlessness.

Carol Adrienne says it in her book, *The Purpose of Your Life*, and she said it during a workshop we were co-teaching: "The Universe is always sending what we need to fulfill our purpose." Our purpose is one overriding intention in our lives, whether conscious or unconscious, and what appears in our lives, is always a miracle. Whatever comes into our lives is our purpose struggling to reveal itself to our conscious mind.

Yellow Light

You can expect a miracle, but don't wait for one. As an old Russian proverb says: "Pray to God and keep swimming to shore."

The challenge is to observe and respond to what is being revealed. It's somewhat easy to accept positive miracles, but what about negative miracles?

While waiting for a delayed plane I heard the following story from a fellow stranded traveler:

> I had reluctantly accepted a job in New Jersey requiring me to move up from Virginia. While driving up the coast to look for housing and begin the job, the traffic was truly jammed the whole way. In places where there was no commuter traffic, an accident had occurred, or construction was going on. When I arrived at the motel the company had arranged for me I walked into the lobby—and walked right out again. This was one dump I would not tolerate.

> While waiting to drive out of the parking lot onto a main street, a well-dressed man came up to my car window, pulled a gun out and asked for all my money and my wallet. It was surreal: he didn't look or feel like the robbing type. I had my wallet on the seat and pulled out some cash to give to him, I refused to give up my wallet. The wind pulled a few bills out of my hand and onto the ground. While he was bending down to pick up the money, I drove away. At that point it became crystal clear to me that this was not the job for me. I had made a terrible mistake in committing to this job. I immediately called the company and told them I was going home.

Sixth Sense

Most often "miracles" are thought of as positive events. A *negative miracle* is not something conjured up by the devil, it is a powerful, life-changing event that involves pain or fear rather than joy and bliss. It is as unexpected and as powerful as a "positive miracle" plus the "negative miracle" can force attention to important areas of life we'd prefer to avoid.

He recognized the "negative miracle" aspect of this experience. Everything that happened had the same message. He knew the minute he said yes to the job that it was a mistake, yet he could not trust that feeling—he kept talking himself out of what he knew intuitively to be true. Because he was looking for a job, and this job showed up, he assumed he should take it. "How can I say 'no' to a job when I'm looking for one?" he asked himself. It took several strong experiences to convince him that his initial intuition was correct.

Human beings are a funny species. When something is not working, when the flow has stopped completely, our tendency is to push harder and do *more* of what isn't working!

The intuitive way is to:

➤ Stop when things are not working

➤ Reflect on what is happening

➤ Begin to move in another direction—be open to new solutions

From an intuitive perspective, things are always flowing toward the fulfillment of our purpose. At any point, your mind, will, and personality can get attached to a particular place or perspective and resist moving on. This creates a negative flow. Both positive and negative flow states are moving toward the fulfillment of purpose.

Intuitive signals are like highway signs along the way, providing information about how far away we are from our destination. When headed toward a particular destination, the expectation is that signs will point the way. If signs for the destination stop appearing, it's a good thing to wonder whether some turn-off was missed. It may be time to check a more detailed map and reroute. The closer to a destination, the more signs appear, giving the details of precisely how to get to where you want to go (unless you're going to New Jersey, where the system is exactly the opposite).

Add Up Your Opportunities

This may be heresy. We really do live in a Garden of Eden where at any moment the needed opportunity is right there, usually right in front of us. Unfortunately, it's hidden to the mind, which believes there is no Garden, only struggling and suffering for every little crumb. As Yoda said in *Star Wars*: "Luke, you will only see it when you believe it."

Tried & True

Maybe, in my wildest dreams, I could imagine that if I discovered some amazing discipline that gave me complete control over my mind and body, like becoming a Kung Fu master (though I couldn't really imagine that, either), I might be able to become so strong I could live a life without alcohol—a life of continual stress from resisting the need and temptation, of course. If you had told me the day would come when I would not drink anymore simply because I no longer had the desire to drink—that the deep, ingrained compulsion to drink was "lifted" from me, was no longer part of who I was—I would have dismissed the idea as insane. Or a miracle.

It happened. Today, I am not afraid to use the word. It is, in my own life, in my own terms, a miracle.

—Dan Wakefield, *Expect A Miracle*

Here's a three-part workout to help loosen your vision and let the opportunities appear. Before you begin, reflect on the following "opportunity" equation:

Desire + Readiness = Quality Opportunity

First, write down the area in your life where you most need an opportunity. Remember, intuition works on real juice, so if you're just browsing and not ready to buy in to an opportunity, your intuition will give you a so-so option.

Second, write down the following three items about your current day's schedule:

➤ One of the scheduled events of the day

➤ Something unexpected that interrupted your schedule already today

➤ Something you'd like to do, if you had the time

Finally, reflect on the following meanings for each of your items. Let the scheduled event you wrote down represent something that will help you be ready for the opportunity. To help you allow the intuitive meaning to surface, try the following questions:

➤ What activity is involved with the scheduled event?

➤ What skills are involved?

➤ What is the result of the activity?

Let the unexpected interruption represent something that you need more of. Ask yourself the following:

➤ What interrupted me?

➤ What was needed?

Let the thing you'd do if you had the time represent the mind-set or the activity where the opportunity will emerge. Ask yourself the following:

➤ If you did the thing you don't have time for, what attitude or mind-set would you slip into?

➤ What happens if I adopt that mind-set now and look at my world?

Tried & True

William Friedman built the Signal Intelligence Service, which cracked Japan's military and diplomatic codes during World War II. His work was so crucial that General George C. Marshall said it "turned the tide of the war" at the Battle of Midway. His philosophy: You can't rely solely on logic to solve tough problems. He urged his code breakers to rely on imagination as well as on more analytic tools. He proved his point by helping his wife and fellow cryptologist, Elizabeth Friedman, crack a stubbornly resistant European cipher. Rather than have her analyze the problem, he asked her to clear her mind and open it to random associations. Before long, she guessed the pass phrase that cracked the code.

Follow Up, Follow Up, Follow Up

Here's where your organizational skills will pay off. Use your ability to develop a system of following up with and responding professionally to the people you meet and the opportunities you encounter. Allow me to offer the following three guidelines:

➤ Articulate your follow-up philosophy

➤ Create a doable system to match your philosophy

➤ Do it, with a large pinch of intuition

Say It

What do you think is important in following up? When others have followed up effectively with you, what have they done? What has made it easy and enjoyable for you to follow up with others? How can you let those you come into contact with know who you are and how you might serve them?

Reflecting on these questions, write down your thoughts and begin to formulate your follow-up philosophy. Whatever you do, make sure you make it part of your philosophy to reach out to new acquaintances *more than once* before throwing out their business card or phone number.

Some people use the magic law of three times, while others keep contacting until they receive a "no, thank you." Be sure to avail yourself of the many wonderful, detailed books on networking and following up.

Set It

Whatever philosophy you decide on, create a system to support it that is simple and doable. Devise ways to follow up that are cost- and time-effective for you; otherwise, you will not work the system.

Do It

The best system has to allow for the intuitive process. At any point, you may have a stray thought about someone you haven't spoken to in many months, or even years. Follow up on that thought. Contact them.

You also may be having trouble reaching someone you want to contact. All of a sudden, at an odd hour, you think of her. Call her. Your intuition may be giving you information about *when* to follow up as well as *whom* to follow up with. Go back to the discussion of "timing" in Chapter 4 to review this concept.

Plan on a Higher Plane

The old way to plan was to write down what needed to happen, prioritize the steps, and then follow the plan. Often, these plans end up in the drawer, never looked at again. That kind of planning process would be great if nothing ever changed. If the world stayed still while the plan was worked, then the plan would remain relevant. The truth is that everything is always changing.

New opportunities and experiences require adjustments in the plan. If the plan calls for working with a certain person on a project, and then that person is called away on a important trip, the plan feels like a failure. Or perhaps, after the plan is established, someone new emerges who has a fantastic yet completely different idea of how to get to where you want to go. This creates such a conflict with the plan that either the new idea is ignored or the plan is trashed.

When the plan is abandoned, motivation is often not far behind. Without a plan, the structure of what to do next can fall apart and the energy to accomplish the goal dissipates.

There's a middle ground between creating and following a detailed plan and going from moment to moment: I call it *Continuous Intuitive Planning.*

We know that intuition works best when there is a strong intention, but traditional planning seems to fly in the face of intuitive thinking. What's needed is a way to maintain a strong intention to set the direction, a structure to focus continuous effort, and room for spontaneity so that new opportunities can be responded to and incorporated into the process easily.

Here are the two guidelines for Continuous Intuitive Planning:

➤ Focus on what you can do, and unload the rest onto the Universe

➤ Make room for intuitive knowing every day

Practical Wisdom

If you want something done, yet you don't have the skill or the time, pass it upstairs. Let the larger force of the Universe get it done.

Ready, Focus, Unload!

This is the basis of intuitive planning: separate what you can focus on right now versus what needs to happen. Most of what needs to happen usually involves meeting the right people, synchronistic events, right timing, and other things you can't control.

From a lecture by a "channeled" being called Abraham, I learned the best technique for intuitive planning. Make the following chart, and fill it in. Look at it every day and keep adding to both sides of the chart or make a new one every week.

Me	Universe
Show up	Provide new clients
Make some specific phone calls	Provide support people
Take care of my health	Provide continuous abundance
Write	Provide publisher for work
Improve my material	Provide ideas
Read	Provide books

This is an example of one of my own Continuous Intuitive Planning models. On the left side is what I can focus on in a single day. It provides a structure for me to get done what I need to and can get done. On the right side are things that I need to happen that I can't control. I know I need them, yet the thought of making all of that happen is exhausting to me and not what I enjoy. Besides, the Universe, having a pretty wide network, does a much better job.

Once I've unloaded all the stuff that needs to be done but can't be done by me alone, I feel free—free to focus my attention on what's in front of me, knowing that when the time comes, the right people and connections will show up. Guess what? It works!

Expect the Unexpected

Something else happens with this planning process. In not knowing when or how the Universe is going to bring the next opportunity, I pay more attention throughout the day. I've ended up meeting very influential and important people in my life in the most unusual places. You may have noticed that most of successful business life doesn't happen in the office. It happens on the airplane, in elevators, in restaurants, while playing sports, and on vacation.

Sixth Sense

Channeling was big in the late '70s and '80s. People who "channel" claim to make contact with a bodyless soul who has wisdom and a positive message they want to share with those of us stuck in bodies here on earth. Since there is no verification of the process, I listen to the message and decide from there whether the information is useful to me or not, regardless of who it comes from.

When you know something is on its way to you, but you don't know when or where it's going to arrive, you pay more attention—you're more excited and involved with everything because you're thinking, "This may be it!" The person you're interacting with may have the answer you need. It certainly makes life a much more interesting adventure.

Here is an Intuition Workout to help you recognize some results from Continuous Intuitive Planning:

1. List in your journal three people you've recently met in unusual ways.

2. Write down the circumstances under which you met, and what was on your mind at the time.

3. Describe the conversation you had with this person.

4. Track the intuitive follow-up. Will this person be a part of your life? Will what this person said to you be a part of your life?

Yellow Light

When you unload tasks to the Universe, you must also unload any expectations or images of how or when it might be done. The Universe has its own timing, and it is impeccable and may be different from what you want.

The Least You Need to Know

➤ Take pride in where you are and in what you do.

➤ Stop doing what drains you, and do more of what energizes you.

➤ When things stop working, look for another way.

➤ Unload burdensome tasks onto the Universe.

➤ Focus on what you can accomplish today.

➤ Expect the unexpected opportunity.

Chapter 7

Making Powerful Choices

In This Chapter

➤ Learn to choose success

➤ Practice intuition exercises for making powerful choices

➤ Learn to use your intuition when playing blackjack

➤ Discover when intuition is not enough

➤ Learn the power of waiting

So what's the big deal about making choices? Each day you make choices a minimum of 10 times an hour, 10 hours a day. That's a minimum of 100 choices every day. With all that practice you should be good at it by now, right? Think again.

A young concierge waitress shared the story of how she picked the winner of the Kentucky Derby the day before the race. She didn't know much about racing, but she did hear about one horse, Real Quiet. The horse was a long shot—14 to 1. Her boyfriend told her she was crazy to bet on it. She chose to put money down on the horse and the horse won. She was quite excited about it.

Several choice points mark her success.

1. She chose to pay attention to the upcoming Kentucky Derby.

2. She decided to bet on a horse she had a "feeling" about.

3. She chose to stay her course, even in the face of negative vibes from her boyfriend.

4. She chose to follow up and took the time to make the bet.

There is one more overriding choice that she had to have made—the choice to be successful. Some people call it luck; I call it *making powerful choices*. In this chapter, you'll discover how to make powerful choices in your life, thus stimulating your intuition in two ways:

1. Intuition will help you make the powerful choices to begin with.

2. Once the choice has been made, intuition works to fulfill the promise of that choice.

What'll You Have: Success or Failure?

I recently spoke to Micki, a good friend of mine. Over the past 10 years she has lived through tremendous changes in her life, including raising four children, getting divorced, and starting her own divorce recovery group. As we spoke, she shared with me how excited she was to have been recently accepted into Columbia University's School of Social Work to begin working on her master's degree.

Micki, who hadn't completed her bachelor's degree until last year, was reveling in how she's accomplished what just a few years ago seemed completely unattainable to her. On top of it all, she's writing a book on divorce recovery and, after struggling with the decision, decided that she just did not have the time to get a job to support her during school. There were too many important projects in her life and she decided that there had to be another way to find the money. She made the *choice* to not work at an outside job while attending school. She then discovered company stock from her mother's estate that had been tucked away somewhere. It amounted to exactly what she needed to cover her costs for the first year of school!

All successful people know this law. Think about it. If you plan your life based on what's in your budget right now, you most likely can't afford to do much. On the

Practical Wisdom

Vision first, money second.

other hand, once you create a tangible vision, resources will flow to support it. Micki did not discover the stock a year before she needed it, when she was applying to school, but rather after she had been accepted and after she made the choice to not get an outside job. She was well on her way, ready to make appropriate sacrifices, unwilling to sacrifice her time and energy, to reach her goal. The need was clear, her choice was clear, and the needed resource appeared.

Choosing success is not a vague or mystical act. It's a master choice that guides all the other choices you make each and every moment. Here are the three stepping stones to choosing success:

➤ Step Up

➤ Step In

➤ Step Out

Step Up

It's a common baseball metaphor: Step up to the plate. Take up the challenge of your life. Decide to go for it—whatever *it* is for you, without knowing how you're going to do it, or even what first steps need to be taken. Stepping up is the internal act of deciding that a life of useless pain and frustration is not for you. You may be surrounded by disabling, disempowering circumstances, but you still have *you*. You can choose to define what success is for you in this situation, and choose it. It may be to survive and move on when possible, or it may be to stand up and walk out of a situation that seems like a dream to everyone else, yet is a prison to you.

Stepping up to your life means taking a good hard look at what is, then choosing something different if you don't like what you see. Choosing something different doesn't require that you know what to do next. To know that something else is possible and that you're willing to discover what that is, is enough.

Stepping up to your life sets a new pattern in motion. It's as simple as asking: "If this is my life right now, what choices do I have?" Imagine if a mail carrier decides to shift his route and deliver the mail in a different order. Even changing one element of the route will change everything. At first, it creates a little chaos. It changes the routine for all those who are used to getting their mail at a certain time each day. The mail carrier may have his own reasons for making the change, and it affects everyone involved.

Step In

Keeping with the baseball metaphor, once you're up to the plate, the next step is to start swinging. The choice made in stepping up has set new patterns in motion. New opportunities and situations now arise spontaneously. Stick to the feeling of what you have chosen and make choices that match. If your choice is to become voluntarily unemployed, supporting yourself through simple living and accrued savings, your choice will be to buy an economical, durable car as opposed to a flashy sports car. If your choice is to live healthier, you may start choosing different food or reorganizing your time around new physical activities.

Stepping into your life doesn't require making big changes or big moves. It's really the little, everyday decisions that will support the movement in your life. In Chapter 6, you learned that all you can do is focus on what can be done right now. Your "right now" will lead you into your future. Choosing success means choosing each moment to act in ways that support your sense of self.

Tried & True

[Celebrated baseball player] Mark McGwire, who topped Babe Ruth (61) and Roger Maris' (62) home run records (1998), visualizes the pitcher throwing the baseball before each at-bat. He also has chosen success and works hard at improving his batting and his physical fitness. "I've never seen anybody that intense," the Cardinals' Howard said, "or someone that can concentrate like that. He hit a grand slam once and when he got to home plate, he seemed a little surprised all these guys were waiting for him. He got back to the dugout and asked, 'How many guys were on base?' He stands there with his eyes closed, and he's already envisioning what he's going to do."

—*New York Times*

Step Out

Stepping up and stepping in are both internal activities. They have set the ball in motion. Now it's time to move. *Stepping out* is talking openly about who you are, what new choices you're making, and what new things you're looking for. Live who you are in a way that lets others know. Through actions, words, and results, your life of success will unfold at a faster and faster pace. By letting others know where you're headed, they'll be able to provide support and referrals.

One note of caution. When embarking on a new path, some people in your life may not be able to share your enthusiasm. In fact, your new path may seem like a threat to them for some reason. Use your intuition to choose whom to share your new choices with. Especially at the beginning of a new endeavor, when it's most vulnerable, be aware that some people may be unable to support your new choices. To try to convince them of the validity of your ideas would only drain you.

Power Choosing

This section provides practical workouts to help you flex your intuitional muscles by making powerful intuitive choices. Each exercise is designed to stimulate a deep sense of intuitive knowing and to bring that to your conscious mind. Some will work better than others for you. Once you become familiar with an exercise by doing it a few times, take it with you for a week and use it every day. At the end of the week, it will be a part of your life and it will require almost no time or effort to sense your intuitive knowledge about something in your life.

Which Path Should I Take?

When you have two or more options and need to decide on one, do the following:

1. Write down the situation and the options you're considering. Number the options.

2. Imagine yourself walking down a path, real or imaginary. Notice the time of day, the season, the weather. Relax as you walk down this path and enjoy the scenery.

3. The path comes to a place where it forks into as many paths as you have options. Number the paths to correspond to the number of your options.

4. Walk down path number 1. This path represents your first option. As you walk, notice what you feel, what you see, what happens on this path, where it takes you. Absorb the experience of walking this path, taking in intuitive information about this option. When you're done, go back to the fork in the path.

5. Repeat Step 4 for all of the paths.

6. Write down your results and digest the information you have received.

After you become familiar with the mechanics of this workout, it's easy to use it every day without having to take lots of time. When I am faced with a choice, I take a deep breath and feel myself moving down the path of taking that choice. Immediately, I know whether it's appropriate for me to make that choice.

When beginning to use this workout, though, it's important to allow yourself some time to get into it. Allow the imagery to take over and note all the sensations and feelings that occur. Even though you may know immediately, as you walk a path, that it's dangerous or uncomfortable, it may still be the choice you want to make. You aren't necessarily looking for the easiest path, but for the one with heart and meaning for you.

Can I Dance to This?

Imagine for a moment that your life is a dance. It has a unique rhythm, differing tempos, many variations. Your life dance interacts, intersects, and blends with the dances around you. You learn from the dances of others, just as they learn from you.

Dance involves movement and constant change. Even when something sad is being danced, there is an underlying connection to the life force. Things end, cycles change, and life goes on while particular parts of life shift and die. Dancing connects us to that underlying life force and allows creative expression in ways words can't adequately describe.

Practical Wisdom

It's got a good beat and I can dance to it. I'll give it a 10!

—Dick Clark, *American Bandstand*

When making life-changing choices (and what choice *doesn't* change your life?), it's always important to check the *danceability* of the choice. When you make a choice, there needs to be room for you to be yourself, to grow, to laugh, to play, to share, and to learn. I sum this all up with the phrase: "Can I dance to this?" That is, does this choice allow my life force to flourish? (The question may sometimes be "How can I dance to this?" when the situation is set and you need to walk through it.) If not—if it feels overly restrictive, or if there is no room for movement and growth—is it worth it? Will what you gain be worth the energetic price to be paid? Only you can answer that question, and there is no right or wrong.

Some people dance through the most destructive situations and emerge with tremendous vitality. Look at Nelson Mandela. He kept his spirit alive through 26 years in prison by finding a way to continue his dance. When he emerged from the ordeal, his vitality and personal power were ready for the next challenge.

Who's at the Door?

Before you let someone into your home, you first open the door (or peek through the spy hole) and see who it is. The door acts as a buffer between you and whomever is on the other side. It gives you time to decide whether to let them in or keep them out.

You can use the same system for checking out opportunities before moving on them. Intuition anticipates and guides (remember our warning lights from Chapter 2), so when a new opportunity comes knocking, your intuition already has a sense of the quality of this opportunity and whether it is in alignment with your life goals.

When an opportunity presents itself to you, take a moment to pause, then imagine that the opportunity is on the other side of a large door, ringing the doorbell. As you imagine yourself approaching the door, ask yourself: "Who could this be?" and "What do they want?" Open the door in your mind's eye and notice:

➤ How you feel

➤ Your immediate response to what is on the other side of the door when you open it

➤ Who or what is standing there

➤ Your comfort level with walking through the door

Ask them: "What do you want?" Ask yourself: "Is this for me? Will it help me achieve my goals?"

After a little bit of practice, all of these workouts can become a part of your normal thinking repertoire. Whenever a new situation presents itself to you, you will have easy access to your intuition, on the spot. They take less than a minute to use and can be done anytime, anyplace. The key is to practice them enough so they become part of you. You'll then have established a link allowing information from your intuitive self to flow to your conscious self.

Practical Wisdom

Not every acorn that falls from the oak becomes a tree. Not every opportunity that comes into your life is right for you. Check it out intuitively. Pause, then ask: How does it feel? Is it for me?

Applying What You've Learned

Now we're going to walk through the previous workouts using two specific situations:

➤ Deciding between two or more job opportunities

➤ Deciding whether to leave or stay with a current job

These can be adapted to fit any decision-making situation.

Decisions, Decisions

1. Create a column on a piece of paper for each job opportunity. These may be jobs that are being offered to you, career choices you're considering, or perhaps educational opportunities you're choosing between. Label each opportunity with a letter such as A, B, or C.

2. Walk down the path workout and, at the fork, imagine a path for each of your opportunities. Write down your results for each path in the corresponding column. Also write down any personal impressions and evaluations of each opportunity.

3. Imagine yourself dancing with each opportunity, one at a time. Perhaps there is an imaginary partner for each one, or perhaps you're dancing to different music in a different atmosphere for each alternative. Write down your experiences with this exercise in the appropriate column for each opportunity.

4. Now imagine yourself saying yes to opportunity A. Note how you feel. Imagine yourself in opportunity A in six months. Note how you feel. Imagine yourself in opportunity A in a year. Note how you feel. Write your results in column A. Repeat this workout with each of your opportunities.

Now you have a database of intuitive input to add to any analytic input you're considering in making this decision.

Should I Stay or Should I Go?

Let's assume for this workout that you're unhappy with your current situation yet don't really know what else to do. I've stated it as a work-related situation, but it could be anything. Do the following:

1. Write down the situation as you see it—what you're unhappy with and your thoughts on leaving.

2. Imagine that for some reason you had to stay with this situation. Use the dance workout and see what it would take to find something danceable for you in this situation. What could you do to make this situation not just tolerable, but fun and challenging? Focus on one or two elements of the situation that give you joy and imagine a way to expand those parts. Perhaps making this situation tolerable means saying something to someone that you have been avoiding, or perhaps you can begin to take up a fun hobby after work. Write down your results.

3. Now imagine yourself dancing into the unknown, saying good-bye to this situation and moving in a new direction. How does that feel? What parts of you can now express themselves? Where does this lead you? Record your results.

4. Imagine yourself in a hallway with two doors, one marked *stay* and the other marked *leave*. Pause for a moment and then walk over to one of the doors. Open it and notice everything that you see, feel, hear, and sense. Then go to the other door and do the same thing. Write down your results.

5. Sit with all the data for a day or two.

Still Scared to Death?

The intuitive answer is either clear or not. The decision is right in front of you, or not there at all. What you're looking for is the *clear knowing*. Clear knowing doesn't mean you won't have conflicting feelings. You can know what you need to do and still be scared to death to do it, or want the intuitive answer to be something else.

Right now look at what you know intuitively. Whether you choose to act on it or not is another matter and can be put aside for now. What is important now is that you access your intuitive knowing and recognize it, even with the emotional reactions around it.

When To Call 411

If there is not a clear direction or answer, it's time to get more information. If the intuitive knowing is not clear, do not act. If action must be taken, move very slowly, take your time.

Often action is taken toward something desired. Something is wanted and action is taken to get it. The intuitive way is to recognize what is wanted, pause and focus internally, then act from an internal urging. Often the most effective way to get what is wanted is to take indirect action.

When there is no flow, when the next move is unclear, get more information.

Yellow Light

Embracing illusions is not unusual when you're upset. Suppose you're working in a job you hate and the only thing on your mind is finding new employment. If interviews are slow in coming, you may panic. Negative thoughts like "Maybe I'm not going to find a decent job" or "Maybe I'll be stuck in my present position for years" may flood your mind. A pressing need to leave, coupled with increasing doubts about finding a new job, can make you susceptible to misreading new situations and welcoming illusions offered in order to entice you to take a new position. Finding a job, any job, may become more important than finding a good work opportunity. People in this spot usually grab the first offer, overlooking any negatives.

—Richard M. Contino,
Trust Your Gut

The Power of Waiting

The most powerful action one can take is to wait. For those of us raised in Western culture, waiting is often the most difficult thing to do. We are trained to act, to make something happen, to take charge of our destiny, to go out there and get it.

Intuitive skill is more precise. It works on the principles of leverage and timing. You are one person out of many. You have limited power on your own. Using your intuition you can leverage your action so that a small act creates large movement. Acting powerfully at the right time creates the largest payoff.

Think of waiting as part of a sound budgeting strategy. Your budget includes money available to spend as well as available energy to spend. The payoff or profit you're looking for includes an increase of money returned as well as energy generated. If you spend too much money trying to make something happen, even if it happens, the project is a financial loss. The same philosophy is true with energy. If you spend too much energy making something happen and end up depleted at the end of a project, it's an energy loss.

When there is nothing to do, and you wait, you're building your energy resources so that when the time to act appears, you are ready.

Don't Wait Too Long

If waiting comes from the fear of making a mistake, it's not intuitive waiting. The moment to act often comes before analytic validation for taking the action. There is an urge to act, a quiet sense of *now*, that accompanies intuitive timing. As Lee Iococca says: "Unlike fine wine, good information does not age well. If you wait, by the time you act, your facts will be out of date because the market has moved on.... At some point, you have to take the leap of faith. First, because even the right decision is wrong if it's made too late. And second, in most things there is no such thing as certainty."

Hit Me: Blackjack for Fun and Profit

If you're feeling courageous and would like an instant way to practice intuitive skill, you can try playing Blackjack. Playing Blackjack requires money, so real life juice is generated. It can be broken down into a series of yes or no movements, so it's simple. There is no waiting allowed; all decisions need to be made instantaneously, without analytic thought. It triggers greed, desire, and fear, all of the emotional elements that can distort intuitive knowing. If played with awareness and within limitations, it can provide an instant evaluation of your intuitive sense and what gets in your way.

It's not for everyone. The atmosphere is often noisy and disruptive and highly pressured. You may not function well in this kind of setting. It's great to know your limits and to adhere to them. There are plenty of other ways to develop and evaluate your skill.

Here's how to approach the table:

➤ Find a quiet, out-of-the-way table.

➤ Don't drink alcohol.

➤ Practice the following yes and no signals before you arrive.

➤ Completely let go of any analytic tools, including systems of cutting and memorizing cards.

➤ Set a financial limit for yourself, and when you reach it, quit.

➤ As soon as you're done, track in your journal how you did and what you learned.

➤ Decide on one, consistent amount to bet every time—perhaps $1, $5, or $10.

Practical Wisdom

I can remember the day I made that decision, I felt trepidation. I was nervous. I was worried. But I also had a sense of real calm. I walked away from the deal. I made a decision that ultimately what they wanted was not in the best interest of my company; even though I knew politically it would be wonderful. It didn't fit in with the long-range goals of Marvel.

—Margaret Loesch, as President of Marvel letting go of a deal with Disney

And here's how to play:

1. Take a few relaxing, deep breaths.

2. Begin to say the word "yes" to yourself.

3. As you repeat it, allow the feeling of yes to take over.

4. Feel the sense of yes, the smell of yes, the physical sensation of yes.

5. Now let the feeling of yes condense into one movement or feeling.

6. Imagine yes as one simple, unmistakable, internal signal.

7. Repeat the exercise with the word "no."

Now you have your signals, unmistakable and personal. Practice using them for a few days. Say *yes*, then *no*, to yourself and experience the signals.

When you play Blackjack, listen for your internal signal at every decision point—that is, whether to play this hand or not and whether to receive a "hit" card or not.

Watch how your mind, your desire, and your fear override your intuition. Track what happens when you follow your intuitive sense only. Remember, your goal is to pay attention to your intuitive process and practice listening under stressful circumstances. If you win, it will be a bonus and an indication that you are listening.

Practical Wisdom

I asked Doyle Brunson (world champion poker player) what made him a cut above the poker world. "Intuitive sense," he replied. I asked if he thought is was a gift, or something he'd developed. "A gift," he said. He went on to say that he'd had this gift as a teenager, used it to develop the bankroll that would be his working capital in clawing to the top.

What is intuition? It is the sense, not reasoned out through painstaking logic, that a given decision is the correct one. It's an awareness of all the variables without taking the time to itemize them. It is the knowledge that a certain course of action will prevail—win the most or lose the least, insofar as poker is concerned.

—Roy Cooke, from
Card Player (magazine)

The Least You Need to Know

➤ You achieve success by choosing success.

➤ Vision first, money second.

➤ Success is chosen by stepping up to your life, stepping into the challenges, and stepping out into action.

➤ Get better at making intuitive choices by imagining options as paths, and envisioning walking down them.

➤ If a potential choice is not something you can dance to, don't do it.

➤ When your intuition is unclear, wait.

➤ When your intuition is clear but the reasons are fuzzy, act anyway.

Chapter 8

Using Intuition in the Workplace

In This Chapter

➤ Talk about your intuitions with co-workers and bosses

➤ Build an intuitive team

➤ Use intuition when hiring and firing, and during meetings

➤ Learn to love chaos

Intuition is one of the best kept secrets in business. After I had delivered an "end note" speech on intuition at a conference, a member of the audience came up to me with feigned anger and said, "You just gave away all my secrets to success!"

As we spoke, he revealed the seriousness of what he was saying. He had discovered on his own that if he trusted his intuition, he was on target with his work, successful, and seen as a star. Feeling a little like he was cheating because it was so natural and easy, he discussed it with no one. Then along comes this speaker (me) who blows his cover and suggests that everyone can succeed in business by developing their intuition!

There is a magic about life that many business people have attempted to codify, ana- lyze, and control. The magic has to do with the creative process that motivates and guides the growth of innovation and scientific discovery. This chapter shows you how to apply that magic in the world of business. Whether you're an entrepreneur, working solo, part of a large company, or attending school, intuition will be your key to getting ahead.

The Sneaky Truth About Business Decisions

Daniel Isenberg, in a study for the *Harvard Business Review*, spent two years studying decision-making techniques used by senior managers. The managers were all male, between the ages of 40 and 58, and had 10 to 30 years of experience. Eighty percent of those interviewed said they preferred using their intuition, "especially when making complex decisions or decisions involving other people." The same percentage also said something very interesting: that they were the only ones who made decisions that way, and that none of their colleagues did!

Many people use their intuition in business, but are reluctant to talk about it. Its intangible, unquantifiable nature means that it's somehow suspect, something to keep quiet about. Those who trust their gut feel that they're doing something wrong, or at least different from the norm.

Practical Wisdom

"The only mistake I ever made was not listening to my gut."

—Lee Iacocca

Weston Agor, director of the Master of Public Administration Program at the University of Texas at El Paso, has developed a test for intuitive skill and given it to more than 10,000 managers. Agor discovered that "intuition appears to be a skill that is more prevalent as one moves up the management ladder." He's convinced that intuition is a necessary skill for anyone in leadership positions, and that in fact good intuitive skill helps one move up the responsibility ladder. "The findings are unequivocal," he says. "The higher the level of management, the higher the raw ability to intuit solutions, and the more reliance is placed on intuition." He goes on to talk about one of his clients. "Disney's decision to approve the lucrative Epcot Center was a decision based as much on gut instinct as on analytical processes."

If you think about it, it makes sense. Analysis deals with the past. It takes what has happened and sums it up from different perspectives. Trends are important but can only be extrapolated so far into the future before they become useless. Today's rate of change is so fast that not even the fastest computer can keep up. Fortunately, we have intuition, which is a very human ability to sense and feel which ideas can make it in the future.

Learn How To Talk the Talk

The overriding reason to bring intuitive thinking into the workplace more openly is that information is key to success. Intuition brings more information into the decision-making process. The fact that intuitive information is non-analytic makes it challenging, but not impossible, to integrate into corporate structures. In fact, the use of intuition adds creativity, inventiveness, and agility to corporate processes, making them more flexible during times of change.

Following are a few guidelines for actually talking about intuition in your workplace, whether or not you're the boss:

➤ Share your own intuitions

➤ Ask intuitive questions

➤ Deal with resistance through creative listening

➤ Encourage intuition, not emotional dumping

Spill Your Gut

Sharing your own intuitions is always a good opener. Fill in phrases like: "Call me crazy, guys, but I just don't feel right about this decision. How do *you* feel?" Be willing to postpone the decision by pausing for a moment to reflect whether the timing is right. The more willing you are to talk about your intuitions, the more willing the others around you will be.

By the way, while you're sharing, keep track of your intuitions. After a while others will begin to notice that your "feelings" were right, whether or not they were acted upon. You may be the next golden gut in your office!

Ask Intuitive Questions

Get to the intuitive side of issues by asking a few simple questions. The first step is remembering that there is intuitive information available in every person you come into contact with—and they may or may not be aware of it. Your job as facilitator, manager, or leader is to play the role of detective so that intuitive wisdom can be discovered and made part of any discussion.

Practical Wisdom

There are two kinds of intelligence: one acquired,
as a child in school memorizes facts and concepts
from books and from what the teacher says,
collecting information from the traditional sciences
as well as from the new sciences.
With such intelligence you rise in the world.
You get ranked ahead of or behind others
in regard to your competence in retaining
information. You stroll with this intelligence
in and out of fields of knowledge, getting always more
marks on your preserving tablets.
There is another kind of tablet, one
already completed and preserved inside you.
A spring overflowing its spring box. A freshness
in the center of the chest. This other intelligence
does not turn yellow or stagnate. It's fluid,
and it doesn't move from outside to inside
through the conduits of plumbing-learning.
This second knowing is a fountainhead
from within you, moving out.

—Rumi, Sufi poet (1207–73)

Here are five questions you can use to stimulate intuitive thinking among your co-workers:

1. Now that we have looked at the data, what do you really feel?
2. Which options have the most "juice" or vitality? Negative juice?
3. What are you ready to do to move this along right now?
4. What opportunities, people, and events are emerging in relation to this project? What is happening at the periphery? What does that tell us about the viability of this project?
5. Is this the right time to act?

These are very basic, innocent questions that fit within any corporate environment. They throw a net out to discover intuitive sensings of timing, flow, seemingly inconsequential details, and perhaps relevant synchronicities. They are questions with no right or wrong answers and they stimulate discussion. Use these or any variation during your next information-gathering or decision-making meeting—even if it's just with one person—and see what happens.

Deal with Resistance Through Creative Listening

Joel and Michelle Levy, co-authors of *Living in Balance*, worked with folks in the Army, getting them to meditate and build their inner selves. You can imagine the resistance they encountered! As soon as they started their program, someone would inevitably raise their hand and ask sarcastically, "When are we going to start singing 'Kumbaya'?" Joel and Michelle's approach was always non-resistance. "Go ahead and sing it now if you want," they'd say, "and then we can move on."

Tried & True

David Sun and John Tu of Kingston Technologies, a producer of computer accessories, "are quick, intuitive thinkers who've been known to decide to build a product on the 30-second walk between the parking lot and Kingston's front door. Their hit rate—the ratio of successful products to product introductions—is 90%, a phenomenally high number given the fast-changing world of personal computing.

—*Inc. Magazine*, Oct. 1992

Emotional discomfort is a natural response to something that feels new and awkward. Just like learning any new skill, intuition feels awkward at the beginning and some people won't want to even try it.

What happens to someone at work who resists learning to use the computer? When something is important enough to the group, it gets done anyway. We may scream and yell, stamp our feet, and not like what we have to learn, yet we learn it anyway and end up being glad we did. Those leading the way for the new skill can be compassionate for those who are struggling and help them as much as possible.

Change and newness always meet with resistance. If you attempt to bring intuitive thinking into your workplace, many won't like it, won't understand it, and won't want to participate. See this as an opportunity to increase an important component of your own intuitive skill: *listening*. Underneath the resistance you're hearing is a deeply held *value*. They want "the right answer," "to not waste time," or "to take appropriate action." If you can listen for the value they're attached to and address how intuition will support that value, you have made a new friend to intuition and have increased your own skill.

Encourage Intuition, Not Emotional Dumping

When you begin to disclose your intuitions, and ask others how they "feel" about something, some co-workers may begin to complain and whine. There is nothing more draining of creative energy than this.

Here too, you can listen for the underlying value, bring it into the open, and use it as a tool to discover where the "flow" might have slowed or stopped, or for some new solutions. As a leader, you cannot indulge in negativity or judgments about others. Here's an example of a recent conversation among board members of a nonprofit group:

"What's your sense about our next step?"

"[A co-worker] has cut me out of the loop. That wasn't very nice."

"It sounds like you want to be more involved."

"Yes, I miss being a part of the group."

"How about helping out with [a particular project]?"

"I'd love to."

Build an Intuitive Team

The *Wall Street Journal* reported the following story in 1991, the headline reading "We've Got a Hunch Intuition Is In":

"In 1987, Herman Maynard managed a product development group at DuPont's Wire and Cable Division. 'Rational skills were not sufficient to accommodate the rapid rate of growth in the industry,' Maynard explained. He and several consultants began offering customized courses in intuition development and creative imaging. The results were astonishing. 'Our work spread rapidly throughout the organization,' he said. 'One hundred percent increases in productivity were commonplace.' The time it took to develop new product ideas and make them commercially available dropped from three years to three months."

There are three elements to building an intuitive team:

➤ Trust
➤ Listening
➤ Follow up

Earn Their Trust

Trust is not free; it is earned. Like dividends on a blue chip stock, trust pays off in proportion to the amount invested. In developing team members, build trust by giving them room to show what they can do to accomplish the results you want. Set the goal, not the plan. Give them a clear vision of what you want accomplished, then let them figure out how to do it, given the boundaries of the business. This builds their trust in you and yours in them. At check-in meetings, ask:

Practical Wisdom

The idea flow from the human spirit is absolutely unlimited. All you have to do is tap into that well.

—Jack Welch, CEO,
General Electric

> ➤ What are you noticing?

> ➤ Where are you drawn to? What's catching your attention?

> ➤ What are your choices?

Resist telling them what to do, even when you think you know how it should be done, or an easier way to do it. Children don't learn to walk if they're never allowed to fall down.

Remember that the dividends of building trust, competence, and self-confidence will more than pay for your retirement.

Listen

If a team member has a feeling that there's a better way to do something, but can't articulate the new way precisely, many work groups won't or don't know how to support the gestation of what may turn out to be a breakthrough insight. A marketing executive may have an uncomfortable feeling that a particular approach won't fit the potential client, but can't articulate exactly why. Work groups and management need to learn how to encourage, respect, and develop this intuitive knowledge. This requires listening for the intuitive nuggets of gold that may be lost in the confusion.

Practical Wisdom

You can lead in two different ways, by knowledge or intuition. What makes a great leader is someone who uses both.

—Edward Keating, FMC Corp.
Director of Human Resources

Three things to avoid when listening for intuitive gold:

> ➤ Don't ask "why?" When someone comes to you with a great idea or vague sense of something, asking them "why?" immediately puts them in an analytic mode, and they can't access their intuitive mind.

Yellow Light

The immediate reaction of "That will NEVER work!" is a holdover from our toddler years when all we heard was "No, don't touch that," and all we could say was "no." Watch out for automatic reactions of "no" and experiment with another choice.

Practical Wisdom

Since the early '60s, when Harrison began climbing the ladder of corporate power, he has quietly watched his superiors ignore warning signs.

In 1989, E. Hunter Harrison finally got a chance to be heard when an investment group offered him an executive position at Illinois Central.

Now he says: "We do a lot of things around here on gut feeling," said Harrison, president and chief executive since early 1993.

—*Investors Business Daily,*
April 20, 1994

➤ Don't say "That will never work." Even if that's your first reaction, learn to say, "How might that work?" or "What direction might that idea point to?" before squashing even a wildly outrageous idea.

➤ Don't give the answer, even when they beg you. Keep asking questions and encouraging them to come up with their own answers. It may take an extra five minutes of your time, but the dividends of that time will add up to many hours back to you when they're working independently and successfully.

➤ Don't hold on to a "right answer" and wait for them to come up with it. Listen openly to their idea, take it in—then share your idea and collaborate.

Three things to ask when presented with a new idea or approach:

➤ "What is it that you really love about this idea?" Get them to talk about the essence of the idea—hidden in the idea is perhaps a need fulfilled or a talent utilized. While the original idea may not work, the need and the talent can be used to great advantage.

➤ "Tell me the story of this idea. How did it occur to you?" The story behind the idea is often rich with observations and creativity.

➤ "Who or what do you see involved with putting this thing together?" Instead of asking "why," this question helps the idea person use his or her creativity and intuition to round out the idea and bring it to a practical level.

The most important thing when listening is to be sincerely open to hearing the merits of any new idea or approach. It may not change the current direction, but it may set a benchmark or create options for future directions.

Follow Up

Following up has two components: your follow-up and your team members' follow-up. You follow up by tracking what the team member is doing, and how the ideas and intuitions are playing out. The team members follow up by fleshing out their ideas and hunches. If they have a great idea, write it up, work out some of the details, do some research. If they have a hunch about how a situation is going, track it. Were they right? How often are they right?

Here's an example that illustrates all the points involved in creating trust. A credit manager was working with a new client who happened to have an immaculate credit history and appeared to be a good risk. However, every time the credit manager tried to get the client on the phone, he was difficult to find, and every time the manager hung up the phone, he had an uncomfortable feeling about the client.

Eventually, the client called on a Friday afternoon, asking for the product he wanted to purchase to be released and saying that he was putting the check in the mail that minute. Against his instincts, the credit manager complied. Sure enough, the check did not appear in the mail and it was a struggle to receive payment.

Now, if there had been trust between the manager and his supervisor, he could have gone to his supervisor (or team members) and shared his discomfort regarding this client. If the supervisor had been tracking this particular manager's intuitive track record, he could have backed up the manager in his decision and they could have worked together to find another way to serve this client. Perhaps another team member would have made some other observation, which in and of itself might have been meaningless but, coupled with the uncomfortable feeling of the first manager, would have begun to build a picture. More questions could have been asked until the manager felt comfortable with the plan.

Tried & True

Donna Karan, a highly successful clothes designer, looks into her closet at the beginning of every season and intuitively "sees" what is missing from her wardrobe, then designs it. Ninety percent of her designs sells like hotcakes.

—*Working Woman,* May 1993

Too often in companies, the "rules" or "structure" override individual instinct and intuition. When there's no trust, the structure rules and valuable insight and intuition is lost, costing time and money. Structure is important; there's no need to "reinvent the wheel" for every event, but there are moments when large amounts of money or time are at stake and someone's intuitive feel can make the difference between overall success or failure.

Collapse the Box: Have Intuitive Meetings

Whose stupid idea was it anyway that meetings had to be joyless? Why do we buy into that idea when every cell in our body knows that we learn more, accomplish more, and create more when we're having fun?

Fun and joy go together with serious intuitive practices. They do not negate hard work and involvement. When people love what they do, they do more of it, not less. When they are drained by what they're doing, they do less of it or do it less effectively. As you learned in Chapters 3 and 4, intuition functions more fully in a joyful environment. This is not rocket science, nor does it take an MBA to figure it out!

> **Practical Wisdom**
>
> You know what? This work stuff can be fun!
>
> —J. P. Morgan executive

Business meetings have been the butt of jokes for years. They're notorious for being time-consuming and unproductive. Take the risk of adding some joy and fun to the business meetings you conduct and watch the involvement and productivity rise.

Here are a few ways to get started:

➤ *Ask:* Ask everyone how they really feel. It helps to disclose your own intuitive impressions to encourage others to talk about theirs.

➤ *Catch the first impression:* Intuitive insight is often the very first impression that occurs when faced with a new situation. Catching that first impression takes practice. After a new idea or a decision is presented, ask the team members: "How does this smell? How does it taste?"

➤ *Use power moments:* Begin team meetings by asking everyone to take a moment of silence to collect their thoughts about the meeting's agenda and write down a few personal thoughts, experiences, and feelings as they occur. Then go around and ask everyone to mention something they wrote on their list. This simple moment adds focus, depth, participation, and wisdom without taking much time or effort. Try it yourself before going into a meeting and watch how much more involved and prepared you are.

➤ *Encourage intuitive thinking:* Stimulate non-analytic impressions by having some toys in the center of the meeting table. Ask each participant to take one and reflect on how this toy might reflect an answer or new approach to the current situation.

➤ *Force a decision:* Before all the data is assessed and discussed, ask team members to state the decision they would make if they had to do so right now. Make the decision simple. Is it a yes, no, or maybe? What action should happen now, never, or later?

➤ *Distribute journals:* Hand out small notebooks to team members and ask that they record stray thoughts, dreams, impressions, details, and insignificant events surrounding the project. Spend some time during team meetings, or individually, discussing and comparing notes.

➤ *Isolate the unpopular idea:* Ask team members what the "unpopular" information or choice is regarding a current project or situation. Make it safe for them to bring up politically incorrect ideas.

➤ *Encourage reflection:* Encourage reflective and creative breaks. During coffee breaks, draw, use crayons, work with colorful paper. Do something that uses the mind in completely different ways than the busy-work of a normal workday.

➤ *Set up a mind gym at work:* This should be a place with creative tools and toys and quiet space. Like physical workouts, creative and intuitive workouts reduce stress and make things healthier.

Hiring

More money is made hiring the right person—and more money is lost hiring the wrong person—than in any other single business practice. Finding the right fit and then managing that fit is essential to financial success—and intuition can help you do it.

Intuition plays a major role in the hiring process. Following are a few techniques for developing your intuitive skill and using it when considering new hires. (These techniques assume that you have done and will continue to do the analytic side of hiring throughout the process. For example, if there are company guidelines, government regulations, or corporate procedures, follow them.) Once you've narrowed the field to 10 candidates or fewer, follow these intuitive steps before, during, and after each interview.

Tried & True

We were at a particularly difficult time. We needed some help, and this person had a well-known name. Everybody said okay. We invited the woman to make a presentation to our faculty in a setting that we call "grand rounds." It didn't go well, and this was nagging at me. I just didn't feel right with this. But everyone told me to hire her, so I did.

It was a disaster. It wasn't that it was a self-fulfilling prophesy. I didn't set her up for failure. It was horrible. Within four months this lady had alienated virtually everyone in the department. She was bitter and cynical.

I didn't follow my instincts and we paid for this one. Every time I've followed my intuition I've been right.

—Dr. Philip Find, SPAIN Rehabilitation Hospital, talking to Ron Schulz

Before the Interview

Before talking to the candidates, loosen up the possibilities. Instead of looking for an exact replacement for someone, or for someone who fits a narrow focus, open your mind to the possibilities; be willing to see the gifts and shortcomings of your candidates.

Here's a way to determine and acknowledge your biases:

1. Take a piece of paper, draw a line down the middle, and write on one side all the qualities you like in other people.

2. On the other side, write down the qualities you don't like in other people—the things they do that bug you. Draw on your experience at the office, school, or in the field.

3. For each quality you don't like, write down how that quality could support the work responsibilities you're looking for in the new hire.

During the Interview

Your intuition needs to have something to go on in the hiring process. In a short amount of time, you want to determine whether someone has the immediately necessary skills and long term possibilities within the company. Use the following guidelines to get your intuition involved in the interview:

1. Let them talk: Ask open-ended questions and let the interviewee fill in the gap. Don't be compelled to fill a moment of silence—watch their ability to be comfortable with uncertainty.

2. Ask real questions: Use a real-life, decision-making example from their potential job.

3. Listen for the qualities you need for the job: Keep your list of "qualities" handy and listen for them during the conversation.

4. Ask them about their intuitive feeling about the job: End the interview with a question such as: "Does this feel like the right job for you?" or "What is your sense of the fit between you and this company?"

Practical Wisdom

I was taught to never listen to my intuition when hiring—to only go with the "facts." When I was managing a department on my own, it just didn't work. When I decided to try to go with my gut, I started making much better hires. Now I always listen to my gut when hiring, and it's never wrong.

—Joel Namer, Program Director, Practicing Law Institute

After the Interview

After the round of interviews, narrow your choices to three or four candidates. Visualize each one in the job right now, in three months, in six months, and in a year. When you visualize them in the job, notice how they have changed and grown with the job. Pay attention to their learning skills. Don't be wowed by an initial burst of energy; look for longevity and loyalty.

Firing

Honk if you like to fire people. There would not be much noise generated from that bumper sticker. Firing is a job most people find distasteful, at best, and avoid at all costs, at the worst. Still, it is a fact of life that hires are made that just don't work for either the company or the employee, or both.

The intuitive side of firing has one main component: recognize a dead-end when you see it because everyone else involved already does. There are two crucial moments to pay attention to when you are managing others:

1. Right after someone new has been hired: If someone is not going to work out, it is usually obvious within the first 3–6 months. Why torture everyone? Cut your losses and move on.

2. When work behaviors change: Most people don't quit a job they no longer want, they force themselves to be fired. Why play "chicken" with them—it only costs your company money in time, vitality, efficiency, and cooperation. Talk to them and find out what is going on. Sometimes they don't even know that their intuition and work behavior is screaming—"Get me outta here!" You may be able to find a better fit for them, or put them out of their misery.

Sixth Sense

According to the dictionary, *chaos* is a state of disintegration and violent, random events. It is also the term used to describe a modern mathematical theory which relates to large and extra-large numbers applied to business and quantum mechanics. The gist of the modern understanding is that there is an underlying, larger order to things that seem totally out of control in the moment.

What Business Hates About Intuition, and What To Do About It

Where intuition is concerned, modern business is squarely on the horns of a dilemma. On one hand, companies need to maintain a stable, systematic process of planning, implementation, and control. On the other hand, in the words of Ralph D. Stacey, author of *Managing the Unknowable: Strategic Boundaries Between Order and Chaos in Organizations*, it is also "necessary to practice frame-breaking management, in which managers conflict, question, learn, and make new discoveries." The dilemma for business is that "the structures and behavior appropriate for stable management have to coexist with the informality and instability of the extraordinary form of management that is necessary to cope with the unknowable."

In other words, what business hates about intuition is that intuition isn't hierarchical, analytic, or predictable. Even the new wave of quality management and re-engineering (QMR), while innovative, doesn't have room for hunches and gut feelings. Following are some suggestions about how to make the two shake hands and try to get along.

It's Higher Anarchy, Not Hierarchy

Intuitive skill is not based on formal education or years of experience, but rather on insight and awareness. Someone at the bottom of the corporate pyramid may have an intuition that is equal to or greater than someone at the top of the pyramid. Strategically gathering intuitive insights in a hierarchically diverse way can greatly increase the chances for business success. Doug Mellinger, CEO of PRT Group, Inc., shared with *Inc. Magazine* how he leads non-hierarchically. "Instead of asking, 'How can I do that?' Mellinger asks, '*Who* can do that? *Who* knows how to do that? *Who* can help me get that done?"

Asking *who* instead of *how* changes everything. All of a sudden the world is open and available and everyone has value. Instead of the burden being on the leader to make something happen, creativity is triggered to discover who has the talent to do the job. Hierarchy is then turned upside down. The talent is the broad base; the leader is the one who sees it and engages it.

You Can't Pin a Number on It

The main intuition lament in corporate settings is: "Yeah, it works, but how do we quantify it and back it up with data? How do you expect me to go to my boss and say that I don't think we should proceed with a project that we've spent tons of time and money on because I have a gut feeling about it?"

On the other hand, intuitively we can know what to do long before we know why we are doing it. A story gathered by Dr. Marcia Emery, author of *The Intuition Workbook*, illustrates this:

> "I was doing my morning stretching exercises as part of a program called 'Corporate Athletes.' While exercising, I suddenly had a sense that something was wrong and left to go to the area where we had a new product displayed. I found a problem that no one had caught despite all the testing we'd done. By finding the problem, I protected the company from liabilities that would have come from this product.

> "The product's supplier was called in to fix the defect and, after five days of looking at the problem with their engineers and ours, they arrived at a very costly solution. The next day I spent a few minutes looking at the problem and came up with a very inexpensive fix that all the engineers had overlooked."

Unfortunately, encouraging employees to follow up on hunches and gut feelings and communicate non-analytic information has not been a priority for most companies. Many preventable problems run their full course, while the managers involved are waiting for analytic proof before taking action.

What to do? Broaden the spectrum of choices made available to decision makers. Even Alan Greenspan, Chairman of the Federal Reserve, admitted in the *New York Times* that he uses an intuitive approach when determining interest

Practical Wisdom

You are liberated to imagine. Since you don't assume you're the one who's going to have to do things—or even that you're the one who has to know how to do things—you're not limited to considering seriously only the things you know you can do. Start thinking who, and the results are exponentially reinforcing: once you find you can make things happen that you couldn't dream of doing yourself, you believe you can do anything.

—Doug Mellinger, CEO, PRT Group, speaking to *Inc. Magazine*

rates. The narrow indexes used previously did not fully capture the movement of the market and the changing times. If he can do it, so can larger companies.

It's Unpredictable

Intuition is unpredictable in a couple of ways. First, the information and guidance received intuitively may stray far outside the boundaries the company is comfortable with. Second, intuitive information may not be forthcoming when needed. It cannot be relied upon in the same way that analytic data can be. Intuitive information can be developed and incorporated into the decision-making process, but it will never conform to rules and regulations. Learning to wait for the right time to act, allowing key factors to emerge, and changing direction in mid-stream are all intuitive activities that by their nature can't be planned for. Business people must learn to love chaos.

As my friend and colleague Ann McGee Cooper says: "There are at least two ways to approach life, time, and work. One way is the logical, practical, convergent way: define a task and get it done. The other is the innovative, intuitive, divergent way: define a task, then do something else." At first this looks absurd, but on closer look we find that we've all experienced the need for an idea or project to "cook on the back burner" of our minds before it's ready to come together. Every business person knows the importance of good timing. Strategic planning in the current corporate environment is becoming less focused on the details of a three- or five-year plan and more focused on building a collective vision and mission. This allows intuition to play a more important role in both planning and implementation.

As a source of valuable information, intuition is at least equal to analytic data. The methods needed to gather intuitive information require the skills of listening, expanded awareness, and sensitivity to subtle factors. And yes, you can go about your business ignoring your intuition and getting by, but it's like hiring a contractor to fix your leaky roof without considering several bids. You can do it, but it's risky with information from only one source. You might not find the leak!

The Least You Need to Know

➤ Intuition already plays a major role in business decisions—begin to look for it.

➤ Talk about what you know analytically and then talk about how you really feel.

➤ Stimulate the intuition of your co-workers by asking questions about timing, flow, and feel.

➤ When you meet resistance, seek out the values underlying the negativity.

➤ Don't ask "why?" Say "tell me more."

➤ Make business meetings fun.

➤ Check your gut before hiring.

Chapter 9

Making the Intuitive Leap to Your Next Job

In This Chapter

➤ Learn to move at the optimum time

➤ Discover the power of boundaries

➤ Recognize artificial limits and go beyond them

➤ Learn to negotiate intuitively

➤ Learn from the future before it happens

Shari shared the following story about finding her first job straight out of college:

> I had several interviews that, while they went very well, didn't feel right to me. Two very substantial positions were offered and I turned them down. My friends and family thought I was completely nuts. I had no solid prospects other than the two offers I declined, yet neither of them felt right to me. I had a feeling there was something else out there.

> Within two months, I got my dream interview and my dream job offer. That job set the tone for my whole career in a field I am extremely happy with. Had I jumped at one of the first offers, I would never have had this opportunity. It sounds easy now, but I'll never forget those two months of managing not only my own fears, but the fears of my family as well.

When To Jump: The "S" Curve

A window of opportunity opens for a short period of time for every successful shift in our lives. There is usually a gap between the moment of powerful action and the certainty of knowing that that action will accomplish what we want.

In baseball, a fly ball soars out to left field and the fielder positions himself to catch it. He won't know concretely that he has caught it until it hits his mitt. In a trapeze act, one person needs to let go and turn, sensing her partner there ready to catch her, but not certain until it happens. In these situations, the participants can at least use their eyes and their experience to help them. Often in our lives, we can't see something coming yet we sense the need for action.

Success comes with the ability to move with what is sensed, rather than sticking with what is known concretely or waiting for certainty before acting. You can do okay in the stock market following what everyone else is doing, but following everyone else will never create great success. That comes by anticipating the market and leading the pack.

The same rule applies to career moves. The ability to act on what is sensed, before concrete certainty sets in, makes the difference between living your dream and just making a living.

There is a graphic image called an "S" curve that describes the stages anything that grows goes through over time.

The classic "S" curve and its stages.

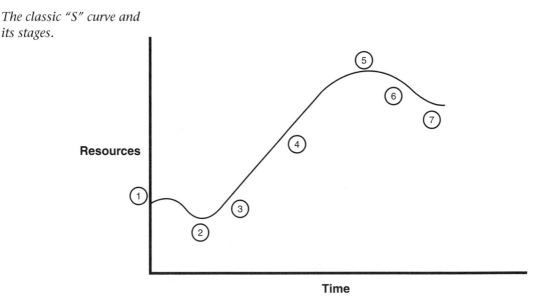

The stages can be described as follows:

1. Initial enthusiastic burst of energy
2. Project requires input of resources to get going
3. Growth begins, the project builds momentum
4. Growth rate increases
5. Peak output, goals accomplished
6. Growth diminishes
7. Project will either find a level of maintenance or stop altogether

What we're interested in here is what the "S" curve says about the best time to make a move for something *new*. The optimum time is somewhere at the peak and before the drop.

If the goal is to maintain steady profits, the time to begin marketing a new product is before the old product peaks. The time to get involved with something new is before completing the current project. The time to quit is just before or right at one's peak.

The best time to get into a stock is at its lowest point, and the best time to get out is just before or as it peaks. Those are the points where the data says the exact opposite. This is why intuition plays such an important role in determining timing.

That point can only be sensed because, until the output begins to decline, there's no concrete evidence that the peak has been reached. The wonderful thing about analytic data is that it provides concrete knowledge and a feeling of certainty. The unfortunate thing about analytic data is that you never know something until after it has already happened. When determining optimum timing, that's too late.

Apply the "S" Curve

In your career you'll go through many "S" curves. Projects, jobs, even completely different careers, will cycle through your life. Your intuition will anticipate the peak of the current "S" curve and prepare you for what is to come.

While speaking to a group of folks who had recently been downsized, I learned that many of them had experienced an urge to dust off their résumés and begin networking before any sign of downsizing occurred. Some of them heeded the call while others talked themselves out of it. Those who prepared made the shift more smoothly, whereas those who didn't had a longer gap to fill between jobs.

Practical Wisdom

Tom Scott, co-founder of Nantucket Nectars, believes that his "cluelessness" at the beginning of running his business helped him do things he never would have done had he *known* more about the business or been taught how to do things *right*.

Practical Wisdom

Any sailor worth his or her salt looks at the telltales flying from the mast, sails, and support lines to see where the wind's coming from and if it might be changing direction. We must look for the telltales in our own lives.

Look for Signs of Change

The move you need to make may not be to leave where you are now. It may be to remain within your current organization or work structure while doing something different. You may need to ask for a promotion, or for new job challenges. Perhaps it's time to go back to school to learn some new skills. There are many ways to begin a new "S" curve in your life.

Here are some tips for what to look for to sense the changing winds in your life:

➤ When it becomes harder and harder to show up for what you're doing, start looking for something new.

➤ When arbitrary, chaos-producing changes in rules, structure, or procedures increase in frequency, pay close attention to your inner messages.

➤ When the same idea keeps showing up in unusual ways, pay attention and begin to explore its possibilities.

➤ If an unusual class, conference, or workshop attracts your attention, attend it.

Practical Wisdom

Don Juan described it well to Carlos Castenada:

All of us, whether or not we are warriors, have a cubic centimeter of chance that pops out in front of our eyes from time to time. The difference between an average man and a warrior is that the warrior is aware of this, and one of his tasks is to be alert, deliberately waiting, so that when his cubic centimeter pops out he has the necessary speed, the prowess to pick it up.

Making the Move

A move to something new is rarely a leap out of nowhere. It's preceded by pursuing new interests, making new contacts, personal preparation, and loss of vitality in your current pursuits. Following the threads of change, paying attention to the more subtle movements in energy will result in a moment where the time to act becomes completely clear. There's an urge, an inner sense of *now*! It will not be risk-free or certain, yet it will be clear, if you've paid attention.

Build Your Launching Pad

Your personal boundaries are often seen as limiting factors, a fence separating one area from another. In developing your intuition, think of boundaries instead as your launch pad, providing both the designated landing and takeoff areas for the realization of your dreams.

Answer the following questions about your current situation:

1. What do you find intolerable in your current position? This might be the money, the people, a specific person, the distance from your home, the hours, the work, or other factors.

2. What is enjoyable about your current position?

3. What do you risk losing if you leave this job? How might you cope with that loss?

Write down three necessary components of a new job. Now imagine that you were offered a job with two of the three components. Under what circumstance would you accept this job? If you found a way to accept the job, then you haven't discovered your true boundary. Revisit the above questions. For example, you might have boundaries to do with salary, length of commute, and job-related travel. If you were offered a job close to home with the right amount of travel opportunities at a lower salary, would you take it? Let's say you'd consider it, if it looked like you would learn something from the job and have opportunities to gain more responsibility. Your boundary is not salary, then; it's job opportunities. What you're looking for is a job that stimulates and involves you.

Once you have identified your boundaries, take one at a time and write it in the center of a piece of paper.

Draw a medium-size circle around the word and in the circle write ways in which you could have this within your current position. What might you ask for? How could this job be changed? How might you change to get what you want?

Draw a larger circle around the first one and write other job possibilities that would support this boundary.

Do this for all three of your identified boundaries.

Sixth Sense

Boundaries establish the area within which we want to create. Just as an artist who works with paints needs a canvas and a writer needs a page, your life needs borders. The borders become powerful points of departure and return. Some boundaries are established through circumstance and some you create yourself based on what you want and what you don't want.

Practical Wisdom

Imagine yourself holding the nozzle of a balloon filled with air. Release the nozzle and imagine what happens. The balloon flies around the room from the propulsion created by the moving air. Air, without the limits of the balloon, just sits there—no propulsion. Air, limited by the boundaries of the balloon, can be a source of power.

Notice how creative and adaptive you can be as long as certain boundaries are kept. Having the boundaries also provides focus and power to take positive action. Knowing that you want to look for a job opportunity within 30 miles of your home makes the search easier to focus on. Having that boundary also helps you focus on what you want to ask your friends and network relationships.

Recognize the edge, the place beyond which you're unwilling to go, as a source of intuitive power for you. In making a career transition, spend a few moments building your launching pad and get ready to take off.

Here is an example of what the above workout looks like on paper.

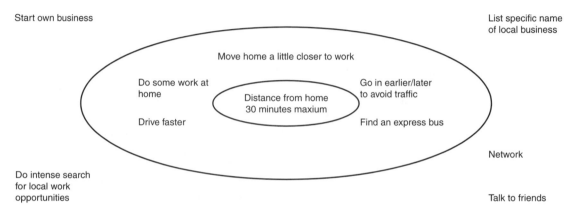

Work out the components of a new job on paper.

Practical Wisdom

Failure makes you better. Ben Stiller, who worked on a film with Mick Jagger that never happened, among other "missteps," says, "You learn more from failure than success." His father Jerry says, "Life is about building blocks."

The Jaws of Life

If the runway represents solid boundaries, the height a plane can go represents our limitations. We can now send spacecraft deep into space, and with the growth in technology, there's no doubt that space travel will continue to expand and break the current limitations.

We often set artificial limitations on ourselves that interfere with our intuition. These limitations are restrictive and unnecessary and need to be released.

Most perceived limitations are the result of faulty thinking, past experience, and training, and have nothing to do with your present circumstance. It's essential for your intuition to flow, to keep the channel of possibilities open.

The "Jaws of Life" are a device for forcing an opening through which a person trapped in a smashed car can be rescued. Let's use imaginary Jaws of Life to keep our possibilities open.

The other night my family and I were discussing the current state of nuclear weapons in the world. I suggested that the only sane alternative was for everyone to disarm. The others involved both jumped on the absurdity and impossibility of my claim. "That's impossible. It will never happen," was all I heard. After several minutes of discussion, I got them to at least admit that at some point in the history of the world it's a possibility, and that if it were done, it would eliminate many problems. At that point, they came up with several creative ideas about what it would take to get to the stage where world leaders would be willing to give up their nuclear arsenals.

It was a perfect example of what I am talking about here. No solution will evolve if the possibility is closed. As soon as the possibility is open, creative ideas flow. Sometimes it takes a real stretch of the imagination and a kind of mind strength to keep a possibility open.

Sixth Sense

A *limitation* is an artificial barrier mistaken for reality. In the game "magic circle," one person is placed inside a circle, which has been drawn around them, and they cannot get out until the circle is erased. If you play the game, the circle is real. If you decide to not play, the circle is artificial. Limitations are very similar. If you see them as real, they stop you from moving forward; if you see them as part of the game, they become tools.

The same is true in your life. The moment you dismiss something as impossible, you have closed the door to intuitive and creative innovation. Holding open the possibility stimulates the flow of creative ideas. Intuition does not like a vacuum, and if there is a need that is unfilled, intuition will fill it with a possible solution.

Getting Out of a Limiting Situation

The steps in the following workout will help you keep the possibilities open:

1. When stuck in a situation or decision, write in the center of a piece of paper the seemingly impossible thing you would like to have happen.

2. Draw a medium-sized circle around the word and write outside the circle all the things that make it an impossibility.

3. Draw a larger circle around the first circle and write outside that one what would happen if it were possible, such as feelings, experiences, or changes.

4. Somewhere on this page or on another, write the qualities of someone who could find a way through the limitations.

5. Next to this list, assess whether you have the seeds for those qualities right now and reflect on what it will take to mobilize those forces within you.

Here is an example of what this workout looks like.

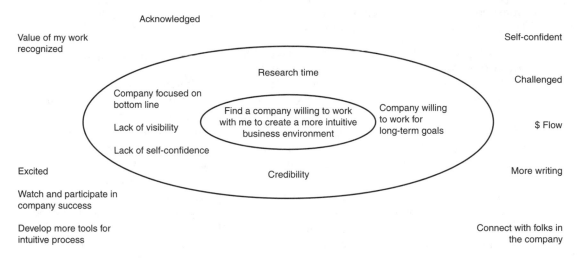

Acknowledged

Value of my work
recognized

Self-confident

Research time

Challenged

Company focused on
bottom line

Find a company willing to work
with me to create a more intuitive
business environment

Company willing
to work for
long-term goals

$ Flow

Lack of visibility

Lack of self-confidence

Excited

Credibility

More writing

Watch and participate in
company success

Develop more tools for
intuitive process

Connect with folks in
the company

Work out the limitations of a situation on paper.

What is discovered most often with this workout is that there's no limit to what you can accomplish, only a lack of focus and commitment to doing what it takes. The real question becomes: "Do you really want to do this?" and "If so, what are you waiting for?"

The ability to see through artificial limitations and discover new solutions and new pathways to achieve goals is a lifetime pursuit. You might live with a seeming limitation for years and then discover it was artificial. The more artificial limitations you uncover and dismiss, the more your self-confidence and personal power will increase.

When we say something is impossible, we are right. Conversely, when we say something is possible, we are also right. Roger Bannister broke the barrier to the four-minute mile forever by proving the "impossible" possible.

When I was in second grade, my best friend was chosen for the special art class and I wasn't. This of course left me convinced I had no talent for art. Twenty-five years later I noticed an art class that grabbed my attention. My first thought was, "I can't do art." Then I said to myself, "Wait a minute; why not?" I took the class and broke through many of the artificial limitations I'd been living with for all those years. These days I actually like what I paint and, bless their hearts, so do my children. It's not something I'm pursuing as a job or lifetime love, but it freed me to express an artistic side I thought didn't exist.

The same thing happened to my brother-in-law. He was told not to sing by a nun in 6th grade. He didn't—for 40 years. He finally broke his silence at one of our family Christmas sing-alongs. He admits to not being competition for Pavarotti, but finds joy in the expression.

124

How many of us are restricted and kept from joy by artificial restrictions imposed by others or, even worse, by ourselves?

The Career Opportunity Formula

A formula for using intuition is:

Intention + Powerful Action = Synchronistic Opportunities

➤ Intention: Whatever goals, or vision of what is wanted, as well as it can be articulated in the present moment.

➤ Powerful action: The most powerful action that can be taken is doing what is needed right now. That may sound simplistic, yet many times the work focus slips to doing something that is way before its time. It may be more glamorous or more fun, but it won't be productive.

➤ Synchronicity: The opportunities, people, and experiences that show up in our life, often with astounding timing.

At any moment there is an intention, whether conscious or unconscious. That intention dictates the next action to be taken. Once the action is taken, possibilities, opportunities, and experiences occur to support and direct fulfillment of the intention. From that point, choices are made as to which path to follow, eliminating other possibilities and creating new ones.

Practical Wisdom

Push the walls of the limitations you perceive. Find out how the limits might be moved, stretched, or released altogether.

For example, imagine you're planning a party. Your intention is to provide wonderful refreshments and create an atmosphere in which your guests will feel comfortable talking to each other, meeting new people, and reconnecting with those they already know. If you have all the refreshment ingredients at your home, the first action may be to prepare some of the food. If you don't have all the ingredients, the first action may be to go shopping.

Having an *intention* sets up what needs to be done next. The intention in this example is not to go out to eat with some friends, it is to have friends over to eat at your home. A different intention would set up different action and thus different opportunities.

Taking the story further to illustrate our formula, imagine that while taking the action to go to the store, you run into someone you forgot to invite, but who would be a great asset to the party. You invite him on the spot and he accepts. That's a synchronistic opportunity. If you weren't having the party, meeting the friend at the store wouldn't have been as significant as meeting him with an intention at work.

Tried & True

Scott had a great job as sales manager for a luxury gift company, but began to anticipate that it was time for a change. His career needed to move on and he wanted to manage new products, but he didn't want to move to a new town. Scott set his intention and began to talk informally to friends and associates about what he was looking for. He was completely happy in his current job and it wasn't a forced situation, but Scott's internal clock was ticking and he felt the urge to move on growing stronger.

It was his wife who noticed the newspaper ad: A luxury gift company was looking for a product manager located in the same town. Within a few months of setting his intention, Scott had the job he wanted.

The above sidebar is a perfect illustration of the career opportunity formula. Scott set his intention, then did what was in front of him to do. He did his job, spoke to appropriate people about what he was looking for, and was patient enough for the opportunity to literally come to him.

The clear and more conscious the intention, the clearer the next action becomes and the clearer and more powerful the synchronicities. There is no value judgment to be made. There are times when the intention is appropriately vague. Some high school seniors may not have any idea of what they want as a career. Good! They may choose to travel, work at many odd jobs, and in the process discover what they like and what they don't. Then their intention will become a little clearer and more focused possibilities will emerge.

Sometimes your intention really comes from what someone else thinks is best for you. In that case, there will be tension and unhappiness. What shows up synchronistically will not jive with one's inner sense. In this case, time needs to be spent in releasing the limitations of the artificial intention so that the personal intention can emerge. We must live our own dreams and make them our own reality. As Shakespeare said, "All the world is a stage." Well, we must each write our own script.

Let's revisit the three main ingredients to the career opportunity formula: setting your *intention*, taking *powerful action*, and anticipating the *synchronistic opportunities* that will result.

Set Your Intention

Setting your intention is like setting an internal thermostat. Set an internal gauge to your sense of what you want or where you're going. Another way of thinking about setting intention is setting and memorizing the combination to a lock. Once you have it memorized, you know it physically as well as mentally. There is a physical sensation of turning the dial to the correct numbers that will open the lock, as well as knowing the numbers. Often, if you forget the numbers, your body will remember the feeling of the turns and the lock can still open.

Yellow Light

Someone else's intention for you can be poison, no matter how well intentioned. If you can identify what *it* is they want for you and distinguish that from what you want for yourself, you'll be able to counteract their poison.

Set your intention in the same way. Memorize it mentally, physically, and emotionally. Then tuck it away inside where it won't be lost. Revisit the career intention you made in Chapter 5 and memorize it now.

Take Powerful Action

Look at what is right in front of you to do. What is ready to be done right now to accomplish your career goal? It may be a phone call, looking something up, getting more information. It's usually simple and very direct. It requires only you. Even if your new career involves many people, your most powerful action is what you need to do right now. It may be to talk to someone about what they are doing, or it may be to have a meeting. Whatever it is, the action to call the meeting requires only you.

Anticipate Synchronicities

Just as ducks line up when they fly, the synchronicities are going to start happening as you follow the formula. The challenge with synchronicities is that you can't make them happen. They are uncontrollable and unpredictable by nature. You can expect them, but you can't know when or where they will happen.

Yellow Light

Looking for the hidden meaning in everything that happens is not intuition—it's superstition. When synchronicities happen, the knowing occurs spontaneously. There is an experience of "something important just happened," even if the whole meaning of it is not clear at the time.

Interview Your Intuition

Interviewing for new jobs clearly requires intuitive skill. How can you know what the job is going to be like by talking to a few people whose positions are different from the one you'll have? You're interviewing the whole company, the potential opportunities for you, and the education you'll receive there as well as for a particular job. You're making a commitment on limited data.

Before the Interview Workout

As soon as you have a time and place for a job interview, begin the following workout:

➤ Do a mental run-through of the interview at least a day before it's scheduled. How does the office or workplace feel? What do you notice? What do you sense about the personality of the interviewer? What are their needs? Compare the actual events to your run-through.

➤ Get to the interview early and sit in the reception area. Take a few moments to notice how you feel being there. Can you see yourself fitting in? Can you be yourself here? Is there room for you and your creativity here? Can you see yourself "dancing" here?

➤ I always love to talk with the receptionist for a few moments. She or he usually has a keen intuitive perception of what's going on, who the players are, and where the group is going.

➤ What can you bring, say, show, or tell to communicate your uniqueness?

Practical Wisdom

Writer Rudolf Steiner explains that the spiritual world from which intuitive information comes is very different from our physical reality. In fact, he says that one of the ways you can be sure that the information is intuitive is that it seems a bit strange or comes in images that are rather odd.

—Sandra Weintraum,
The Hidden Intelligence

After the Interview

➤ Imagine yourself in this job in three months, six months, one year, five years. How do you change? How does the job change?

➤ When faced with more than one job offer, imagine each job as a door. Imagine walking through each door and notice how you feel, what is on the other side of the door, which doorway has power for you. (Review "*Who's at the Door?*" Workout in Chapter 7.)

➤ Compare the actual interview to your intuitive run-through.

May the Best Job Win

The following workout can be done before and after a job interview. Do the first part before an interview to establish what you are looking for, and then compare what you've got with what you want and what is offered.

1. Rate the following qualities as they relate to what you have and what you want. Use a number from 1 to 10, with one being low and ten being high. This will give you an opportunity to evaluate where you are and how far you have to go to get to where you want to be.

2. Rate the following qualities as they relate to what you're looking for in a new job on a scale of 1 to 10, with one being low and ten being high. It's helpful to have two columns. In the second column, write down your existing job or the perfect job and head the third column with the new opportunity.

Job Qualities	Current or Perfect Job	New Opportunity
Challenge	_____	_____
New skills to be learned	_____	_____
Interaction with others	_____	_____
Growth potential	_____	_____
Money	_____	_____
Benefits	_____	_____
Formal educational opportunities	_____	_____
Purposeful work	_____	_____
Creative work	_____	_____

3. Once a specific job opportunity is offered, rate the job in these categories, also on a scale from 1 to 10.

4. Compare your original list with the job offered.

5. Ask yourself whether this job creates a sense of new or positive flow in your life.

6. Use the Applause Meter from Chapter 4.

When You're Stuck

If you're still unclear about whether to take this job or not after all of the preceding workouts, you're either thinking too much or the job isn't right for you. Don't take it too seriously. Make a decision. The most important thing is to get out of the whirlpool and back in the flow, even if it's negative flow. If you take a job that is not right for you—it's not the end of the world. At least you have met some new people and created more opportunities for synchronicity to work.

Sixth Sense

Julian Gresser, in his book *Piloting Through Chaos*, discusses *negotiation* combining two definitions of the world. He speaks of negotiating both as a way of getting what is wanted and as a way of traversing difficult terrain. We negotiate our way through mountain trails and swampy lagoons to arrive at our destination.

Intuitive Negotiation

Sometimes the opportunities available at any given moment aren't in complete harmony with what we intended. The ability to *negotiate* then emerges as a necessary skill. Do you take what is offered from the universe without question? Do you close the door on an opportunity that does not fit the mental images?

Remember the career opportunity formula? It went like this:

Intention + Powerful Action = Synchronistic Opportunities

Let's extend this formula of Intention + Powerful Action = Opportunity and add the element of negotiation and synchronicity. It would look like this for all of you math wizards:

(Intention + Synchronicity) × Negotiation = Reality

Translated into English that means: What you want, combined with what shows up, gets transformed through the process of negotiation into reality.

When the synchronistic opportunity that appears is not what you wanted, you find yourself with an opportunity to negotiate. You can accept and work with what is offered to you or you can hold out for what you want. Often the former is the wisest path to take.

Synchronistically, I just caught up with a client who had come to see me for intuitive counseling several years ago. At the time she "thought" that her future success was down the path of finding the right man to marry. Intuitively I felt the exact opposite, and told her so. She left extremely disappointed and visited other "intuitives" who gave her similar advice. Taking the opportunities that were offered to her instead of holding out for what she thought she wanted led her to get Masters and Ph.D. degrees and to make a valuable contribution in the field of education.

She is a different person now than she was when I first met her and she is still looking forward to meeting a man she can truly share her life with, yet her view of herself and of who Mr. Right is has grown. She originally thought that finding Mr. Right was her career path, yet she discovered other talents and skills when that path did not create satisfactory results.

On the other hand, this chapter opened with a story of a woman who knew what she wanted and did not take what was first offered. She landed her dream job by waiting for the one she wanted.

These two stories illustrate the core intuitive skill of decision-making—how each situation is unique with no set answers or formulas. Ultimately, it comes down to how you respond to what is in front of you.

To negotiate intuitively you do need to know what you want and what you don't want. You need a clear, articulated intention. Yet, if it doesn't happen—if the opportunities just don't materialize, what are you going to do? The intuitive approach works with two elements simultaneously: holding on to what is intended and staying open to the current opportunities. This allows you to negotiate a path from where you are to where you want to be in a creative, innovative way—using what is available, refining and adapting what you want, while staying true to your inner core which will tell you when you are giving up too much or are stuck with an intention which has no life.

All of this changes the formula for career change discussed earlier into a kind of chemical formula where the elements are constantly moving back and forth, interacting and changing each other:

> Intention + Powerful Action = Synchronistic Opportunities

evolves to

> Intention + Synchronistic Opportunities (flows back and forth with) Powerful Action + Refined Intention

To negotiate intuitively requires clear, articulated intention. You have to know what you want and what you don't want. Then, when something is offered to you that has some of the elements of what you want, you can negotiate.

In the process of intuitive negotiation, we remain open to the following:

➤ Learning something new about what we really want.

➤ Changing our view and thus our intention of what we really want.

➤ Allowing the situation to affect us in deep and personal ways.

➤ Staying clear about our focus.

➤ Remaining firm about basic intentions.

➤ Perceiving creative solutions and new opportunities.

We truly navigate through the terrain of the opportunity. Here are the guidelines for intuitive negotiation:

➤ Articulate your intention before beginning any negotiation.

➤ Ask for what you want.

➤ Listen to and understand the other points of view.

➤ Release your personal attachment to the outcome of the negotiation.

➤ Be open to creative solutions.

Mr. Bubble and Your Future

You walk through this world only seeing what is right in front of you, yet your life has a past, a present, and a future. Imagine that you're walking through a huge sphere, yet you can only see the two-dimensional line you're walking on. All around you there are forces, events, and opportunities waiting to be encountered.

A developed intuition helps you sense the broad range of dimensions that can't be seen through the linear line you're walking. It can also help direct you to get there. For example, you may be walking in a garden that is filled with cactus. You hate cactus and want to get to the roses. "Where are the roses?" you say to yourself. "Why can't I get to the roses?" Little do you know that if you keep walking, the roses are right around the corner. The park is larger and has more dimension than you can see at any one time. Most parks have maps, so you can know how to get to the roses.

In life, intuition can be the guide. Where is the kind of life you're looking for? Probably right around the corner, yet you can't see it from where you are. Your intuition can guide you if you pay attention to the signals.

Here's a workout to help develop the intuitive ability to sense the future:

1. Imagine yourself surrounded by a bubble. Imagine the bubble as large enough to be comfortable, yet small enough to feel. Inside, the bubble is filled with your personal energy, including your intentions, desires, needs, fears, and purpose—the whole essence of who you are right now.

2. Imagine the future in a bubble separate from yours. Fill that bubble with the essence of the future even though you are consciously unaware of what it is.

3. Bring these bubbles together so that they barely touch. Notice their initial interaction with each other. Are they attracted to each other? Do they seem compatible?

4. Blend the bubbles slightly and allow the future bubble to catalyze your bubble. Ask yourself how you have to change to blend with this future. How might the image of the future change as you enter it?

5. Slowly, perhaps over several days, allow the future bubble to blend with your present bubble, penetrating and changing each other as they blend.

6. Write down all your thoughts, feelings, and images as you go through this workout.

7. Pay attention to what happens to you, synchronicities and opportunities, over the course of this workout.

Practical Wisdom

The world is not fixed but is in constant flux; accordingly, the future is not fixed, and so can be shaped. Humans possess significant tacit knowledge—we know more than we can say. The question to be resolved: how to remove the blocks and tap into that knowledge in order to create the kind of future we all want?

—Joe Jaworski, *Synchronicity: The Inner Art of Leadership*

Return to Your Intention

You may find a "perfect" job, but if it doesn't fit your dream it may waste your time. Compare each job opportunity to your life goals and ask yourself if this job will bring you closer. A dance/aerobic instructor was offered an acting job, which was considered by many to be a dream job. For him, it was not. He wouldn't be able to dance, which was his love. He said no to that job, and the following week was offered a full-time job as a dance instructor—just what he was looking for.

The Least You Need to Know

➤ Begin to move toward something new before the present job or project has peaked.

➤ Opportunities for change happen with intuitive clarity and without concrete certainty.

➤ Determine what career opportunities you want by looking at your boundaries and releasing artificial limitations.

➤ Keep open to synchronicities and use them as highway signs toward your future.

➤ Prepare for interviews intuitively.

➤ When what you want is not offered, be open to creative solutions.

➤ Be sensitive to how your desired future is preparing you for it right now.

Part 3
Growing Your Money Tree

Can you feel the power building? You're ready to allow wealth into your life now, and this book is ready to deliver. Part 3 offers effective tools for using your new intuitive green thumb to grow your money tree as tall as you want. You'll begin by getting crystal clear on your financial goals, understanding how your intuition will help you, and then swinging into action to find your power support team.

Then the real fun begins. You'll learn how to apply your intuitive skills to fatten your investment portfolio and enhance your entrepreneurial flair—and then how to take a power break to refresh your batteries and make sure you spend your wealth wisely.

Chapter 10

How Much Money Do You Want?

In This Chapter

➤ Discover what you can't live without

➤ Open your mind and your wallet to unlimited possibilities

➤ Establish a vision for your ideal lifestyle

➤ Find out what it'll take to get there

➤ Set and seed your financial intention

How much money do you want? What will it take to live your dream? Until you know how much is enough, you won't know what to ask for, and no one will know what to give you.

Yamoah, a Ghanaian veterinarian, noticed that the dogs she was treating were malnourished because their owners couldn't afford expensive imported chow and weren't feeding their pets properly. She began experimenting with recipes and is now Ghana's sole producer of pet food, selling about two tons each month.

What she needed to get started was $6,000 to buy a food dryer. Although banks were reluctant, she eventually got her loan, started her business, paid back the loan, and continues to support herself and the dogs of Africa. She knew what she needed and asked for it. She had to ask for it over and over again before she got it. Knowing exactly what she needed made her asking more powerful and eventually successful.

This chapter will help you define precisely how much wealth you want and make sure that it's in sync with who you are and where you're going. You'll learn both to unchain your desires and to act in balance with your lifestyle. Workouts to get you firmly on the road to wealth will finish up the chapter.

Know Your Bottom Line

You were born into a certain *suit* of wealth. In fact, the word *investment* has the word *vestment* in it, which means *clothing*. Whatever that suit is will haunt you your whole life unless it's examined and consciously changed.

Sixth Sense

Making an *investment* involves doing something now which you hope will grow in value and return to you more in the future. It is most often used in relation to investing money in the hopes that it will return more to you later, and you can also invest time, attention and talent knowing that the payoff will occur later.

Here's another way to think of it. Imagine for a moment that you were born into a pond of water, the same pond that your parents were living in at the time of your birth. That pond may be large or small, polluted, or clean. The pond represents the level of wealth lived and accepted as reality by your parents.

If the pond remains unexamined, you can swim around it for your whole life and never change it. It becomes a particular comfort level of wealth that fits, like a suit of clothes. It may not fit with your personal destiny, it may make you very uncomfortable, yet still it persists until consciously released.

I knew a man who was born into an extremely wealthy family. When I met him he was deeply in debt to the IRS and had no income, yet he lived in a penthouse apartment, wore wonderful clothes, schmoozed with influential people, and somehow got by, eating out in wonderful restaurants and vacationing in exotic places.

Meeting him helped me see the phenomenon I'm talking about here. No matter what he did, his life stayed at a certain level of comfort—one that wasn't in alignment with his soul, but one that was in alignment with his family and childhood. He was unhappy, unable to release the hold his ingrained lifestyle had on him. When I last saw him, he was beginning to change his lifestyle to match his real life situation. I don't know what happened to him; I only hope he discovered how to use his true wealth of caring and insight and incorporate it with a wealthy lifestyle.

I've met other people who live very comfortably on low incomes. Their lifestyle is simple, and their needs more than adequately cared for by the income they produce. Usually there is something in their lives that deeply involves them and utilizes their creativity. Their wealth *is* their creativity and it is abundant.

You have a bottom line below which you won't go. To build your wealth, you must first take a look at the pond you were born in and decide whether you want to stay there or change it. And while you're at it, it's a good idea to do a little digging into your family's financial habits.

Follow Your Financial Family Tree

Go through your family tree, as far back as you can. Find out as much as you can about how each section of your family built and used its wealth. Give each section a number from one to ten indicating how they valued each of the following categories:

➤ Earning money

➤ Spending money

➤ Inheriting money

➤ Saving money

➤ Sharing—giving money

➤ Passing on money

➤ Losing money

Now do the same for yourself.

While doing this, you'll discover many impressions about what your family values, whether it's money or something else. Pay attention to all the information you gather along the way.

Yellow Light

Things are only as important as your mind believes them to be. What you decide to change, what you decide to do differently is based on your beliefs. As you look at your financial history, look at the whole experience without judging the beliefs of those who have gone before you. They were doing the best with what they had.

Sketch Your Financial Pond

This workout suggests that you sketch a picture. For some of you, that might cause a ripple of fear and insecurity about your drawing ability. Back in the first section of this book I shared my fear of drawing, so I readily empathize but won't let you off the hook for at least giving it a try. Remember that no one has to see this but you and that drawing helps access your intuitive mind. Take a deep breath, acknowledge that you are no good at this drawing thing, and do it anyway—you just might surprise yourself.

To discover the size and shape of the financial pond you're currently living in, try the following workout:

1. Write your name in the center of a piece of paper.

2. On the left side of your name write: Income stream. Sketch an image that represents the flow of money into your life. Where does it come from? Many sources or one? What is the rate and level of flow? Draw it flowing into your name.

3. On the right side of your name write: Outflow. Sketch an image representing the flow of money out of your life. Where does it go? How is it used? What is the rate and level of flow?

4. Around your name write words that describe your thoughts and feelings about money: What it does for you, what it allows you to do that you love, what it costs you in terms of time, effort, and creativity.

Compare this sketch with what you learned about your family financial tree. What's the same? What's different?

Reflect on what you now know about your financial bottom line and how your current life reflects historical choices and circumstances. Keep your pond sketch handy—you'll need it again a little later on.

Expand Your Horizons

Your sketch should give you a sense of the size and shape of the financial pond you're living in. Now ask yourself the following:

➤ Do you like it?

➤ What do you like about it?

➤ What about it do you want to change?

➤ How do you want it to change?

Perhaps you're happy in your current pond, with just a few adjustments. If so, by all means choose it and live it fully.

If you want to change ponds, though, you can. Expanding your horizons like this involves using the resources you have wisely and creatively, going beyond the perceived limitations.

Practical Wisdom

For every native-born American who becomes a millionaire, four immigrants become millionaires! People come to this country with a vision for what they want. Their determination to attain their goals allows them to overcome any perceived obstacle or limitation. The energy to immigrate is often matched by the energy to succeed.

Those limitations come in many forms. Education, skill, and resources are a few of the physical limitations used as excuses for staying stuck in an unsatisfying financial situation. Time, effort, and fear are mental and emotional reasons for staying stuck.

Walk yourself through the following workout to break through what's limiting you from growing financially:

1. Write down your current monthly income.

2. Double it and write that down.

3. Reflect on how it would change your life to have that much money flowing into your life. Imagine the new responsibilities as well as any freedom or new options it would mean for you.

4. Double that figure and write it down.

5. Reflect on how it would feel to have that much money flowing through your life. Try it on as a lifestyle. Let your imagination walk you through all that you might feel emotionally and all that would change about your life physically.

6. Keep going until you reach the amount of money that begins to make you feel bloated and uncomfortable.

7. Now, write your name in the center of a piece of paper. Write the final figure on the left of your name. Sketch an image of that amount of money flowing into your name. Imagine several sources it might come from.

8. On the right side of your name write words and word phrases representing how you would use the money. Where would it go? What goals, projects, adventures, and lifestyle would it flow into?

9. Reflect on the life you would then be living. How would it feel? Write these feelings, thoughts, and images around your name.

Practical Wisdom

Don't let money separate you from reality. Here are a couple of folks who suffered that fate.

William K. Vanderbilt, worth $200 million when he died in 1885, said, "I have had no real gratification or enjoyment of any sort more than my neighbor on the next block who is worth only half a million."

Edith Wetmore was born into a wealthy family and lived on $6,000 a day. She died a spinster in 1966 and had never entered a grocery store until she was more than 80 years old. When a friend took her to an A & P, Miss Wetmore didn't have any money, not even a penny, in her purse, so her friend had to pay.

California Dreamin'

In the financial pond sketch you created earlier in this chapter, you established the "seeds" of your ideal lifestyle. On the right side of the page you drew all the things and places you want your money to flow to. In the following workout you will put all of this together to create a vision of your ideal lifestyle.

Begin with your sketch in front of you and follow these steps:

1. With a different color pencil or pen, circle the things you have already begun doing in your life. On a second piece of paper, write a paragraph on each of these items describing how you'd like to see these activities grow. Give each a value number from 1 to 10 representing how important it is in your life. Write down how much time per week you'd like to spend involved with these activities. Give each a ballpark budget figure.

2. With a new color, highlight the activities that already have resources, contacts, and skills to get you started, although you have not started yet. On your second piece of paper, write a paragraph on each of these that tells the story of how you will incorporate these activities in your life. Include how much time you want to spend on a weekly basis, and give a value of importance to these as well. Give each a ballpark budget figure.

3. For the remaining items, those for which you don't currently have resources or contacts to get started, highlight with a new color. On your second piece of paper, write a paragraph on each of these describing how and when you will incorporate these into your life. Write about how much time per week you want to be involved with these activities and give them a value number. Give each a ballpark budget figure.

Look carefully at what you have created. Does it work? Is there enough time in your life to accomplish everything? Are you willing and energized to live this life? If there's any part that feels overwhelming, write another paragraph about it.

Live with this image for at least a week, looking at it daily and changing it as necessary. For the final product, you want a vision that feels expansive, challenging, wonderful, practical, and doable.

Practical Wisdom

To become the lord and master of your existence instead of a tormented slave helplessly buffeted by events, listen to that tiny inner voice sleeping in the depths of your mind and give it more freedom to express itself. The more often you repeat the formula, the more powerful it will become and the more surely it will guide you. This is your intuition, the voice of your soul. The road to your secret power.

—Mark Fisher, *The Instant Millionaire*

Get Real

How does one get real in the world of intuition? On the one hand, there are unlimited possibilities; on the other hand, our world is filled with physical limitations. We know we can ignore those who say "That will never work" or "Get real!" At the same time, though, you want to avoid "magical thinking" or fantasizing that can derail real life.

The balance point is in you. See yourself as the leverage point. You don't have to do everything yourself; there can be tons of help and support around you. But you remain the leverage point, translating your vision into reality through your sense of responsibility, focus, leadership, and management.

Although these concepts may seem similar, they each provide an important tool for manifesting your dream:

➤ *Responsibility:* The ability to put your whole self in (kind of like the hokeypokey) an activity, owning up to the consequences for you and the others involved. Live with the fact that everything you do creates ripples that affect everything and everyone.

➤ *Focus:* The ability to concentrate fully on what you're doing, right now.

➤ *Leadership:* The ability to inspire others to get involved in the accomplishment of your vision and to work toward enhancing and improving their lives in the process.

➤ *Management:* The ability to coordinate the accomplishment of specific tasks related to your vision.

You don't need to do all of the "doingness." You do need to be willing to step into the responsibility of what you want to accomplish and to focus on the tasks at hand.

Tried & True

You have to force yourself to spend some time away from the hustle and bustle of your job in order to get down to reality again. If you don't spend enough time doing that, you can lose hold of the reins and get into all kinds of trouble.

—Richard Abdoo, CEO Wisconsin Energy, *Fortune*, Aug. 1992

To help you bring your vision into focus, grab that pond sketch you made earlier in the chapter and do the following:

1. Go back to the left side of the page and circle or underline with a different color pencil the sources of income that are already flowing into your life. On a different piece of paper, write a paragraph about how that source can increase.

2. In another color, highlight the sources that relate to resources and possibilities that are alive in your life right now, yet not producing income. On your second piece of paper, write a paragraph about how those resources and possibilities could become actual streams of income. How much of your personal energy and time would be required to maintain them?

3. With still another color, indicate the sources that are not currently a part of your life. On the second piece of paper, write a paragraph about how each of these could happen. (Don't use the "lottery" as an option!) How much of your personal time and energy would be required to initiate and maintain them?

Getting real about your vision doesn't mean you should limit your imagination. It is intended to give it more substance and to paint a real picture for yourself about how much time, creative energy, and personal resources are required to support it. Your job is then to make focused choices on where you want to put your energy. As you make focused choices, the Universe will respond by providing opportunities and support along the way. There will always be help, more help than you can imagine. That help happens all the time. Focus and responsibility give that help tangible goals so the results can be seen.

> **Practical Wisdom**
>
> Money often costs too much.
>
> —Ralph Waldo Emerson
>
> I've never been poor, only broke. Being poor is a frame of mind. Being broke is only a temporary situation.
>
> —Mike Todd

Complete the Circle

The reality is that your life is not linear, but circular. What you love to do will support what provides income so you can do what you love.

Look at your sketch again. This time draw connecting arches from items on the right side to the connecting items on the left side. These arches represent the feed lines between what you are doing to what you are receiving.

On your second piece of paper, write a paragraph for each arch describing how what you love to do will feed and nourish your income streams. It may not be a direct link like: "I work eight hours a day to make enough money to pay my bills." It may be something like: "Taking a long walk every day gives me the inspiration to make good investment choices," or "Spending time with my children puts every-thing else I'm doing into a proper perspective."

Put It All Together

Put all of this together with the following imagination workout. After each step, closing your eyes will help you open your mind's eye:

1. Imagine that you are in the center of a positive stream of energy. Positive energy is entering into you, filling you, and then you send it out into the world to seed future energy that will come back to feed you.

2. Imagine a chunk of money coming in to you. Allow it in, let it fill you, then send it on. Send it on to something that will grow and support future nourishment for you and others.

3. Imagine an hour of time coming in to you. Allow it in, let it fill you. Use the hour for your nourishment. Notice how your use of this hour feeds and nourishes future nourishment for you and others.

4. Imagine a creative idea coming to you. Allow it in—notice the energy and vitality attached to it. Let it nourish you. Now use it in a way that will provide future nourishment for you and others.

Set Your Dial to Dollars

Practical Wisdom

Money makes money and the money that money makes makes more money.

—*Poor Richard's Almanac*

Setting your financial intention will lock a piece of your creative energy to a very specific income goal. That lock acts like a homing pigeon on its way to a prearranged destination. The pigeon may go through rough weather, dangerous territory, smooth sailing, and warm breezes, yet nothing will deter it from going home. Neither seduction nor adversity will alter its course. Once you set your intention, the wheels are in motion. It may take months or years to attain, but you're on your way. Everything that happens in your life from that point on is guiding you toward your goal.

Just yesterday a friend was telling me about how something he'd been trying to complete for more than two months had just fallen apart. His assistant had failed to do something and the whole project needed to start over.

Instead of panicking or getting angry, however, he just picked up the phone and talked to someone involved in the project and discovered that there was another way—a quick way, one that was complete in about 20 minutes! If the failure hadn't happened, he never would have found this new way that helped not only him but his colleagues as well.

Decide on your income goal. What amount of income fits and supports your lifestyle? Follow these steps to set it:

1. Imagine a thermostat and set it to a number.
2. Make sure that number feels comfortable. It may be a little stretch from where you are now, yet still comfortable.
3. Imagine the thermostat in your heart. How does it feel? Is it still comfortable?
4. Leave it there, untouched.

Just like the homing pigeon, you may find yourself in challenging circumstances, yet your direction will never vary. Something inside of you is now directing you to your goal. You can't always consciously know the purpose of particular events right away. Remember that intuitively we know *what* before we know *why*.

Plant Your Money Seeds

Now that you have set your intention, it's important to sow it, to make it real by planting seeds that will bear fruit. Let's do a little gardening.

Seed Capital

Take 10 percent of the income you have set as your intention. Divide it by 12. That's how much money you need to spend on seeding your dream life every month. Here are some examples:

If your financial intention is $75,000, your yearly seed money is 10 percent, or $7,500. Divided by 12, that's $625 to invest in yourself every month.

Using the same formula, for $100,000, your yearly seed money is $10,000 divided by 12, or about $834.

For $500,000, your yearly seed money is $50,000, and your monthly investment in yourself is $4,166.

Now let's calculate your seed money:

Your financial intention is: $_____

Move the decimal point one place to the left to calculate your yearly seed money: $_____

Divide that number by 12 to get your monthly investment in yourself: $_____

Tried & True

John Wendel, a porter to John Jacob Astor for many years, did what his employer advised him to do and put his savings in land. He was so diligent in this task that his portfolio of Manhattan real estate was worth $100 million by the time it reached his last descendants, two reclusive sisters named Ella and Rebecca.

Create a budget for your seed money. It might include investments, networking groups, education, coaching, training, physical fitness, health revitalization, retreats, sports, or whatever you deem necessary. Be creative about ways you can use that money to seed your positive future. Don't include anything that is strictly maintenance in the budget such as rent and telephone bills. Your seed budget is all about building a positive future for yourself. Diversify it, get the most out of that money and have fun spending it. As you budget and spend it, know that you're seeding your future wealth.

If your seed budget is truly impossible for you to spend, you have aimed too high in setting your financial intention. Go back and reset your thermostat. Take the journey a little slower. Once you reach a more reachable goal, you can move on and build the next phase.

If your seed budget seems possible, but a real stretch, breathe in to it. Most people have a difficult time spending money on what they consider non-essentials. If you're not willing to invest in your future, who will? What is more essential? Try this for one year and note what happens.

Seed Time

Take a look now at how many work hours you spend every week. Multiply that number by 10 percent. The resulting figure is your seed time. For example, if you work 50 hours per week, your seed time is five hours. Spend five hours every week seeding your dream life. Budget your time. It may include research, education, networking, physical fitness, writing, reading, or meditating. It has to be time spent supporting your dream and your personal development. Entertainment time with friends is important but doesn't count for seed time.

Practical Wisdom

Most business people would not mess up half as much if they just took a few minutes to close the door and do nothing for a little while.

—manager interviewed in *Executive Female*, Nov. 1996

If you can't take 10 percent of your time and spend it on yourself, without sacrificing family or relationship time, you're working too much. Rethink your work schedule.

Try seeding your time and your money for one year and watch your results. If you aren't happier and wealthier at the end of the year, I will personally refund the money you spent buying this book.

Setting your financial intention and seeding it with time and money is the most powerful action you can take toward creating your positive future. This is it, right here. Do this, and all else will emerge. If it's too uncomfortable for you to do it, do it anyway. Don't think about it too much, just do it. If you need to start small, do it.

The most important thing is to do something toward your positive future. The longest journey begins with a single step.

The Least You Need to Know

➤ Your financial "comfort zone" is based on family history and can be changed.

➤ Look realistically at your current financial flow and decide if you want it to change.

➤ Imagine your ideal lifestyle and determine the financial flow necessary to support it.

➤ Get real about your ideal by outlining the responsibilities and focused energy necessary to live it.

➤ Set an imaginary, internal thermostat to your financial goal.

➤ Devote 10 percent of your time and money to seeding your dream.

Chapter 11

Being Yourself and Doing What You Love

In This Chapter

➤ Discover your most important asset

➤ Take your place among history's greatest

➤ Learn why it's important to take your whole self to work

➤ Develop a daily practice that keeps all of you present

➤ Discover the power of love

➤ What to do when you don't know what to do

Merrill-West Publishing was developed when James Wanless wanted to publish his own writings. Discovering that he couldn't do it himself, he started a small company. With three full-time employees and 20 "extended corporate family members," otherwise known as outside contractors, it's one model of future business structures. In his words, "We are committed to fiscal success and to producing excellent products, but each of us is also encouraged to further his or her own vision and skills. Our company is a 'whole-person' workplace. Emotions are valued, communication is open, and we support frequent time-outs—from nap breaks to beach walks to vacations and sabbaticals—to let body and spirit regenerate."

Sound like a dream job? I have good news and bad news for you. The good news is that there can be successful business environments that support and honor individuals with a creative, stimulating, and challenging workplace. The bad news, at least for some, is that it requires individuals to know who they are and to be self-motivated. No more "just tell me what to do and I'll do it, then go home" thinking. When you show up at work, you have to show up with ideas, energy, awareness, and focus. If you don't, you're of no use to the project. The new world of business requires communication skills that go beyond asking for the next assignment and gossiping at the water cooler.

This chapter focuses on the most important asset you have and one that grows in value the more you use it: *you.* You have the ability to continually generate money, ideas, and energy. You're a non-stop creativity machine. As you learn to love yourself, love your talent, and love what you do, you will never be poor. Intuition follows love and, as you'll discover in this chapter, money follows it, too.

You Are Your Résumé

Have you ever met someone and immediately trusted or not trusted him? Of course you have. Everyone has. A key component of our intuition is its ability to immediately sense safety and trustworthiness. As a child, you were a master perceiver of people, yet were also barraged with cultural stereotypes, prejudices, and social rules that confused your intuition. For example, as a child, you may have felt completely yucky when Aunt Smoochie came over and kissed you, yet you were told to be nice and entertain her. It could have been that you were just not in the mood for hugs and kisses, yet what you wanted wasn't important. It also could have been that Aunt Smoochie was untrustworthy in some way, you felt it, yet you were stopped from acting on your intuitive feeling.

This kind of thing happens over and over again in childhood and pretty soon our internal people-reader and personal safety-meter are completely confused. It takes careful detective work, awareness, and retraining to put the pieces back together. In the meantime, life goes on.

When you go in for a job interview, sales call, or clothes shopping, whoever speaks to you immediately sizes you up. Perhaps their intuition is covered over with bias about race, age, sex, appearance, and other factors, and they won't see the real you. Perhaps you are good at presenting an image that they like, yet that isn't the real you. This is the stuff our culture has tried to deal with by making rules and laws, a poor substitute for a developed intuition. Until more people trust what they know intuitively and recognize their bias and fear, the rules will be used to make some of the decisions, although rules are sometimes used to justify personal fear.

The solution is simple: Be yourself, trust yourself, look for mutually beneficial fits.

Tried & True

Stephen Balogh, former general manager of a $100 million Raychem unit who became vice president of human resources, had to find a way to display human talent as added value rather than "a drain on resources." He developed the idea of championing a culture where employees recognize that it is their responsibility to develop their careers, and it is the managers' responsibility to attract and develop talent. He promoted the idea that learning and working are one and the same thing.

Take Your Whole Self to Work

Many people hang their wisdom on the coat rack before they go into work, then pick it up on the way out. This is sometimes due to habit, and sometimes due to a work environment inhospitable to personal involvement and creativity. Whatever the case—change it now. You owe it to yourself and to everyone else to keep connected to your soul, your wisdom, your true self, as much of the time as possible.

Take Your Place Among History's Greatest!

From the moment you breathed your first breath, you have been unique. There is not another being like you on earth, nor will there ever be. When you breathe your last breath, that will be the end of the story. You will no longer exist in this form, ever. The particular combination of genetics, environment, personality, and opportunity that takes the space you live in will only exist as long as you keep breathing. While completely unique, you have equal value to every other living being—that means Einstein, Michael Jordan, King Tut, Cleopatra, Geronimo, Lao Tsu, the Dalai Lama, and anyone else you can think of!

Practical Wisdom

Every second we live is a new and unique moment of the universe, a moment that never was before and will never be again. And what do we teach our children in school? We teach them that two and two make four and that Paris is the capital of France. We should say to each of them, "Do you know what you are? You're a marvel. You're unique. In the millions of years that have passed, there has never been another child like you."

—Pablo Casals, master guitarist

151

Think of the world as a huge park. Each flower, tree, blade of grass, trail, bird, body of water, and everything else that makes up the park is important. Each thing plays a part in creating the whole. If one thing decides not to live its life fully, the park as a whole suffers. Imagine, if the oak tree decided to only grow halfway, the reduced shade would change how the squirrels and birds lived, to name only one element that would be affected by the oak's decision.

When you decide not to be fully present in what you're doing, everyone you come into contact with, either directly or indirectly, is shortchanged. Based on the universal law of reciprocity, when they are shortchanged, they tend to shortchange you in return by not sharing their full selves with you. According to James Redfield in *The Celestine Prophesy*, we are here to share love. When love is shared, everyone grows and is energized. Sharing anything less results in a control drama that depletes energy.

Practical Wisdom

This is what human conflict has always been about, at every level: from all the petty conflict in families and employment settings to wars between nations. It's the result of feeling insecure and weak and having to steal someone else's energy to feel okay. When you appreciate the beauty and uniqueness of things, you receive energy. When you get to a level where you feel love, then you can send the energy back just by willing it so.

—James Redfield, *The Celestine Prophesy*

The Secret Universal Law of Adaptability

The reason most people leave their wisdom at the door before going to work is the feeling that their wisdom won't be welcomed. They have the impression that what they really know, what they perceive, isn't wanted or won't be accepted by the powers that be and their co-workers. It somehow feels safer to reduce yourself to fit the box provided at work and give up being involved. Sometimes that decision is made before starting a job. School is also a place where it seems easier to leave your wisdom at the door before going to class, then pick it up on the way out.

When you know and experience the validity of the Universal Law of Adaptability, you will be more careful with your wisdom and won't leave it hanging around. The law itself is very simple: Everything adapts to the present condition.

What that means is that when you go to work without your wisdom, and you shrink yourself to fit either a real or imaginary box to work in, everything around you adapts to that. Your life, your opportunities, your ambition, how others treat you, and so on. If you keep your wisdom with you, even if you go into an environment where it's not accepted or honored, eventually the environment will adapt to you. Opportunities, ambition, and how others treat you will grow to match you. It may not happen overnight, but it will happen. It may mean that the current environment may have to spit you out because you don't fit, yet another environment more suited to you, your talent, and your wisdom will emerge.

This challenges the part of us that wants to be nice, congenial, fit in, and be a team player, yet I know you have either experienced the truth of what I'm saying yourself or by witnessing someone else.

My mother used to say: "The squeaky wheel gets the grease." And she was right. I would sit in complete embarrassment while she would walk into some bureaucratic situation and begin asking for what she wanted—to be treated with respect and to have her questions answered. She was never rude or disrespectful to anyone, but she never gave up what she wanted in order to make it easier for their system or to just play by what she considered ridiculous rules. She almost always got what she wanted.

The other side of the Universal Law of Adaptability is that when you want to change, the first thing encountered is resistance. You need to persevere through the initial barrier that wants to keep things the same.

Workout: Our Daily Bread

There are three simple things to do to stay connected to your wisdom in all situations. They're simple, but not easy. They don't take much time and can be practiced daily. Daily practice makes it easier to do them when you really need to, when the pressure is on. They are:

➤ Breathe

➤ Open yourself to joy

➤ Look for the open door

Your Daily Breath

Breathing instantly connects your unique self to your body, and to the present moment. Although we breathe all the time, often it's something that is done completely automatically, with no awareness. When in an uncomfortable situation, most people go unconscious, their breathing becomes shallow, and their behavior goes on automatic pilot. At that point, they'll either fight to force their way or acquiesce to please and disappear. Either way, the situation won't get the benefit of their wisdom.

Breath is sacred. It is the first act of life. Every living thing breathes, and that breath vitalizes each unique configuration of molecules into life. Remembering your breath reminds you of your uniqueness and brings your mind back to your wisdom. It isn't always comfortable, yet it is always powerful.

Practice breathing for five minutes every day. Watch and count your breath. It's very simple, yet it's something that can save your life and your integrity.

Breathing is something everyone does all the time, yet it is rarely actually practiced. Breathing initiates all bodily functions: digestion, circulation, absorption of nutrients, healing, and much more. To breathe correctly means to fully release the carbon dioxide with each exhalation and to breathe in the full capacity of oxygen with every inhale. Let each breath begin at the base of your lower back, allowing your abdomen to fill with air, then the lungs and the upper chest. Exhale completely, pushing the last bit of air out of your belly before beginning again.

The Joy Faucet

If breathing connects you to your uniqueness, joy connects your universal wholeness. Intuition connects you as an individual to the larger whole. Joy is the natural state when those two lines of connection are plugged in. Think about it, have you ever heard of someone feeling sad about being one with the universe? No. When that feeling happens, it is always joyful. Joy is something that we are always connected to, yet not always conscious of, like breathing. If breathing is what keeps us as individuals alive, joy is what keeps us in relationship to the rest of life. If we are not experiencing joy, at least some of the time, what's the point?

The good news is that joy is always available. Imagine a joy faucet connected to your heart. Imagine turning it on and allowing joy to flow into you. The ease with which you can access joy validates my point that it's as available as air and just as essential.

For practice, spend a few moments each day, remembering to turn on the joy faucet. Just before you walk into work is a good time, as well as before you meet up with family and friends.

Look for the Open Door

If you've done the preceding two workouts, this step comes naturally. Having your mind and soul connected through breathing, then linking up with universal wisdom by turning on the joy automatically puts you in a state of mind where you can see new options. You will at least be able to see where the energy of the situation isn't flowing and where there might be an opening.

What blocks the ability to see new options is wanting things to turn out a certain way. That prevents the flow of joy and focuses attention on forcing something to happen, even if there's a better alternative right in the room.

Practice looking for open doors by asking: "Where are the opportunities in this situation?"

The Lights Are Bright on Broadway

Love, like joy, is more than an irrational emotion. Love describes the whole experience of being connected to oneself and connected to the whole. Love and joy go together to make up the electricity of life. When you're plugged in to love, anything is possible.

The other plug, fear, is actually being unplugged. Nothing seems possible, there's no energy or vitality, only fear. When you're plugged in to love, you don't experience that it's up to you, alone, to accomplish something. There is always help and a sense of guidance. When unplugged, and in a state of fear, the experience is one of having to do it all by yourself, no help, no support, all alone.

Practical Wisdom

By consistently choosing love rather than fear, we can experience a personal transformation that enables us to be more naturally loving to ourselves and others. In this way we can begin to recognize and experience the love and joy that unites us.

—Dr. Jerry Jampolsky, *Love Is Letting Go of Fear*

When plugged in, energy is on, vitality is flowing through your system, connecting it to an even larger source of energy. When unplugged, energy is off, no flow, no juice. What's often referred to as just an *emotional state* of joyful or fearful, is our ability to sense our relationship to ourselves and the whole. Because the analytic mind doesn't acknowledge the validity of emotions, this vital ability to *plug in* to universal energy has remained a secret for the successful.

Tried & True

My businessman friend knows that his business is better when his relationships are better, whether they are with customers, vendors, or employees. He knows that relationships are built on reaching people as people, not as digits.

He tells the truth. He says what he knows in his heart to be true, and people believe him because they want to believe him. He solves most problems by helping people find solutions. He understands the spirit of business, holding the belief that everyone in the same business shares a common bond and wants to have that bond reinforced, person to person.... No matter what anyone tells you, when you lose business, it's almost always a relationship problem. Good relationships and personal connections can come only when you abandon the patterned thinking and language of business.

—James A. Autry, *Love and Profit*

I think of "love" as Broadway. In New York City, the streets are laid out in a very easy-to-follow grid. From north to south there are numbers and streets, and from east to west there are avenues with numbers and names. Then there is Broadway. Broadway winds itself through the city cutting across from the west side to the east side, then splitting into two streets, then joining again way downtown. It completely confuses the grid.

We like to lay our lives out in order. We want security, stability, and regularity. Then comes love. Love zigzags through our lives opening us to opportunities and experiences we would never allow if we were focused solely on order. Through loving other people, loving activities, loving animals, and so on, our lives become rich and diverse.

Intuition Follows Love...

A colleague of mine, Sharon Franquemont, author of *You Already Know What To Do*, has said for years that "intuition follows love." What she means is that when you're engaged in activities that are meaningful and enjoyable, intuitive insights will also be present. If you're doing something without that feeling of joy, it's highly unlikely that intuitive insight will be noticed.

Grocery shopping isn't one of my favorite activities and often it's done under time pressure. I have my list, go in and get what's on it, and leave as quickly as possible. When in that "rushed" state of mind, I have had many moments where I notice something, like the mustard, but then decide that because it's not on my list, we don't need it. Invariably, when I arrive home, my husband says, "Did you get the mustard? We are all out." Then another trip to the store is necessary. When I can shop in a more present state (breathing and feeling joy), it's easier to pick up on those messages and get the things we need that may not be on the list.

The same holds true in our business lives. Rushing through the day to complete a certain number of details and tasks overrides intuitive impressions, and thus opportunities and information that don't fit the schedule but that may be incredibly valuable.

Do what you love. If you can't do something you love, find something to love about what you're doing. Enjoy the people, the environment, the creativity, the money, something—and really let yourself enjoy it.

... And So Does Money

More than 40 years ago, Jim Henson majored in Home Economics because he loved to make his puppets. He continued doing what he loved and created a concept and a business—The Muppets—that's still going strong today, supporting those who work there and bringing joy and entertainment to millions of people, young and old.

Can you imagine being his parents and watching your son devote his life to puppet-making? If they were not creative themselves, they might have often wondered if their son was ever going to amount to anything.

Anything is possible and any work that is loved can become something you can build a satisfying and abundant life around.

If you love what you do, you will keep finding ways to do it better, and you will keep learning from what you're doing. I even encountered a street beggar once who clearly loved what he was doing. I asked him what he loved about it, while I happily gave him some money. He said, "I get a thrill out of connecting to people who are shut down, and getting them to open their heart, just a little." He begged with no shame. Even telemarketers do better when they find something to love about what they do. It comes through in the first nanosecond of the phone call.

Tried & True

H. J. Heinz started canning pickles at the age of 12 in 1856 and later became the founder and CEO of Heinz & Co. He managed his "model" factory with the credo, "Heart power is better than horsepower." Understanding that money and success follow love, he offered his employees lots of amenities, rare at the time, such as having a manicurist come in regularly to provide manicures for his female employees.

Inch by Inch, Row by Row

Joseph Campbell has been quoted as saying, "If you see footprints in front of you, you are not on your path." Each of us has a unique trail to blaze. The best advice is to take it one small step at a time.

1. Look around in your life for something you love and begin spending more time doing it. It may be something you only have a few minutes for each day or week, yet as you give yourself permission to do it and love it, your joy connection will grow. You may love reading the paper but feel that you have to do it in such a hurry most mornings that you no longer enjoy it, it has become a chore. Stop for a moment and remember that you're doing something that you love. It costs no time to enjoy what you're doing already. Savor the moment. Store the feeling.

Practical Wisdom

Sex is not love, although sex can be loving.

Money is no substitute for love, although money follows love.

Power is not loving, although love is powerful.

You may not have someone to love in your life, but you can still love your life.

2. Let the feeling you get from doing what you love spread to other activities in your life. Once you allow the feelings of joy and love actively into your life, you can fairly easily spread them around. Spread it to loving the act of shaving or washing your face. Spread it to doing the dishes and taking out the garbage.

If you follow these simple, little steps, when the big challenges come, you will be ready. When something completely awful happens, a part of you will start immediately looking for the open door.

When in Doubt, Smile

When you hit a wall and don't know what to do, rejoice! That is the moment that your intuition has the best chance to provide real guidance. Most of your time is packed with plans and calendars. With every minute filled, there is no opportunity for your intuition to break through and reveal its best wisdom, even to yourself. Getting to the point where there's nowhere to go, things have stopped, red-light time, is a golden opportunity. The next time you are there, smile. Pause, take a deep breath, and remember to enjoy the moment. It may not last very long, but that moment of enjoyment, in the midst of uncertainty, no matter how brief, opens the door for something new. You may not recognize it right away, but it will be there, growing, and sometimes when you least expect it that new opportunity will reveal itself to you.

The Least You Need to Know

➤ You present the "real you" to others, whether you know it or not, and you recognize what is "real" in others.

➤ Being your whole self at work will create new opportunities.

➤ You are a unique being, and the world needs you to do the job of being you— don't worry, the environment will adapt to you.

➤ Daily practice to improve being you involves breathing, opening to joy, and looking for the open doors.

➤ Intuition and money follow love.

➤ When in doubt, smiling opens new opportunities.

Chapter 12

Building Your Dream Team

In This Chapter

➤ Discover the power of working with others

➤ Maximize your strengths and minimize your weaknesses

➤ Learn to intuitively hire professionals

➤ Learn when to spend more than you think you can afford

➤ How to use your intuition when working with business colleagues

➤ Catch and use your first impressions

➤ Network with the Universe

Ishi was the lone survivor of the Yahi, a Native American tribe, in the late 1800s. He grew up afraid of white people after watching the massacre of his community and the forced isolation of the seven surviving members of his tribe. For more than 40 years, they lived in the backwoods of California, far from white civilization, until all, except Ishi, had died. By now a master hunter and tracker, he avoided white people altogether and grew progressively lonelier.

Finally, the loneliness was too much for him. In 1908, he gave up and threw himself on the white man's road, fully expecting to be shot or hung. For him, it was better to be killed than to continue living without a community.

The group he happened to throw himself in front of included a sympathetic sheriff who brought Ishi into town and introduced him to Dr. Kroeber, a young anthropologist. Kroeber recognized the gift that was in front of him. Ishi became a part of Dr. Kroeber's family and Ishi's wisdom and insight was not lost with his tribe. Dr. Kroeber's wife, Theodora, wrote Ishi's story to share with the rest of us.

This story illustrates the fact that no one does anything alone. We are designed to be social. We can live without all the "things" of life, yet we cannot live without each other. We are leaves and branches of one tree, life forms sharing one ocean, different pages of one book. However you look at it, we need each other and we serve each other.

This chapter is about how to use your intuition to work effectively with others. In your endeavors, you will need to pick a team of people to help you realize your goals. You'll also interact with many others informally who will help in a wide variety of ways. Realizing that you may have to spend money before you make what you want, this chapter helps you choose wisely on whom to spend it. Finally, you will learn to "network"—not just with people but with the Universe.

Practical Wisdom

Every manager concerned with wisdom knows it's often necessary to make the journey with the learner. To accompany is, first and foremost, to be present and attentive; this can actually be more important than actively intervening in learning. To the extent that the management of a company encourages learning, it needs companions, coaches, mentors, and guides. Accompanying, more than any other learning skill, justifies the learning manager's presence within the organization.

—Robert Aubrey &
Paul M. Cohen,
Working Wisdom

Star Power

Whether you work alone, as an entrepreneur with a small staff, or work with a large company, you are the center point of a large network. Think of yourself as President of Your Life. You have people around you with assigned tasks: advisors, supporters, and friends. Your success in achieving and fulfilling your aspirations depends on your ability to manage your team. Most teams are informal. There may be no money involved or lots of money involved. All of those involved in your life, from the person who bags your groceries to your accountant and stockbroker, help make your life easier and can be much more than mere "temporary employees." They can be "points of light" in your life, bringing necessary information, ideas, new opportunities, friendship, and pleasure. Remember, intuition flows on the wavelength of love. When you like and admire those you do business with, the chances of success increase tremendously.

Complete the following workout to get an idea of how many people you have working for you. Take a piece of paper right now and put your name in the middle. Think of the people in your life who help make your life work. Make bigger circles for those who are in your life every day in important ways, and smaller circles for those who support you less often.

As you complete this workout, it will become clear that there are more people than you can fit on one page. The circles go on and on. Here is a sample of how this workout looks on paper:

Example of "clustering" to determine your network.

Now, go back to each circle and give each interaction a number on a scale from 1 to 10, using the following key:

➤ 1–3 designates a negative, unsatisfying or difficult relationship. This relationship is difficult either emotionally or technically. Perhaps you don't like the service you receive, or perhaps most interactions require effort and several explanations before the relationship is right.

➤ 4–6 designates a neutral, nondescript relationship. The job gets done, yet there is no relationship. It is a neutral interaction, perhaps you don't even know the name of the person who provides the service.

➤ 7–10 designates a positive, effective relationship. Most of the time you enjoy dealing with this person or business. If something goes wrong, you can talk to this person or someone at the business. The work is done to your satisfaction, and you have a more-than-superficial sense of whom you're doing business with or feel some kind of personal tie to those involved.

After completing this workout, look at what you have. Notice the overall trends in your circle of support. If more than half of the relationships are negative, you may be the problem. Perhaps you haven't been clear enough in communicating your needs. The most courageous way to handle negative support relationships is to talk with the other person and ask how they feel about working with you.

Have a conversation about how the working relationship might be improved for them as well as for you. Ask them directly how they like working for you and be open to hearing the truth. If you aren't satisfied with their work, they are most likely not satisfied working with you.

Practical Wisdom

Never let a problem acquire so much importance in your eyes that it traumatizes you.... If you do this, you will find the truth and the intuition that you will need to guide you through life. You will also find that thing so rare on earth: love for whatever you do, and love for others. That is the dual secret of true wealth.

—Mark Fisher, *The Instant Millionaire*

There may be some working relationships that you're ready to terminate. Before walking away, give yourself the gift of learning something before you do. Talk to the group or person, let them know you're taking your business somewhere else, and let them know why. Be constructive in your comments and open to having a real conversation. It may or may not happen, but you will walk away with a fuller sense of completion.

If you have just a few negative work relationships, you most likely have some emotional or political ties to them that give you the impression that you're powerless to change them, so you just put up with them.

If you have mostly neutral relationships, you're not paying enough attention to what's going on in your life. There are tons of opportunities passing you by every day. Start paying more attention to who serves you coffee, who sells you the newspaper, who cleans your clothes. It only takes a moment to have a conversation, share a smile, and it can make your day as well as someone else's.

Choose Your Points of Light

Begin to look at everyone in your life as someone you exchange energy with, not just money or time. Each transaction has an energy component. Energy works under the laws of love and creativity, which are completely different from the laws of the balance sheet.

Most people live under the mistaken assumption that energy is a *zero sum* transaction. A zero sum transaction is one where there's a finite amount of resources and one party will get some and the other party will get the rest. At the end of the day, the balance will remain zero, with those involved dividing up the resources.

The law of creativity has a different kind of math. In the creative process 1 plus 1 equals infinity. If this sounds completely crazy to you, think about being in love and think about having a creative idea. Think about it. Have you ever been in a rotten mood, completely upset when you received a phone call from someone you've been wanting to talk to, and, instantly, you're in a great mood? Not only did your mood change, but now you have energy! After the phone call, you're motivated to accomplish what you couldn't find the energy for before the call.

It works with creative ideas too. When you're turned-on by a creative idea, you can work on it for hours, not feeling the least bit tired.

We will work with this concept even more when dealing with investing money, but for now it's enough for you to realize that each human transaction has the potential to give you energy. When the transaction generates energy, both you and the others involved receive energy. There are no limits and no losers. Instead of zero sum, there is abundance. Instead of having to divide up the energy, like counting out the money, there's plenty to go around with more to spare.

Who you choose to work with is important, so choose with an eye to talent and interactive chemistry. Do you want to work with someone who depletes the creative force? Do you want to work with someone who supports the pool of abundant energy?

Practical Wisdom

Being grown up doesn't have to mean leaving all our positive childhood traits behind. Victor H. Palmieri, who was brought in to help rehabilitate Mutual Benefit Life Insurance in New Jersey, said, "Strategies are okayed in boardrooms that even a child would say are bound to fail. The problem is, there is never a child in the boardroom!"

When choosing a support person in your life ask yourself:

➤ Is there vitality?

➤ Can I talk openly with this person about my concerns?

➤ Does he or she answer my questions directly?

➤ Is he or she interested in my success and the success of the project?

➤ Am I interested in this person's success? Do I want to see him or her grow?

If more than one of these questions are answered with a no, it's time to rethink the relationship. Decide whether you want to continue with a neutral relationship, which really has a negative pull of energy when compared to a relationship that generates energy. A negative or neutral support person is like a dripping faucet. You may not notice it all the time and it may seem too insignificant to fix, yet it's constantly losing energy, 24 hours a day/7 days a week.

No one is perfect and no relationship is perfect. We are not looking for perfection here. Every relationship has issues to work out, disagreements, and tension. While conflict may seem worth avoiding, it actually solidifies and deepens relationships. The energy it takes to avoid a conflict drains a huge amount of resources.

Things that stop and slow energy flow between people:

163

➤ Avoiding the truth

➤ Slanting opinions to meet the perceived needs of others

➤ Fear of criticism or rejection

➤ Fear of unjust punishment

➤ Low self-esteem

➤ Obligation

What you can do to increase energy flow:

➤ Tell more of the truth

➤ Listen to others without immediately criticizing or critiquing their ideas

➤ Stop using anger as a weapon—don't punish unjustly

➤ Accept and take responsibility for the consequences of your actions

➤ Notice and appreciate the gifts of those around you

Tried & True

Ann McGee Cooper, author of *You Don't Have To Go Home from Work Exhausted*, lists 15 childhood character traits used by many business leaders:

1. Seek out things that are fun to do, or else find a way of having fun doing the task at hand.
2. Jump from one interest to another.
3. Be curious and eager to try anything once.
4. Smile and laugh a lot.
5. Experience and express emotions freely.
6. Be creative and innovative.
7. Be physically active.
8. Constantly grow mentally and physically.
9. Take frequent risks, don't be afraid to try something you aren't initially good at, and don't be afraid to fail.
10. Rest when the body says to.
11. Learn enthusiastically.
12. Dream and imagine.
13. Believe in the impossible.
14. Don't worry or feel guilty.
15. Be passionate.

From Black Holes to Suns

Draining energy patterns between people are based on need. Mutually energizing patterns are based on support. It sounds simple, and it is. The fix can take a lifetime or a moment, so don't get down on yourself if this next workout doesn't work right away.

Transforming an energy-draining pattern of need into an energy-enhancing pattern of support, as delightful as the result is, is often difficult to do. Like quitting a bad habit, releasing addictive behavior and turning your life toward an upward spiral, requires intention, action, grace, and timing.

For the grace and timing, try prayer. The following workout will take care of the intention and action phases:

1. Identify a relationship that is draining energy from you. For example: "Nothing gets done when I'm around person X. All the focused energy seems to dissipate and then drain."

2. Write down what your intention is for this relationship. Write down what you'd like it to be. For example: "This relationship could be stimulating and focusing for both of us. I would like to see us both accomplish more, individually and jointly."

3. Use your imagination to remember the "drained" phase of this relationship. Pretend to be with the person right now and feel what it feels like to be around him or her, at the relationship's worst.

4. Write down what you need, want, or expect from this person in this state. For example: "I want this person to tell me what to do. I want him or her to decide the direction we should move in."

5. Write down things you could do that would take care of that need yourself, or take care of it in some way that doesn't involve the other person. For example: "I could decide what I want to do, without waiting for him or her. Even if the person doesn't agree, the energy would move more clearly and cleanly."

6. Ask yourself if there's a way to support the other person, to use more of his or her vitality and energy. Write it down. Example: "As I do what I see is necessary, it frees him or her to do what he or she needs to do. We both feel better and more energized, as opposed to trying to guess what each other thinks is the best thing to do."

7. Use your imagination to see the relationship functioning with this new behavior. How does it feel? Is there more energy available for everyone? Is it possible to love and appreciate who this person truly is and the gifts this person offers?

Yellow Light

Every time you hear yourself say or think, "I can live with this," you are going in the opposite direction of your intuition.

Write down your images and your results. Keep track of how the relationship evolves over time. As I said before, the need to need is hard to give up. The fear is that if we don't need others, they won't stick around to give us the attention we want.

When a relationship is based on need, it is difficult for love to also be present. The need drains everyone. Once the need is out of the way, love emerges spontaneously. A relationship based on love, whether professional or personal, will generate vitality for all.

Use Your Points of Light

Using your support group is easy. It doesn't mean asking for their help all the time, sharing your problems and concerns, or emotionally dumping on them. It does mean acknowledging them as people when you interact and letting them know what's happening in your life—the successes and the concerns—as it seems appropriate. Be open to listening to what's going on in their lives, too. The most important part of the interaction is to be open to sharing energy with them, boosting the energy for both of you. New jokes, updates on mutual friends or interests, quick stories, and odd events and observations are great ways to keep the relationship a point of light.

Power Up Your Points of Light

Nothing pulls energy out of a relationship faster than obligation and expectation. As soon as one part of the relationship focuses on what the other part should be doing, the relationship moves in a downward spiral of energy. The reason most people don't develop relationships or aren't open to sharing more of who they are with others is the fear of obligation. The thinking goes like this: "If I develop a relationship with the person who sells me coffee in the morning, chances are he'll start telling me all of his problems. Then I will feel obligated to somehow help him, which I can't do. It's better not to start at all."

Tried & True

In *The Celestine Prophecy*, James Redfield summarized what most of us know intuitively— that relationships based on domination and manipulation can be immediately energizing but quickly become draining and unsatisfying. Relationships based on trust, love, and respect generate mutually beneficial energy.

It is true that people tend to bond through their wounds, as Carolyn Myss explains very clearly in her book *Why People Don't Heal*. What starts energy on a negative spiral isn't the pain of life or even the sharing of it, it's the expectation that someone else can help us or that we need to help others. As soon as a relationship steps into the realm of "you owe me/I owe you," it's doomed. This sets up all kinds of "control dramas," in the words of James Redfield, and energy begins to spiral downward.

All this may seem quite esoteric and abstract to some, yet as your intuitive awareness increases, your sensitivity to subtle energy dynamics will increase. An athlete will be more sensitive to how her body feels than someone who never exercises. She'll notice muscle tension and strain before it would register to someone else. Similarly, those who are intuitively aware will sense when something does or doesn't feel right, before someone who isn't intuitively aware.

Having that intuitive edge is a huge benefit when preventing business and personal relationships from moving in negative directions.

On the other hand, to serve others to the best of your ability, generates energy. Have you ever been at the right place at the right time to help someone in a time of need? Was it a drain of energy? No. It was a blessing—it gave you energy. Has someone ever helped you through a rough spot with no sense of obligation or "owing?" Was that a drain of energy? No. It was a blessing—it gave you energy. When we are present and available to what's needed in the moment with those we come into contact with and we freely give what's needed, energy is generated.

Empower those around you to be points of light in your life by following these simple steps:

➤ Share yourself with them

➤ Learn about their lives

➤ Say what's on your mind when with them without expectation

➤ Listen to what comes back to you

➤ Take action only when it's effortless

Sixth Sense

Control dramas are the ways people attract attention and energy in self-defeating ways. In *The Celestine Prophecy*, James Redfield summarized them as follows: "Intimidators steal energy by threatening, Interrogators steal it by judging and questioning, Aloof people attract attention by playing coy and "hard to get," and Poor Me's generate guilt and a sense of responsibility for them through feeling victimized."

Practical Wisdom

When you do something for someone else, make it a habit to do it without the expectation of something in return. If that isn't possible in the situation, don't give at all.

Practical Wisdom

To give is to receive is the law of Love. Under this law, when we give our Love away to others, we gain, and what we give we simultaneously receive. The law of Love is based on abundance; we are completely filled with Love all the time, and our supply is always full and running over. When we give our Love unconditionally to others with no expectations of return, the Love within us extends, expands, and joins. So, by giving our Love away, we increase the Love within us and everyone gains.

—Dr. Jerry Jampolsky,
Love Is Letting Go of Fear

Don't Hesitate To Delegate

If something you're doing is a constant drain of energy, it may be time for you to delegate it to someone else. As your particular talents and gifts emerge, it becomes clear where you excel. Certain tasks generate positive energy while others just create drain. Avoiding the tasks that drain only makes it worse. It is better to leverage what you do well by doing it more, and unloading or delegating what drains you to someone who loves it and develop a "point of light" relationship with them.

Avoid the Neutral and the Negative

The quickest way to fail is to continue doing tasks you're good at but that generate zero positive energy. I've met hundreds of entrepreneurs who spend most of their energy doing administrative tasks, because they "have to get it done and they can't afford to pay someone else to do it," and then they wonder why their business fails. Any successful business person knows how to follow and generate positive energy. It usually involves doing what gives them positive energy and delegating the neutral and negative energetic tasks.

You may be nervous about talking to others about your ideas, yet that's where the positive energy is. It may feel safe and important to write letters and take care of administrative tasks, yet it's neutral energy and thus nongenerative. You may be involved in a creative task, such as writing a book. It may not be generating income, yet it generates creative energy and positive flow, which will lead to generating income. Even if it requires doing a job that creates income in order to spend time doing something that is creative and exciting, do it.

Try your hand at the following workout to help you put these ideas into practice:

1. On the left side of a piece of paper write a list of all the tasks you have done over the past three days. Go over that list and put a check mark by those tasks that generate positive energy. Put a 0 by the neutral tasks and a minus sign by those that drain energy.

2. Now, go to each of the tasks marked with a "0" or a "–" and imagine outsourcing those tasks to others. Imagine spending more of your time doing what generates energy for you. How much more income will you make when that happens?

The way to break the cycle of negative flow is to focus on positive flow. Spend your time and energy on tasks that have positive flow and it will increase. Spend your time and energy on tasks that have negative flow, and negativity will increase.

"Fire" Clients Who Drain

If you work as a consultant or in a service business, you may have clients you need to "fire." They may be more trouble than they're worth. How many clients do you work with who drain your energy? It's okay, in fact, it's a positive step to fire them. Don't attempt to change them or judge them. Acknowledge to yourself and to them that the working relationship isn't working, for them or for you and recommend that they find someone else. Perhaps you can even make a recommendation. It may be that their needs have changed since you started doing business or that your needs and services have changed since you started doing business with them.

Practical Wisdom

I am a forceful, strong personality and I like to be in control. In my position, I have been given a lot of power. But I firmly believe that the only thing to do with high power is to give it away. To delegate ultimately gives you the greatest leverage. One of my early reviews at Alza said, "Jane is full of hubris." I had to get the dictionary to see what hubris meant: "arrogance" and "self-pride." I learned from that because I didn't know how other people were seeing me. I've since learned to back off, to listen, and to keep in mind the impact I have on people.

—Jane Shaw,
President and CEO of Alza
Corporation, in *On Our Own Terms*

Be Impressionable

In general, Western culture and Western business focus on results. When business people meet for the first time, the emphasis is on how the parties will benefit from doing business together. In Eastern culture and Eastern business, the focus is first on relationship and process, then on results. In general, Eastern business people want to know who they're doing business with. In the West, if it looks like someone can get the job done, that is good enough.

Yellow Light

Every negative relationship drains you twice. The energy spent in the relationship drains you, and the energy missed by not spending that time in positive flow is lost.

Both systems have their strengths and weaknesses and would benefit from incorporating aspects of their counterpart. The danger of the Eastern approach is that it can degenerate into judging people by their family history, for example, rather than on future potential. The danger of the Western approach is that the lure of quick money or quick results of any kind, can overlook integrity. That is how business deals and sales get made on outward appearance rather than on inward substance.

Intuition can help cut through all of these issues very quickly, and the following is a workout to help you. By trusting and working with first impressions, many headaches and heartaches can be avoided. Your first impression is usually a felt sense about the person you're meeting. It may be very clear to you, or it may take some practice to catch it. Intuition doesn't stop after the first impression. Throughout the developing relationship, intuition can help guide its speed and direction. Here is how to do it:

1. When first meeting a potential business partner, employer, employee, professional, or anyone else, ask yourself the following questions:

    ➤ How do I feel about this person?

    ➤ Do I feel comfortable around him?

    ➤ Do I feel power coming from him?

    ➤ What can I learn from him?

2. If you decide to proceed and develop the relationship further, ask these questions:

    ➤ Is she answering my questions?

    ➤ Is she listening to me?

    ➤ Do I understand completely what the deal is?

3. If you have invested a certain amount of time and energy into a relationship and you begin to feel uncomfortable at any point, don't abandon the relationship, ask more questions and get more information. Be cautious about getting more involved, and proceed slowly. Trust your internal warning system and when you experience anything like a deep sinking feeling, red flashing lights, penalty flags, continual energy drain—back off. When you back off and seek to slow down, watch how the other person responds.

Tried & True

What got me into the most trouble, and what led to my mistakes in hiring and choosing investors, was that I didn't stick to my gut feelings. I didn't know how much I knew about running my company, how good I was at it. As it took off, I ended up deferring decisions to more-experienced businesspeople, believing they knew more than I did. That proved to be my downfall.

—Gregory G. Graendel, *Inc. Magazine*, July 1994

4. Watch your "wanting" vs. "receiving" quotient. When something is wanted, really wanted, it can override intuition. The problem isn't what's wanted, the problem is in deciding that what's wanted is going to come from a particular source. Once the mind locks on a target, it becomes more difficult to access intuitive knowing. Hold on to what's wanted and release the perceived source. Remember, what you want could come from any number of sources. Your attachment to one particular source may be blocking intuitive flow. Ask these questions to get back on track:

> ➤ Am I any closer to what I want?
> ➤ Where is the positive flow?
> ➤ What are my options?
> ➤ Is what I'm receiving energetically equal to what I'm giving?

Your first impressions are a great source of information. Write them down to keep track of how they play out. If your first impressions are difficult to grab, keep asking yourself how you feel when you are around someone. The first impression won't just disappear, it will continue to be part of the relationship and can be grasped at any moment.

My Lawyer Is More Intuitive Than Your Lawyer

The professionally skilled people you work with can help you tremendously with your success. Traditional professionals like lawyers, accountants, brokers, health specialists, financial planners, sales people, and fitness trainers, as well as consultants and specialized professionals worked with regularly or periodically can make the difference between success and failure. They can take over tasks that are time consuming and not enjoyable to you, and they can provide important assistance exactly when needed.

They become your core team. They know you, your goals, your needs, and they're there to serve you. Successful people surround themselves with talented and accomplished people. As the mother of Nido Quebein (a successful entrepreneur, consultant, and motivational speaker) said to him: "Walk with powerful people and it will rub off."

Professionals are usually people you want to develop a long-term relationship with. Here are some steps, beyond working with first impressions, to help capture your intuitive insights about the professionals you work with:

1. Begin with your first intuitive impression about this person by asking:
   - ➤ How do I feel about this person?
   - ➤ Can he deliver what I need?
   - ➤ Does she like her work?
   - ➤ What can I learn from him?
   - ➤ Does he listen to me?
   - ➤ Are my questions answered to my satisfaction?

Tried & True

A woman interviewing a potential financial advisor didn't understand what he was telling her and felt that she was somehow "stupid" or just not interested enough in her finances to "get it." In other words, she thought that she was the problem. I suggested that the problem was the financial advisor and not her. If her questions could not be answered clearly and comfortably, interview a few other advisors before making a decision.

2. During the conversation, ask a few questions that will give you a deeper sense of who this person is, or at least who this person thinks he or she is, such as:

   ➤ What do you hope to accomplish with this project?

   ➤ What do you love about what you do?

   ➤ What is your overall mission?

   ➤ If you could change something about your job, what would it be?

3. Once you have an impression, sit with it. It will either be positive, negative, or neutral. In some cases, it may be completely clear that this is someone who just doesn't fit in with what you're doing. In other cases, there may be interest and some positive energy, yet doubt or confusion. Reaffirm what you want to accomplish and get more information about this person. Meet with the person again, have others meet with the person, ask questions, learn more. Keep looking for the intuitive green light or red light about this person, as he or she relates to your project or goal. Wait until there's a sense of positive flow between the two of you before proceeding.

4. When working with professionals who specifically focus on helping you achieve financial success, it's imperative to pay attention to how they deal with money. There will be fees for the services you receive. If they're not receiving adequate compensation, you won't receive adequate service. If they don't talk directly about money and financial issues, they may be uncomfortable dealing with money and success. Money is a form of energy. When professionals are uncomfortable asking for their fees, talking about compensation, and explaining the financial part of their work—watch out. Their own personal issues about money and success may interfere with their ability to provide you the best service.

Don't Be Cheap

The first thing not to be cheap about is working with professionals and getting the help and advice you need for your success. The sooner you work with others, the sooner you will be successful. Remember, no one does it alone in this world. The sooner you gather your team and have them working for you, the sooner you will reach your goal. Think of your team of professionals as your audience. They cheer you on, lift you up when you're down, give valuable feedback when things are not going well, and acknowledge your successes.

Yellow Light

Watch out for professionals who can't talk directly about fees, money, and compensation. They're struggling with their own money issues, which you may not want to help them solve.

Practical Wisdom

When a customer buys a low-grade article, he feels pleased when he pays for it and displeased every time he uses it. But when he buys a well-made article, he feels extravagant when he pays for it and well pleased every time he uses it.

—Herbert Casson,
from *Forbes Scrapbook of Life*

Aldonna Ambler, a highly successful entrepreneur and consultant to aspiring entrepreneurs, recommended hiring an administrative assistant at a time when it was definitely not affordable. Her argument was persuasive, and I knew intuitively she was right, so I did it. I paid someone else before I paid myself, and it helped me in ways I would never have imagined. Just having someone else to be responsible for, to manage, to keep busy, made me take myself more seriously as an entrepreneur. It was harder to let things slide. My assistant became a friend and advisor, helping with marketing ideas and adding much positive energy to my endeavors.

There's no doubt that many people who become wealthy do so by saving and investing their money, finding bargains, and working with professionals who are talented and "on their way up," whose fees are lower than those who have already made it. On the other hand, skimping on professional fees or buying less expensive stuff that doesn't have the quality you want, will ultimately drain your energy.

Tim, a friend who owns his own successful business in New York City, shared with me how he found a lawyer he needed when purchasing a new home. First, he met with someone close to his home, convenient, and knowledgeable about real estate. Then he met with a very high-powered, well-respected and well-known law firm. The first person felt comfortable to him. The whole interaction was low-key, simple, and informative.

Practical Wisdom

Before saying no to spending money you don't think you can afford, ask yourself: "Is this an investment that will build my future wealth?" If so, you may want to find a way to spend what you need to.

In Tim's mind he thought: "Yeah, but does this guy know what he is doing? No one really recommended him to me, I found him myself, how good can he be?" Then Tim went to see the high-powered lawyer. He had to wait to see him, there were many phone interruptions during their conversation, and Tim left feeling unimportant to this lawyer. After reflecting on his choices, Tim went with the first lawyer. He felt right about that guy and let go of his need to be validated in his choice by choosing the person many others had chosen before. He was completely satisfied with the outcome of his choice.

Become an Intuitive Networker

Many of the business contacts you make will come from more informal sources. People you meet at conferences, lunches, networking meetings, and through friends will form the bulk of your contacts. The business cards add up. How can you possibly stay in touch with all of them? How can you determine who to stay in touch with and who to let go? Intuition plays a key role in successful networking.

Here are the intuitive guidelines to power networking:

➤ When at a gathering of people talk to whoever attracts your attention.

➤ When there's no more positive energy in the conversation, move on.

➤ Be open to talking to whoever comes up to you.

➤ Be yourself—share your dream, your current needs, your talents.

➤ Wherever there is shared positive flow of energy, follow up with notes, email, phone call, or something else. If there's no positive flow, let it go—don't force it.

➤ Look for synchronicities: mutual friends, interests, and so on.

➤ Don't attach an outcome to any meeting—that is, don't fantasize about what meeting a particular person will mean to you.

➤ If you think of someone "out of the blue" call or email that person—follow up no matter how long it has been.

➤ Make a habit of going to networking meetings on a regular basis—provide ways for the Universe to bring you the people you need to meet.

➤ Network with your points of light.

Networking is as old as humans. Every time people get together, there's networking. From tribal times to campfire times to royal court, networking has provided a way of cross-fertilizing with others, renewing visions, and changing directions. It is a time to be open to opportunity. A time to let go of a particular track you might be on and allow new input, creativity, insight, and energy. One phrase someone might say to you could inspire your next project.

Practical Wisdom

People are so accustomed to viewing the business world in warlike terms that even when other players are both competitors and complementors, they tend to see them as only competitors and fight against them.... According to McGraw-Hill CEO Joseph L. Dionne, "In 10 instances when we created an electronic version of the print edition...demand for the print version grew, too."

—Adam M. Brandenburger & Barry J. Nalebuff, *Co-opetition*

Network with the Universe

While networking provides ways to gain energy through interacting with other people, networking with the Universe allows you to interact with the unknown. Remember, your intuition connects you to a vast network of resources. Chapter 6 discussed continuous intuitive planning—the same principle is at work with networking with the Universe. Open yourself to unknown possibilities by consciously asking the Universe to supply what you need but can't do. Be open to receiving powerful partners.

When I was writing another manuscript on intuition, I decided that finding a publisher was something I wanted to happen, but I didn't want to spend the time it would take. I wanted to focus on my writing, and I unloaded the task of finding the right publisher onto the Universe. About two weeks later, I received a fax from Alpha Books/ Macmillan asking me to write this book. How's that for universal service?

Message in a Bottle

Here's a little workout to help you network with the Universe:

1. Draw a line down the middle of a piece of paper.

2. Title the left column "Me," and write the results you wish to achieve.

3. Title the right column "Universe," and write what you need to accomplish your dream but can't provide for yourself.

4. Imagine sending the message out to all the corners of the world. Imagine that exactly the right resource, whatever it may be, hears the call and begins to mobilize toward you. It may take time, it may be instantaneous—you can't know that. You can know that it is on its way to you in a form you may least expect.

5. Be grateful. Thank the Universe for making the connection you're unable to make yourself.

6. Continue to do the tasks that you can do to further your dream. Don't wait for the Universe, but be open to receiving its abundance.

Inter-Networking

Think of what you've just done. You have networked with the entire world in a matter of moments. Sound ridiculous? Just think of the Internet. It's almost like a physical manifestation of that intuition TV we talked about in Chapter 1. We now have the electronic technology to accomplish what would have seemed ridiculous just a few years ago. The Internet is a powerful tool for networking with the Universe. I encourage everyone with a dream to set up a Web page. Give the Universe a golden opportunity to link you to those around the world who might share your vision and help achieve your dream. What is happening electronically has been happening intuitively and spiritually forever. The Internet just makes it easier and quicker for the Universe to respond to your requests.

The Least You Need to Know

➤ Positive energy between people is a signal for a mutually beneficial relationship and negative energy between people is a signal to change or stop a business relationship.

➤ Pay attention to those you interact with regularly and make them part of your success.

➤ Delegate work you don't like to others and fire clients who drain you.

➤ Trust your first impressions of new people, especially when hiring consultants.

➤ Don't be afraid to spend money at the right time for the right purpose.

➤ Expand your network to include the Universe.

Chapter 13

Intuitive Investing

In This Chapter

➤ Learn intuitive exercises for all parts of the investment game

➤ Read the signs and signals for success and failure

➤ Discover your best investment opportunities

➤ Develop impeccable intuitive timing

➤ Learn the 10 secrets to successful intuitive investing

If this book came with a packet of seeds that could literally grow into money trees in your back yard, would you plant them? If the steps included simple, effortless tasks like choosing the right site, preparing the soil, planting the seeds, and watering and nurturing them, wouldn't you give it a shot?

To someone who knows nothing of plant biology, the turning of a seed into a productive plant is magic. To someone who knows nothing about the laws of prosperity, getting rich looks like magic.

If you want to invest, find out first if you enjoy the process. If not, get out. Let someone you trust manage your money and build your wealth for you. Look back to Chapter 12, which discusses hiring professionals to help you care for your financial garden. Invest your time and effort in something you *love*: sports, art, collecting, learning. Whatever you love will pay off in unimaginable abundance.

Practical Wisdom

When it's time to move on a particular stock, I get chills up and down my spine and feel a heightened sense of energy.

—Gary Markoff, vice president, Smith Barney

My husband is a financial planner. He works for American Express Financial Advisors. He also trusts and uses his intuitive abilities. We have learned from each other over our 20 years together and have helped each other trust and follow the intuitive path. Much of what I share in this chapter comes from watching how he invests for us and for others, plus intuitive workouts we use specifically for the investment process. I also have used the insights of other professional friends and experts who are involved in financial markets and are committed to trusting their intuitive process.

This chapter is for those who want to do better with their investments while using more of who they are in the investment process. If you feel stuck in your investing, this chapter will help. If you want to explore whether investing is something that might be enjoyable for you, this chapter will help, too. I'll cap it off by showing you 10 secrets to successful intuitive investing.

Chills Up Your Spine

At a dinner one evening, a woman claimed to have discovered a foolproof method for predicting market trends through complex computer analysis of various indexes. After listening to her for a while, I realized that as she collected data, she waited for her intuition to signal her. When it did, she knew how to act on it, giving all the credit to the data she collected. When pressed, she admitted that, after looking at the trends, a pattern emerged and suddenly she knew what was going to happen next.

Tried & True

Jack D. Schwager, talking to a highly successful trader for his book The New Market Wizards, recorded this nugget:

"Q: I still don't understand your trading method. How could you make these huge sums of money by just watching the screen?

"A: There was no system to it. It was nothing more than, 'I think the market is going up, so I'm going to buy.' 'It's gone up enough, so I'm going to sell.' It was completely impulsive. I didn't sit down and formulate any trading plan. I don't know where the intuition comes from."

Everyone has an internal sensing mechanism. When it's time to act toward a desired outcome, the internal mechanism will use anything available to get the message relayed. In other words, from mounds of information, or perhaps in spite of it, a clear knowing emerges. Information analyzed in any form acts like an oracle, triggering the internal, intuitive "AH-HA!"

Everyone develops their own system and style for accessing intuitive wisdom. Here is the very simple intuitive pattern underlying all strategies and analysis applied to investing. The following sections discuss each of these in detail.

1. Choose to play.

2. Gather intuitive information.

3. Gather information intuitively

4. Recognize opportunity...

5. ...and act on it!

6. Stay with your commitment.

Choose To Play

Let's say you've decided to increase your wealth through investing in the stock market. Pick an area you're interested in. Set some financial goals. And try the following workout to determine whether it's the right time.

Imagine two doors. Door #1 is marked "Time To Invest", and Door #2 is marked "Not Time To Invest." Take a deep breath, release it and walk over to Door #1. Open the door and notice what you see behind the door, how it feels, what you sense. Breathe in the atmosphere behind Door #1. Close the door and walk over to Door #2. Repeat the steps. Ask yourself: "Which door do I want to walk through now? What will I need for the challenge?"

Practical Wisdom

I just wait until there's money lying in the corner, and all I have to do is go over there and pick it up. I do nothing in the meantime.

—James Rogers, interviewed by Jack D. Schwager in *The New Market Wizards*

Sixth Sense

An *oracle* is a divination system where you ask a question and then receive an answer from an external source. The most common oracle is flipping a coin to determine whether something is "yes" or "no." A more complete discussion of oracles will be found in Chapter 22.

Tried & True

Observation number 8 out of 42 market wizardry observations:

"How can good trading require hard work and yet be effortless? There is no contradiction. Hard work refers to the preparatory process—the research and observation necessary to become a good trader—not to the trading itself. In this respect, hard work is associated with such qualities as vision, creativity, persistence, drive, desire, and commitment. Hard work certainly does not mean that the process of trading itself should be filled with exertion. It certainly does not imply struggling with or fighting against the markets. On the contrary, the more effortless and natural the trading process, the better the chances for success."

—Jack D. Schwager, *The New Market Wizards*

Gather Information Intuitively

Gather, sift, weigh, and absorb information. It doesn't really matter what kind of information is gathered, only that you enjoy exploring this information, that you become extremely familiar with the language, and that you have a method for integrating it. This is where "work" may be done, yet if you love what you're integrating, it will be creative work.

You will enjoy learning. Mathematicians and analysts love numbers, artists love style, psychics love synchronistic patterns, astrologers love planets and their inter-relationships. Investors may combine two or more areas of interest: technology companies and numbers, fashion apparel and seasonal buying patterns, home-building patterns and weather conditions. This is the arena where most of the techniques, analytic tools, and systems develop. As long as you get involved, keep learning and pay attention, the specific system is irrelevant.

Practical Wisdom

Ask yourself periodically: "Am I still having fun? Am I learning something?"

Instead of reading the paper or other sources of information for specific content—browse and scan. Allow yourself to be distracted by a seemingly irrelevant article and read it. Imagine the back of your mind open as you absorb analytic information. Make a point to read, listen to, and watch unusual stuff. Don't stick with a pattern of news, magazines, and shows. Break out and get information on stuff you'd never normally watch.

Gather Intuitive Information

Actively engage your intuition, make sure you allow room in your decision-making process for intuitive wisdom. It does not take more time, it takes a shift of attention. Use one or more of the workouts in this book to directly access your intuitive knowledge about specific decisions. Don't go further with anything until it "feels" right.

Tried & True

Although Peter Anderson calls himself a "numbers kind of guy," he also feels strongly that an investment manager has to pay attention to his intuition. "I trust my instincts a lot," said Anderson, Senior Vice President of Investments, for American Express Financial Advisors. "When things don't smell right, I start asking a lot of questions. If the answers are not satisfactory and if I feel I should sell a stock, then I do."

" I trust my gut more, not less," said Anderson. "I've made good decisions and good money doing it the past 27 years. One can narrow the odds by hard work and analysis, but there is a sixth sense to this business, and it has helped me to avoid trouble."

—Peter Anderson, interviewed by *Investors Business Daily*

Recognize Opportunity

Catch the moment of ripeness. At some point, the timing will be right. An opportunity will appear that brings together the desired goal and the information researched. An intuitive, inner feeling of rightness will occur. This is where intuitive alertness pays off. For investors, it may look like an opportunity too good to be true, yet there it is. The money is effortless, the opportunity is easy. There will be an inner urge to act. This is intuitive gold. This is the step that can be brushed aside and overlooked in technical approaches.

Here's a workout that flexes your intuitive skill for recognizing opportunities. I call it The Internal Beeper.

Practical Wisdom

When specific bits of information pass your consciousness three times within a short period of time, pay attention. Synchronicity may be giving you a message. Somehow three times is the magic number. When something grabs you three times, do something about it. I call this the "Law of Three."

Beepers are everywhere. They have become a modern urban signal for immediate attention. Close your eyes for a moment, take a deep breath, and imagine your own internal beeper. Your internal beeper is designed to signal you when there's a financial opportunity in front of you. Set your internal beeper to either "vibrate" or "beep." Place it strategically so you will recognize the feeling or sound. You will be the only one who gets this signal, it's your sign to wake up and pay attention.

Act on Opportunity

Do what's in front of you to do. This step marks the difference between those who excel and those who just get by. The ability, the courage to act on what you know, intuitively, without having to wait for analytic validation, creates success. This is where the heat is.

Practical Wisdom

See if you can differentiate between what you want and what you know. Wanting has urgency and longing. Knowing is neutral; it just *is*. It isn't *predictive* knowing that we're looking for here—it is knowing what *is* right now.

Do what's natural—let the action you take be in complete harmony with the moment. Don't resist it. When snowboarding, would you turn and go uphill? No. When canoeing, would you go against the current? No. The speed of the flow may be fast or slow, rough or smooth—that's where skill and experience play a part. Your role, once you see where the flow is going, is to go with it without resisting.

At the same time, your eye is on your goal. There's a specific place you're going at the bottom of the snowboard hill and while canoeing, you don't want to ram into the rocks, instead, you want to steer around them. Being "in the flow" means responding to the terrain you find yourself in.

Close your eyes, take a deep breath and feel the flow of the moment you're in right now. Let yourself get into the same rhythm and speed. Let go to it and pay attention to what's required of you.

Commit to Committing

Follow up. Initiating action is only another beginning. Follow progress, watch for signs of change. Stay in the game long enough to harvest your results. Don't panic. This is another step requiring intuitive skill. When to get out, when to stay, how to know.

Complete this intuition workout to learn to recognize your own intuitive feeling. Before making a move, imagine it first, walk through the action mentally and emotionally, and notice how you feel after you've done it.

If you make a mistake in a trade, you'll know it almost immediately. Whether it's the mistake of buying something or not buying something, your gut will tell you without the need for numbers verification. You will feel the sinking, empty feeling of a missed opportunity. The right trade feels neutral, clean, smooth—in the flow. If there's too much hype—too much excitement—it isn't your intuition at work. If you can change immediately, do it. Follow through on your commitment to trust yourself, follow your intuitive path, and follow your decision. If you make a mistake, do what you can, then don't look back—keep going or you'll miss the next opportunity.

Use Everything, Including the Secret Ingredient

A friend of mine had a grandmother who shared 99 percent of her favorite recipes. She always left out one or more secret ingredients that made the dish "hers." In the world of investing and wealth producing, most experts talk about the technical, analytic, hard work elements of the business. They know there's a secret ingredient but often even they can't describe what it is. Something magic, something some people seem to be born with.

This book reveals the secret ingredient. It's the intuitive process. It's something everyone has on his or her shelf, they just don't always know where and when to use it.

Use everything for your success and fulfillment. Use the analytic techniques and use the intuitive techniques. Find a blend that will create a magic recipe for you.

The following section walks through the details of stock-market transactions and adds intuitive workouts with each step. Practice these and your intuition will become as skilled as your analytic mind.

You Pay More, You Get More

Much of the beginning of this book is focused on defining your goals and setting your financial intention. It is vital to have all of your investment strategies, decisions, and planning in alignment with your life plan. The clearer the connections between your investments and your life goals, the more successful they'll be. For example, if your goal is to grow enough money to purchase a home, your investments will build faster than if your goal is to

Practical Wisdom

A trader describes a typical conversation with her assistant, whom she is attempting to train to trade:

"OK, Steve, what's your game plan for today?"

"I think I'm going to buy wheat today," he says, explaining his reasons for the trade.

"That's great!" I say, trying to encourage him.

At the end of the day, I ask him, "Did you buy the wheat?"

"No," he answers.

"Well, what did you do?"

"I watched it go up."

—Linda Bradford Raschke, *Trader*

Yellow Light

Attempting to "make" things happen is the most counter-productive and counter-intuitive behavior.

save money for some unknown that might happen. Your intention and clarity adds power to your decision-making and focused action. And, if that home purchase is part of a larger personal vision, it will happen even quicker.

If buying a home is really the dream of someone else, it will be difficult to achieve. You will have to make it happen and apply a force of will to create it, at a high price of personal creative energy.

Review the workouts in Chapter 10 on setting financial goals and reaffirm them now.

Dig for Pay Dirt

Any effort we make has two components. It addresses a current situation and sets something in motion for the future. If someone is on an assembly line making widgets, she is taking care of the current need to put together the widgets and she is making an hourly wage with which to take care of her household needs. Someone raising children is managing the daily needs of the children and seeding her future interests, skills, and abilities. There's always something going on in the present and the future. Investing is no different. The investment addresses a current need and aims for an increase in future value.

Your best investments will address a current, relevant need or interest and build a bridge to your ideal future. For example, the purchase of a home is often the biggest single investment a family makes. It provides a current place to live and an investment for the future.

There are an infinite number of investment arenas filled with opportunities for living your dream, fulfilling your purpose, and keeping busy and productive. Where is it most obvious for you to invest? Ask yourself these questions when deciding whether to get involved with an investment area:

➤ Do I want to learn more about this area?

➤ Is this involved with a part of my life I enjoy?

➤ Do I have history with this area? Is there a natural understanding based on my family, past, or inclinations?

➤ Does it fit in with my overall values in life?

➤ Can my energy make a positive difference in this arena?

To take this workout another step, after answering all the preceding questions yourself, try on a particular area and see how it fits. Let your body tell you whether or not it's a good fit. If it feels like a comfortable old shoe, you may want something a little more exciting. If it feels just slightly daring and a little outrageous, it may be the perfect fit. You want something that is comfortable to you and yet helps stretch you into where you're going.

You might want to begin with two or three areas you are considering getting involved in, say Internet stocks and sportswear. "Try them on" and compare the different intuitive imagery and feelings that occur. Is one more comfortable than the other for you? more interesting?

What you really want to know is if this area has juice? Is it hot? Is it a place where you can get in and make good decisions for yourself?

Boat Rocking? Watch the Horizon

You can apply intuitive methods in specific ways to pinpoint market trends, whatever market you're working in. The following techniques are specifically designed for working with the stock market, and can be modified to fit any situation requiring attunement to the future. Remember the first section of this chapter where the overview of intuitive functioning is outlined. The following workouts are ways to gather intuitive information. What you're looking for is a feeling of flow and rightness. You want to build a strong internal feeling, strong enough to act on when the tension is mounting and others are advocating different ways.

This intuition workout assists you with broad forecasting. Once or twice a year, sit down and map out the overview for the specific market trend you're involved with. If you're in fashion, use this workout to map trends in styles, colors, competitors, and so on. If you play in foreign currency, use the map to view worldwide currency trends, and so on.

Tried & True

Women may be more intuitive. I certainly feel that I can see patterns that other people can't, but I don't know if that's because I'm a female. I think it's often more acceptable for a woman to rely on intuition than it is for a man to do so, and intuition certainly comes into play in trading. For example, when I'm watching the price quotes, I never say something like, "Oh, the market is down exactly 62 percent, I have to buy right here." Rather, I might think, "Gee, it looks like we've corrected enough and the price has stopped going down, so I'd better buy."

—Linda Bradford Raschke, *Trader*

Give yourself at least a half hour of quiet time to complete the workout:

1. Spend about five minutes breathing quietly and create an open space in your mind. If it works better for you, hold a pencil up and look at the point for five minutes. Focus gently on the point of the pencil, not staring or straining, just looking.

2. Close your eyes and imagine a blank chart. The left, vertical axis represents growth and the horizontal, lower axis represents time.

3. Imagine the names of the months of the year either across the top of the chart or along the bottom, beginning with the current month.

4. Watch the line of movement as it moves through the months. Without mentally interfering with it, allow it to show you what's going to happen over the coming months.

5. Open your eyes and draw what you saw. Keep it as a reference chart and check its track record.

Yellow Light

The secret to intuitive investing is to keep the throttle that controls timing and action internal to you. Learn from others, but follow your own inclinations.

This workout can be done with specific stocks you're following as well as with overall market trends. The proof will be in watching how accurate you are. At first, you may not want to base many of your decisions on your graph, but as you see how well it predicts the trends, you may want to consult it more often.

Intuitive Planning Revisited

When planning a road trip, it's useful to know ultimate destinations and general guidelines, but it's no fun to plan all the pit stops along the way. You want to allow room for serendipity and synchronicity. The same philosophy works in financial planning. With a rigid plan, many unexpected opportunities are missed. With a loose, unfocused plan, the ultimate destination may never be reached. The purpose of a plan is to establish benchmarks to compare actual performance to desired performance toward your goal.

Each of you has a comfort zone of planning that works for you. Some investors use their investment plan to help them know when they're off track. If someone has a system that works for them, and they watch themselves drifting farther and farther away from their system, it's probably time to get back to basics, or take a break. Laziness and looking for shortcuts is setting in and that is not intuition!

For your next intuition workout, use the Intuitive Planning Model from Chapter 6. Here it is, redesigned for planning an investment strategy:

1. Take a piece of paper and draw a line down the middle. On the left side write your name and on the right side write "The Universe."

2. Under your name, list all the things you can and will do. Make sure that they are things you really can do in the immediate future without intervening steps. For example, my list includes: Pay attention, stay informed in my areas of interest, follow movements, act on opportunities, and keep my spending focused.

3. List all the things on the right side that you want the Universe to do. List all the things you want to happen, yet can't control, can't make happen, or can't force. For example, my list includes: provide big financial opportunities, bring optimal stock choices into my view, bring competent professionals to my attention, and so on.

Do whatever planning feels good to you and add the intuitive planning model. Keep it handy and keep handing over to the Universe that which you want but can't control.

Yellow Light

Shortcuts and sloppiness are not intuition! When you find yourself looking for a quick fix, watch out. You're most likely tired or off your track and need a break.

Picking Stocks Through Intuition

Here are two power workouts for using intuition to help pick stocks. They work equally well for beginners, seasoned investors, and experienced intuitives. In fact, beginners have a slight edge, they'll be less likely to second guess themselves. Remember first to do your homework, know your playing field, and have your goals.

These workouts will build intuitive skill as well as provide important information along the way. Once you feel confident, your internal timing meter will take over and you won't need to workout to get in tune with your intuitive process. Keep it handy when you get out of sync with the market.

And now, let your intuition be your guide.

You Sure Can Pick 'Em

Begin with a stack of note cards and a list of at least three but no more than five stocks or trades you're considering making. Then do the following:

1. Write the name of each stock on one note card. Be consistent and write on either the lined or unlined side of each card.

2. Turn the cards over so that you can't see what you have written on each one and mix them up.

3. Close your eyes and take a few deep breaths. Imagine connecting with a universal source of information. Create an image and a feeling of flow from this source into you.

4. With the cards still face down, pick one.

5. Close your eyes and imagine the movement of this stock over the next one to three months (or whatever time period fits your investing routine).

6. You can imagine a graph or simple arrows pointing up, down, or straight across.

   You may imagine the words up, down, or neutral. As you become comfortable with this workout, the information may come in more detailed images and feelings.

7. Write your results on the blank side of the card. Don't look at the name of the stock yet.

8. Repeat steps four through six with each of the remaining cards.

9. Now look at your results.

10. Notice how you feel when you see the name of the stock and compare it to what you visualized.

11. Keep track of how you do.

Don't attempt to guess which stock is on the card. Allow the information to come to you in any shape or form. This is a non-analytic workout. What you're looking for is unbiased information. Do this workout with three to five new stocks every day and you will become a master at sensing the growth energy of stocks as soon as you hear their names.

For the advanced version of this workout, allow more information to emerge with each card by allowing images, feelings, and physical sensations. The more information the better.

Tried & True

My husband and I used this workout religiously when the stock market did its dance in September 1998. The guidance we received helped us navigate through the market transition with just a little deep breathing and complete effortlessness.

Getting In and Getting Out

Use a variation of the previous workout to intuit timing for investment moves:

1. Write the names of three to five investment picks, one per index card.

2. Turn them over and mix them up.

3. Pick one, close your eyes, and ask yourself: When is the right time to get into this investment?

4. Wait for your answer. You may sense the words now, later, or never You may see a date or a picture of a calendar with a dot or point on a date. You may see a clock or other timing device that indicates when to act. The skill is in not anticipating or making any images appear. Allow your intuitive mind to provide non-analytic information. You are under no obligation to act on it—see it as more information and use it to help make your decisions. Track it for accuracy and improvement.

5. Now do the same for investments you are already in and are wondering when to abandon.

Back to the Applause Meter!

In Chapter 4 you developed an intuitive "applause meter" that told you whether or not something has positive energy for you. Use it when making stock decisions.

Tension You Can Learn To Love

When clothes shopping I can be impulsive. The impatience becomes unbearable and I either leave or buy something that works but isn't just right. Thankfully, my daughters are better shoppers. I have been through excruciating (for me) shopping trips where they said over and over again, "It's not quite right. Let's keep looking." The amazing thing to me is that they did eventually find the perfect fit with the perfect look at the right price.

The tension would build, and all of us would want to quit and go home, but the need for the outfit for a specific event encouraged us to just stop, get something to eat, then keep going. It was often just at the point of giving up that the right outfit appeared. Suddenly, complete peace. A feeling of rightness and elation.

The same principle is at work when developing impeccable timing. Just before the rightness is an incredible amount of tension. The height of an in-breath has the most tension, just before the relaxing exhalation. In a flowing river, the current gets very strong just as the water is flowing into deeper, calmer water. The master trader may never be comfortable with that tension, but he or she knows how to stay with it until the tension resolves itself and the answer becomes crystal clear.

The next time you feel compelled to get in or get out of a situation, wait. As long as you're internally questioning to yourself: "Should I stay or leave? Is it time to get in or get out?" Don't do anything. Live with the tension and see what happens. When you feel like you don't know what to do, but something sure needs to be done—wait. Hold steady with the tension and watch. There will come a point where the energy shifts and the path is clear.

Here's a quick intuition workout: When you're feeling particularly tense, take a few moments to breathe. With every inhalation repeat the word "be" to yourself and with exhalation repeat the word "present." You can also use "open" on the inhalation and "space" on the exhalation. Just five minutes of focused breathing will help get you back on track. If the tension persists, take a walk and continue breathing with the focus words.

Intuitively speaking, decisions don't really get made; they make themselves. Something is either right or not right. If it's right, there is no decision—it is clear. If it's not right, there is no decision—the path is clear.

Avoid False Profits

There are many investment newsletters that promote get rich quick opportunities or promote doom and gloom future scenarios. Don't get caught up in fear-based philosophies. Intuition functions on the premise that we are collectively creating the future by the actions we take today and the attitudes that guide those actions. The intuitive approach is hopeful and puts its money on human ingenuity, creativity, and faith in a larger vision everyone participates in.

In reading the newsletters and advice columns, take in the information and be discerning about what to use and what to throw away. Gather the insights of the voices of fear and get rich quick without buying into the underlying philosophy.

Ten Power Pointers for Intuitive Investing

Here are 10 investing tips which summarize the intuitive investment of this chapter. Memorizing them will help you develop and apply intuitive skill while making successful investments.

1. *Never bet someone else's strategy.* It's okay to learn from others and get information but if they have a strategy that works for them, let it work for them. Develop your own. Take what looks the best to you from everyone you meet and allow your style and strategy to emerge. Once you discover what works for you—stick with it. Your intuition will learn continuously from every encounter, every transaction, whether you enjoyed it or not.

2. *Stay in flow with the market.* Keep your focus on the market movement, not necessarily on what everyone else is doing. Free yourself from either following or leading the pack—your goal is to stay in flow and let intuition be the guide.

3. *If it's obvious to you—it's a gift.* Usually the way we miss opportunities in this business is by saying, "It looks too good to be true," and then not doing anything. Too often we think that everybody else must know something that we don't, and I think that's a critical mistake.

4. *Know how to let go without giving up.* There will be times when a strategy or an intuition won't work—it won't pay off the way you wanted and expected it to. Let go and move on. Learn from what happened without beating yourself or anyone else up.

5. *Deserts are part of the terrain.* When you're off—no blame, it's not personal—just take a break. When I'm wrong three times in a row, I call time out. Then I paper trade until I think I'm in sync with the market again. Every market has a rhythm, and our job as traders is to get in sync with that rhythm.

6. *Tension needs to be managed, not avoided.* Tension is the physical and emotional experience of expanding creative energy. Get used to it. Learn to work with it. Nothing is born without creative tension.

7. *Prayer does not work.* "God isn't a market manipulator," says Mark Ritchie, commodities trader and author of *God in the Pits*. God provides plenty of opportunities yet won't change what is happening to suit your needs. It's up to you to get in flow with God's plan, not the other way around.

8. *Keep learning, and keep growing.* The market is constantly changing. Don't get stuck in one system, one perspective. Keep moving. It takes 20 years in one field to begin to understand its true value.

9. *Live your life and your investments will follow.* Linda B. Raschke stopped trading just before the crash of '87—not because of a vision—because she was ready to take a break and had a personal opportunity she wanted to follow up on. It "just happened" to get her out of a difficult market swing. (Jack Schwager, *The New Market Wizards*)

10. *When you start looking for others to validate your moves, get out—or at least rethink your position.* As Linda Bradford Raschke writes, "Seeking out other peoples' opinions on a trade is a sure sign that the trade should be liquidated."

The secret to intuitive investing is to keep the throttle that controls timing and action internal to you. If you get involved because of someone else's enthusiasm, yet it has no relationship to you, the investment is doomed. It may be a great idea, but for you it won't work. The timing will be off or you will need your money out for something more important to you and you won't be able to get it without a loss. Do what you need to do to keep the handle of decision-making internal to you.

The Least You Need to Know

➤ Intuition will use anything handy to get the message to you, even analytic data.

➤ Establish an "internal beeper" that will sound when you need to pay attention.

➤ Intuition knows. It does not think.

➤ All the training in the world won't make up for the inability to act at the right time.

➤ Insert intuitive workouts strategically, while implementing a traditional investment plan.

➤ The right time to act often occurs after some heavy tension.

➤ Memorize the 10 Power Pointers for Intuitive Investing.

Intuitive Entrepreneurship

Daryl Maddeaux grew up in Canada and discovered early that he loved building with and balancing rocks. He built forts and even snowmen out of rocks. Over years of experimentation and play, he learned to balance large rocks on top of smaller rocks, creating stunning works of art that made people open their minds to consider what is truly possible.

As an adult, Daryl has created a full life around his art. He teaches various groups, including children and business people, sells photographs of his balanced rocks, receives spontaneous donations from passers-by when he does his art on public beaches, sets up balanced rocks for special events, and has his own Web site (www.RockonRock.com).

Daryl lives an abundant life. He has the precious commodity of time to do what he loves, makes more than enough money to meet his needs, and contributes to the well being and creativity of others.

This chapter helps you use your intuition to determine if you're an entrepreneur, as well as how to successfully work *for* an entrepreneur. It'll help you find and pick the ideas you want to work with, and to use your intuition from start-up to going public—including tips on how to intuitively structure your business.

The Entrepreneurial Spirit

Successful entrepreneurs let their lives support them. Rather than asking "What kind of job can I get?" an entrepreneur asks "How can I make the money I want doing what I enjoy?" or "How can I turn this into a business?" The ideas, opportunities, and contacts evolve out of their lives.

Practical Wisdom

According to U.S. government statistics, in 10 years, half of all those working in jobs today will be working in jobs that have not even been invented or defined yet.

Entrepreneurs are the hunter–gatherers of our culture. Plopped down in an environment, they look around and see where the food is and go get it. The skills of tracking, sensing, hunting, and harvesting are very much alive in the entrepreneur.

The difference between those who look for a job and those who look for opportunities is this: Entrepreneurs don't change themselves to fit their environment—instead, they use the environment to meet their needs. Those who look for a job come into an environment and see what they need to do to fit in. They are more willing and able to adapt and change to fit the on-going structure.

Both have their advantages and disadvantages. Your task is to discover which pathway makes you most comfortable.

Tried & True

"When I was working for someone else, I always fell in the middle to low range of employee competence," recalled Tom Scott of Nantucket Nectars. "We loved the water, so we started a business delivering groceries and supplies to boats in Nantucket Harbor." That was the summer of 1988, when Scott was just 22 years old. It wasn't until his partner, Tom First, suggested that they start selling their drinkable fruit concoction that the partners transformed themselves from delivery boys into something completely different. Both pursuits involved something that they loved; one just turned out to be about a thousand times more lucrative.

—Ron Lieber, *Upstart Startups*

Try the following workout to discover the fruitful hunting grounds in your life:

1. On a piece of paper laid sideways, write your name in the center of the paper.

2. Around your name write words that represent all the things you do in your life. Write at least 20 things you do on a regular basis, from the most basic and sustaining to the most exciting and stimulating. Leave a little space around each item.

3. Go to each item written on the page and come up with an idea of how this thing that you do could become a business.

Repeat this workout every week for at least a month, coming up with different business ideas for some of the same items, and coming up with different things that you do. This will center your perspective in the middle of your life. You will begin to see the business opportunities in the most mundane aspects of your life.

For example, everyone brushes their teeth each day. What business could be developed from that? Perhaps you just discovered the joy of kayaking. What business could be developed around that? Let your creativity and ingenuity have some fun.

At some point one will really click. That's the one to pursue.

Are You Willing To Live 100 Percent?

Entrepreneurs walk a narrow path. To some it looks like they're workaholics, and sometimes they may be. The majority just loves what they do—their lives are their work. What they do is who they are. They think about their business most of the time and don't keep to a regular work schedule. Work is fun for them, so it's a form of recreation and creativity as well as how they make a living.

Entrepreneurs put their whole selves into their lives. That's what it takes to be successful. Most people hold back. A reserve of life energy is maintained rather than letting there be 100 percent continuous flow.

Tried & True

Buckminster Fuller lived fully. For much of the first twenty-some years of his life he was unhappy, doing work he didn't enjoy and feeling pushed and pulled by the needs of others.

In his late twenties, he took a year off from life. For one year, he didn't speak to anyone. After that year, his life completely changed. He was now willing to be fully himself. It was then that his inventive mind began creating and developing the fantastic ideas he later shared with the world. His sleeping habits reflected his lifestyle. He would rest when tired by taking 20–30 minute naps several times during the day, and he never slept more than a few hours at night. And one of the wise things he said was: "Don't let yourself get caught in the crossfire of information. Do your own thinking."

Try this workout to gauge the amount of life force you hold in reserve:

1. Take a few deep, relaxing breaths and close your eyes.

2. Imagine all the life force energy available to you. You may experience it as a breeze or feeling of wind moving through you. Perhaps it feels more like a beam of light or electricity or an engine humming.

3. Imagine yourself in a typical situation in your life—work or personal. How much of that energy do you allow to flow in that situation? How much do you screen?

Remember that the purpose of this workout, and all of them in this book, is not to judge yourself as doing it right or doing it wrong. The purpose is to clearly view who you are and how are you using what you have. You can change if you choose to, yet there is no need. Discovering whether entrepreneurship is or is not your life is a valuable thing. Either way is a win because it allows you to more fully choose the life that will work for you.

Entrepreneurs Create Connections

Roger Frantz, Ph.D., an economics professor at San Diego State University, describes normal business function as a grid. Vertical lines represent consumer needs and horizontal lines represent businesses serving those needs. The points where the lines cross represent business transactions where needs are met, business transacted, and money made.

Entrepreneurs, in Dr. Frantz's model, are able to intuit the space between the on-going transactions. They have a gift of seeing what needs are not being met and perhaps have not yet been defined as a need. They then go about creating products and markets to establish new points on the grid. Intuition is the ability to see what no one else is seeing, or, seeing what is there in a different way. Entrepreneurship is also the ability to see and sense the future—what needs will be emerging.

For example, there is a need for people to go from here to there. Automobile makers and airlines are just two of the businesses serving those needs. Amy Nye Wolf put together the fact that more people are flying than ever before and they need something to listen to along the way. Thus, "Altitunes," the airport music store, was born.

> ### Practical Wisdom
>
> When *Pittsburgh Magazine* came out with its annual "Best of..." issue, Tom Baron leafed through it and noticed that a national chain was given the title for the city's best Mexican restaurant. "It was just ridiculous that a chain was the best that his town had to offer," Baron recalls. At that point he knew he had found his golden opportunity. He called his friend Juno Yoon, who was ski bumming in Colorado, and told him that their next business endeavor had been found. Baron saw what was missing and decided to fill the gap with Mad Mex, Mexican restaurant.

Consumer needs   Business serving needs ⟶

↓

need to get from here to there

Automakers

Altitunes

Airlines

Roger Frantz's Entrepreneurial Grid.

Federal Express is a classic example of seeing a need that actually helped pull the rest of the culture into the future. In the best scenarios, entrepreneurs sense future needs and trends that will help move the culture into a positive, healthy, abundance-for-all future.

Tried & True

[Charles] Hess claims that in business as in sports the intuitive players exercise wide-angle vision, spotting new opportunities all over the place, while their less creative counterparts merely concentrate on racking up high profits by focusing narrowly on the bottom line. He cites Larry Bird and Wayne Gretzky as highly intuitive models that executives should pay attention to. He even quotes to his clients *Time* magazine's 1985 cover story about the pair: "Their most uncanny power enables them to see and play the game several moves ahead of the moment, comprehending not only where everything is, but also where everything will be." This statement, says Hess, coincides perfectly with my view of intuition in business.

—Roy Rowan, *The Intuitive Manager*

Larry Bird has also made the transition from player to coach, demonstrating the ability to expand and transfer his intuitive skill.

Intuit New Business Ideas

If you want to practice getting new business ideas, try the following workout:

1. Read a particular newspaper column in the business section every day. Make sure it's something that interests you, such as advertising, high tech, or industrial.

2. Read another section of the newspaper daily—one that is completely unrelated—the obituaries, the weather, a particular sport, social, entertainment.

3. Play a little game with yourself inventing a fantastic story of how the information in the two columns might be related.

4. Do this regularly and pay attention to ideas, hunches, and insights that emerge.

5. Keep an idea journal, writing down your ideas, hunches, and insights in a particular notebook or keeping a handy file on articles of interest, ideas on napkins, and so on.

6. Review your notebook monthly.

This type of workout builds new mental connections associating all kinds of data with the intention of pinpointing spaces in the economic web. You will recognize a hot idea by its shear simplicity and elegance. If you find yourself wondering why somebody else hasn't thought of something, be sure to follow up—that's a sign of a winner.

Here's another workout, borrowed from San Diego State University's Dr. Frantz, to help you get out of the analytic mindset and into the intuitive mindset:

1. Write in your journal or on a piece of paper a sentence that describes your desire to find an entrepreneurial gap to fill.

2. Hold a pencil in your hand, point side up, and gaze at it for one full minute. Do not stare, relax your eyes, breathe naturally, and just gaze.

3. After the minute is up, write down any ideas, thoughts, or images that come to your mind.

4. Look at what you have written and notice if there's a business idea revealed in what you have written.

Yellow Light

Entrepreneurs, by definition, are doing something new. Whether they are discovering a new way to do something that is established or defining a whole new market, they're turning the status quo upside-down. The most common automatic response of others to a new idea is a flat rejection—so be prepared!

How Does Your Garden Grow?

If you know the business you want to create, great. The following workout will provide the intuitive information to help you stay in touch with the day-to-day needs of your growing idea:

1. Take a few relaxing breaths and close your eyes.

2. Imagine that you're standing in front of an open plot of ground. A plot of ground that is ready to be planted with something. Notice the surroundings, the weather, and the season.

3. Imagine that you're holding a seed in one hand. Feel the size and texture of the seed. You may or may not recognize the type of seed. Notice the weight and color of the seed. This seed represents your entrepreneurial idea.

4. Plant the seed in the plot of ground and stand back. Watch it grow. It will grow to a certain stage and stop or pause. Note the image and feeling of the plant at the pause.

5. Take a deep breath and watch the plant continue to grow.

6. Notice as many details as possible about the plant and how it grows.

7. When the image is complete, open your eyes and draw a sketch of what you saw. Draw the image where it paused and where it ended.

You now have an intuitive blueprint of how your business will grow and what you need to do to nurture it. Where the plant paused parallels where your business is right now. Where the plant image stopped represents where your business is headed in the future.

The two images make up two focal points to help determine your next steps: where your business is right now and where it's going.

Take a few minutes right now to reflect on where your plant paused. What does it need? What kind of care and nurturing will help it continue to grow? What is it capable of producing at this point?

Let the image of the growing plant stimulate insights and information about what you can do to support the growth of your business at this particular time.

Spend a few moments weekly visualizing your growing seedling. Keep a log sketching the image of the plant and writing notes on what it needs, what you can do to provide it, and what you can expect the plant to produce for you.

Practical Wisdom

At the beginning of a business, just like at the beginning of a growth cycle of a seed, not much can be expected in return for the efforts you're making. Just as it's unrealistic to expect a seedling to produce fruit or flowers, it's unrealistic to expect a seedling business to give much back to you.

Entrepreneurs, Start Your Engines!

Intuition will provide four key elements during the start-up phase of your new business:

➤ Affirm and energize your intention

➤ Stay alert for new and unusual opportunities

➤ Warn you of impending doom and danger

➤ Trigger impeccable timing

With just five focused minutes a day, you can direct your intuitive signals and set them up to provide all four power keys. Here's how to do it.

Affirm and Energize Your Intention

Once the vision of your business has been established and your overall intention set (see Chapter 5), identify three or four main goals you want to accomplish within the next three to six months. Begin every day checking the intention gauge and reaffirm your short term goals by doing the following:

➤ *Seeing them.* Imagine yourself actually accomplishing the goals. See yourself putting the finishing touches on, receiving the call or the contract, or whatever image goes with the accomplishment of your goals.

➤ *Feeling them.* Imagine how you will feel when the goals are accomplished. Let the feeling become completely familiar and comfortable to you.

➤ *Allowing them.* Imagine how you will change in the process of achieving these goals. Begin to make the changes necessary now. For example, if achieving your goals will require you to be a decisive leader, begin to be that now.

Once you have the images clearly in mind and body, this exercise will take no more than three minutes.

The Opportunity Patrol

Once you have affirmed your intention, take a few moments to identify the specific needs of your new company for today (or for this week). Write down the needs and keep it somewhere where you will see it all the time.

Every time you're on the phone, meeting with someone, having lunch, buying something at the grocery story, at the health club, keep your list handy. In every conversation you have, mention at least one of these needs. Let the people you talk to know what you need and then be open for how they might be able to help you. Use everything that happens to you as an opportunity to have one of your needs met.

Of course, the idea is not to be obnoxious about asking for help all the time. Be sure to return the favor by asking about their lives and seeing if there's a way you might be able to help them.

The Doom and Gloom Patrol

Your internal alarm system will save you hours of time and untold amounts of money if you remember to turn it on and listen to it. Here are two ways to do it:

➤ Sense the central location of your intuitive alarm. It may come from your gut, heart, head, or someplace else. Imagine a switch near that location with a switch for "alarm off" and "alarm on." Every morning turn your alarm to on. Know that when you do, every time you get close to doing something that will jeopardize your business, you will know it.

➤ When facing a big decision, check your alarm system manually. Go to the image of the switch, make sure it is turned on and check to see if the alarm is making any movement or noise.

Practical Wisdom

Asking for what is needed or wanted allows the answer to find you. Replace the image of searching for an answer to one of staying still and allowing the answer to discover you.

Practical Wisdom

The key to timing isn't to filter or shelve the little messages that float through, but to keep a part of your mind open to receiving them. Make the little messages an important part of your "in file."

Practical Wisdom

There are a lot of good management books out there that tell you to say, "I don't know a lot," or "I'm not sure, but I'll go get that answer for you," or to constantly remind yourself that you're in a support position to everyone that you manage, that you're essentially their servant.... If you vocalize this stuff often, not only will people think that you're just a regular person, they'll actually feel like they can contribute to the process of solving the problems that come up in every business every day.

—David Gardner, founder of Motley Fool, Internet Investment Advice, speaking to Ron Lieber in *Upstart Start-ups*

Trigger Impeccable Timing

Being at the right place when you need to be there and acting when the moment is potent, are the keys to entrepreneurial success. Both involve intuitive skill. Here is the Golden Intuitive Rule for developing impeccable timing: *Whenever something comes into your mind related to your business in any way, act on it within 24 hours.*

It actually will take no time as part of your morning intuitive tune-up. It is a 24/7 awareness that comes as you do all the other tune-up workouts.

By the way, "acting on it" may simply mean getting more information, talking to someone, putting in a phone message to someone—not necessarily purchasing 1,000 boxes of toilet paper or renting the warehouse.

Intuitive Pitfalls

Entrepreneurs have two intuitive weak spots: arrogance and greed. Having struggled through many naysayers and finally received their rewards, entrepreneurs can fall into self-destructive patterns, which will block their intuitive flow.

Arrogance

Entrepreneurs often have difficulty letting those around them be intuitive. They have been the creative genius and the organizational motivator who has had to fight the forces of resistance to get their idea to reality. They've learned to trust their intuition the hard way—by bringing a new idea to birth. By the time they've made enough money to build a team, they've forgotten that others have intuitive insight, too.

The same is true of maverick managers in large companies. Somehow they made it through the corporate maze to get their successful ideas realized. There were so many naysayers and critics that they could no longer tell when someone had good advice and insight.

Greed

Entrepreneurs also have difficulty sharing power. They've done it themselves for so long they can't allow too much creativity to go on without their involvement.

The Antidote

The result of both of these weak spots is an organization that is running on one person's energy rather than the full synergy of the whole. Here is what you can do about it:

➤ *Stop being the hero.* See yourself as "the wind beneath their wings" rather than the lone eagle. Your job is to support and make their flying possible. Ask yourself: "What can I do to support the team to run this company?"

➤ *Ask different questions.* Ask "Who can do this?" rather than "How can I get this done?" Shift the sense of responsibility off of you and onto the Universe. Asking "who" opens the door to many possibilities that you don't have to do yourself, once you find and involve those who will do it and do it better than you.

➤ *Use and share intuitive tools.* Look back at Chapter 8 and use the tools for intuitive team meetings. And look ahead to the following section on intuitive business structures.

Can There Be an Intuitive Business Structure?

Most businesses use intuition, yet don't structure it into their systems. For entrepreneurial endeavors, it's essential. Working with a small staff where everyone has broad job descriptions and is actively learning how and what to do encourages the creative and spontaneous use of intuition. The smart entrepreneur will capitalize on this and openly make intuitive thinking part of the business system.

Practical Wisdom

Forget the hero stuff. Do it together. Stuff doesn't have to be so hard.

—Doug Mellinger, Founder & CEO PRT Group, Inc.

Practical Wisdom

Characteristic #3 of the antiheroic organization: Give up being a hero and, suddenly, you don't always have to perform like one. You don't have to supply all the energy, all the ideas, all the emotion. You don't have to fear that if you stop, so will everything else. When it's all about you—the cult of the CEO—you've separated from others. Being a hero is lonely. As an antihero, you get to be a part of what you've created.

—Doug Mellinger, founder, PRT Group, quoted in *Inc. Magazine*

Intuitive information is ignited in a business setting by having a shared vision and shared service values. The most important role of the founder/leader is to continually communicate, support, and promote the vision and values with every member of the team. This establishes the clear intention of the business and magnetizes opportunities. The structure needs to allow for the harvesting of those opportunities.

There are three different skill sets required simultaneously when establishing an entrepreneurial business. Each uses intuition in different ways:

➤ Creativity

➤ Innovation

➤ Consistency

Each set of skills releases and needs different amounts of energy. Each one is accessed in completely different ways and requires a specific environment. Creating a business system that supports all three is the task of the new entrepreneur and his or her team.

Creativity

The word *creativity* barely describes the importance of this level of business thinking. This is where whole concepts, ideas, processes, and products are generated. Creative business thinking actually comes up with new stuff, new directions, and new products. True creative thinking requires deep intuition. As you can probably guess, the best environment for this type of thinking is not a 4' by 8' office with no windows—although it can be and has been done.

With a strong shared vision, anyone in the company is in a position to gather intuitive insight that is creative and generative. Someone in the field, in the office, or even a sub-contractor may come up with the next fantastic product or service idea. This is the most difficult intuition to harness because it can happen to anyone, anywhere, anytime. It also takes time to evaluate and decide which idea to go with. There usually are not enough resources to explore all the ideas that are generated, so decisions need to be made early on about ideas focused on future needs. That requires intuition, too.

Practical Wisdom

My image of an intuitive corporate leader is of a singing troubadour—someone with an open heart and loud voice who wanders around the company singing songs and telling stories. The message of "this is who we are" and "this is what we are about" comes through in a variety of creative, inspiring ways. The individuals and teams are then encouraged to fulfill the destiny and mission of the company in their own creative ways, continually renewing the company vision through their actions.

Here are some beginning ideas to stimulate your thinking on how to make intuition an important part of your entrepreneurial process:

➤ Educate your team about the intuitive process.

➤ Encourage them to use it.

➤ Create an "Intuitive Information" reporting system—where ideas, thoughts, and impressions don't have to be backed up with data right away.

➤ Develop a non-hierarchical system to receive and evaluate new product ideas.

➤ Provide room and time for those who come up with ideas to develop and research them before they are evaluated.

➤ Take regular reflective retreats, clearly separating the creative/generative function from the managing function.

➤ Reward those who provide new ideas generously and consistently.

Practical Wisdom

Over this last decade, pioneer research into such areas as biological evolution, chaos and catastrophe theory, self-organizing systems, and fluid dynamics has revealed that natural and abrupt, nonlogical changes from ordering to reordering and from disorder to order are found everywhere in nature... Individuals engaged in the creative process encounter exactly the same kind of vacillation between disorder and order that occurs in cells and other natural systems.

—George Land and Beth Jarmon, *Breakpoint and Beyond*

Innovation

Innovation is the ability to improve what's already in place. Something gets done, and there's always a way to improve it. This is a different kind of creativity than described previously. Innovation works with what's already there. Combining the need for functionality with efficiency creates innovation.

Innovative ideas come from those who are using the system or the product. They know best what's not working and how it might work better.

Most continuous improvement systems are based on analytic data and look to improve cost base and time issues. An important role intuition can play is to allow for the incorporation of non-analytic data into the improvement process.

Practical Wisdom

Once someone discovered that a seed could be planted intentionally to grow food, it focused thousands of minds to pursue the invention of tools and techniques to make the process more efficient. Generative intuition planted the first seed, innovative intuition developed the tools to do it better.

It's obvious to most quality improvement managers that what needs improving is efficiency. But what if you wanted to improve the quality of life for the employees? What if you wanted to improve life for the community? Might those improvements have a positive influence on company profits? Of course they would. Someone has to set the vision for which definition of "quality" will be used.

Intuitive thinking can be used to imagine what areas might be improved and how it might impact the future of the company. Analytic thinking has become so narrowly focused that it misses incredible opportunities and essentials for future sustainability.

Consistency

Delivering products and services, maintaining the flow of information, and receiving benefits and salaries—these are just a few of the business functions that need to be done consistently. Different skills and attitudes are important here. Deadlines, consistent systems, and procedures make consistency happen. At first, it doesn't look like there's room for the intuitive process, yet there is.

Intuition plays the important role of anticipating problems before they grow. In any system there will be unique situations, inconsistencies, and red flags that require intervention and special attention. Sensing, anticipating, and acting before problems get going requires intuitive skill.

In one company I worked with, the executive secretary was nicknamed "Radar," because she filled the role of company "sensor" so expertly. She can sense trouble or opportunity from a letter or phone call, way before any hard data was available.

Practical Wisdom

The *intuitive nudge* is the person who consistently says: "What if this or that went wrong?" and they turn out to be predicting the future. This person is a great office manager, meeting planner, or trouble-shooter. They may personally feel like their intuition is usually negative, but the truth is that they're receiving information that can help prevent problems.

Listen for the Starting Gun

The two Toms from Nantucket Nectars shared this story:

> "We once went into a meeting with someone who had gotten hold of some market research data from Ocean Spray. She said that they had tested guava as a flavor and decided that the name evoked negative images for people. We looked at each other and said, 'Okay, we're making it.' Now, it's one of our top sellers."

As Tom Scott said so eloquently about the importance of trusting your gut feel: "You can feel what your stomach wants."

You will discover your own timing signals through experience. Pay attention to the signals, pulls and signs that work for you. One image I use is of a horse race. Thinking of a specific situation, I imagine the horses lined up at the starting gate, ready to go, yet waiting for the signal. If it's time to act, the horses are off and running, if it's not time, they're in their stalls, waiting.

Hook Your Bungie to an Entrepreneur

There are dozens of stories out of Silicon Valley about people who have successfully strategized their early retirement by working with entrepreneurs. Their strategy was basically to work for a lower salary with high stock options for start-ups. If the start-up made it, so did they.

Many people worked as administrative assistants, office managers, even warehouse and shipping operators, and became millionaires before they were 35. At that point, they can retire or start their own business. It often takes working for several start-ups before the right one comes along, or before the stock options add up to enough to retire on, but the strategy has worked for many and can still work for you.

You need a sense of adventure, a willingness to put your whole self into manifesting someone else's dream, and an ability to adapt and flex in constantly changing conditions.

The rewards, even if the monetary ones don't work out with every endeavor, are invaluable experience, deep, long-lasting relationships (it's like being at summer camp), and respect for what it takes to build and run a business.

The choice often means choosing a lower salary now for potentially high rewards later. Set your intention to discover the right entrepreneurial opportunity and watch what the Universe brings to your door.

Practical Wisdom

Good timing is like good love-making. Techniques might bring you the opportunity, but nothing less than total immersion in the process and non-attachment to results will reveal the moment for appropriate action.

Practical Wisdom

When working for an entrepreneur, you may have as much experience as he does. The entrepreneur needs you to be honest and compassionate. After all, he's staking his life on this endeavor while for you, it's only a job.

Here are some tips for your intuition when deciding to work with a start-up:

➤ If the dream doesn't make sense to you, forget it, no matter how enthusiastic and well-connected the entrepreneur may be.

➤ You have to trust the entrepreneur like you'd trust your best friend, after all, you're putting your fate in her hands for awhile.

➤ Use the joy meter. Can you dance to his tune?

➤ Are you avoiding your own dream by working with hers? If so, watch out, you may sabotage yourself by picking the wrong startup.

➤ Is it a learning environment?

➤ Will your gifts and talents be developed and utilized?

The statistics tell us that more people are working for small to mid-sized businesses than for large companies, and the number of small businesses is growing every day. Sure, not everyone will make it, but some will make it big. It's an exciting time to be alive and to be involved with creative endeavors. The possibilities and business opportunities are astounding. Anyone who thinks that all the good ideas are taken has not opened his eyes.

If you're young, or for any other reason can work without having to make a big, regular paycheck, take the plunge into entrepreneurship. You don't have to do it yourself, you can be part of a team. Hitch your energy to someone's dream, and give it all you've got.

The biggest obstacle to success is the fear of failure. I actually feel sorry for those who succeed early and often in life. For them, failure becomes an ultimate disaster that must be avoided. Self-esteem becomes attached to success.

Those who fail early have learned a great secret to success. Their self-esteem isn't attached to whether they succeed or fail. What matters is playing the game—getting up when down, starting over when things fall apart. Those who have experienced failure may not like it, but they don't have to fear it. Knowing how to fail is an asset worth acquiring, so set out to fail. Take on something that is impossible, put your whole self into it and learn what you can. Who knows? You might just discover that the impossible is, after all, possible.

Practical Wisdom

He had burned everything there was to burn within him; he had scattered so many sparks to start so many things—and he wondered whether someone could give him now the spark he needed, now when he felt unable to ever rise again. He asked himself who had started him and kept him going. Then he raised his head. Slowly, with the greatest effort of his life, he made his body rise until he was able to sit upright with only one hand pressed to the desk and a trembling arm to support him. He never asked that question again.

—Ayn Rand, *Atlas Shrugged*

The Least You Need to Know

➤ Entrepreneurs ask, "How can I make money doing what I want?" rather than asking, "What job can I get?"

➤ Entrepreneurs live fully—not working to exhaustion—and working in ways that generate more energy.

➤ Entrepreneurs see the holes to be filled in the current system.

➤ Find new business opportunities by keeping an idea journal.

➤ Intuition will help a start-up operation by affirming the intention of the business, staying alert for new opportunities, warning of impending danger, and triggering impeccable timing.

➤ You can also be successful by working for an entrepreneur and being part of a winning team.

The Power Break

The deal was set. She was approved to receive the station license from the FCC. After two years of strategizing against 11 competitors, Dorothy Brunson was about to take control of WGTW-TV. All she needed was to confirm the loan the bank had already approved. Suddenly, however, the bank was absorbed by a larger bank, and her loan was canceled. She had to sell everything she owned and still find investors to help her finance the station. Dorothy had hit the wall.

Wilma Mankill is Chief of the Cherokee Nation in Tahlequah, Oklahoma. Her inspiration to lead her nation out of poverty has enabled her to thrive through childhood illnesses and manage poor health in adulthood. She hit the wall when she was almost killed in a head-on car collision—and was horrified to learn that the driver of the other car, who was killed instantly, was a dear friend.

Henry Heinz hit the wall when his partner committed to buy the entire cabbage and cucumber crop of Woodstock, Illinois, in 1875, for pickling. It was far more than they could afford. By the end of the year, they declared bankruptcy.

Each of the above heroes hit the wall and went on to achieve success in his or her own endeavors. This chapter is about engaging those painful moments with humility, courage, and insight. They are often intuitive messages couched in chaos, pain, and frustration. They are also opportunities to gather wisdom from new sources and expand inner resources. You'll learn how to take a 15-minute "power break" and how to keep learning from the moments when all seems lost.

Hitting the Wall

"Hitting the wall" is a natural part of life. It happens every day in little ways and often in bigger ways periodically throughout life. Outside and inside forces stop the flow of movement and then what? Whatever the response to hitting the wall, it will set the tone for the next phase of activity.

In your lifelong pursuit of personal wealth and success, you will hit the wall several times. Some spectacularly big, others more minor. They are part of the process and often contain the most extraordinary gifts.

The term "hitting the wall" comes from what many marathon runners experience when they reach around the 20 mile mark of a 26-mile or 385-yard marathon race. At that point, the ability of their bodies to create physical energy is completely exhausted. Their resources of water, oxygen, and sugar are completely depleted. The only thing that keeps them going is will power and an internal source of energy martial artists call "chi."

In every endeavor, there is a wall. A place is encountered where barriers of all sorts pop up and thwart the process. It's an important and natural part of any process. If anyone tells you that he has a system that eliminates "down time," he's lying. For any true progress to be made, times of rest and integration have to happen.

Joseph Campbell spent his life studying myths from all cultures. He discovered that all myths have a core pattern that describes the human journey to greatness as well as the mythical journey. In very basic terms, the three parts of the journey can be described as follows:

➤ *Begin*: Decide to do something.

➤ *Fail*: Struggle with the challenge, and fall.

➤ *Emerge transformed*: Continue the journey as a changed person.

What he is reminding us is that people can't change who they are without letting go of who they thought they were. That process involves a shift, with various amounts of pain associated with it. One thing it absolutely contains is hitting something that causes a turn, a stop, a reason to look around for something new.

Here are two productive ways to approach the wall:

➤ *Creative recombining:* For something new to emerge, two or more existent things combine. The process is as old as sex, and equally exciting. Divergence, confusion, and dispersion have to happen for different concepts to blend. When you hit the wall, think of it as a sexy new thought knocking on the door of your brain, which is overly focused on some worn out task. Let go to the dispersion and enjoy being part of the new creation. Imagine that! Have a love affair with the Universe. Think of the possibilities!

➤ *Intuitive danger sign:* The wall can also be a sign of EXTREME DANGER! The only way to stop yourself from making a huge blunder is to pull the plug. Think back on the past few weeks. Have there been warning signals you've ignored? Little red flags on the field you haven't paid attention to? Now is your chance to reset and get back on course.

Here is a three step workout to help you plug back in:

➤ *Recommit to vision.* Take a deep breath. Close your eyes. Imagine the horizon. Somewhere on that horizon is where you're headed. Somewhere on that horizon is your vision, your dream. Hear the call of that vision. Feel its attraction. You are moving toward that vision, nothing can stop you.

Practical Wisdom

Sandra Campbell, fiction writer, can find herself suddenly disconnected from the material she is working on. "I can no longer hold it inside me to play with it. I can't find it." It's a devastating feeling, somewhat like what it felt to be "lost" as a child.

Practical Wisdom

E. F. Schumacher's three purposes of human work:

1. To provide necessary and useful goods and services.

2. To enable every one of us to use and thereby perfect our gifts like good stewards.

3. To do so in service and cooperation with others, so as to liberate ourselves from our inborn egocentricity.

➤ *Push the reality reset button.* Pause for a moment, step back from the whole situation. What have you been focusing on? Where have you been putting your efforts? What isn't working? Take a few moments to realign with the flow, with reality. Let go of your focus and be present to what is happening.

➤ *Look for the open door.* Look around and notice if there is energy flowing in any other direction. Is there another option or another way to approach your goal? Pause for a moment and assess the possibilities. Where is the flow? Where is the open door?

Take a few deep breaths, open your eyes and write down any helpful information from this exercise.

Know When To Fold and When To Hold

One major unproductive way of handling the wall is to keep banging your head against it. When stuck, a deep urge from way back in the brain emerges saying: "When in doubt, try harder." Very few things are as unproductive. Put it in the same category of deeply confused human wisdom as:

➤ If you're late, drive faster.

➤ If you're hungry, eat more than you need.

➤ If you're tired, drink coffee.

➤ If in pain, pop a pill.

➤ If stuck in a traffic jam—blow your horn.

Our culture supports a counter-intuitive attitude toward life. Instead of listening to our bodies and our senses, we ignore them and override them. The cost? A pretty high price of sanity, health, and often success.

Try something different. Take another path. Listen to yourself and trust that you know what's right for you if you can just listen to it.

Some sure signs that it's time to wait and slow down are:

➤ Things stop working

➤ More energy is expended than created

➤ There is frustration at every turn

➤ No one answers the phone

➤ Three trades, business deals, or opportunities in a row don't work

➤ You're irritated at the slightest mishap

➤ Your dog doesn't get walked enough

➤ Your plants are drying up and dying

➤ Your children don't want to be around you

➤ You've forgotten how to have fun

➤ Your jokes aren't funny

➤ You have no time for a manicure

➤ You have no time to exercise

Tried & True

Native American Sister Jose Hobday's Seneca mother taught her that "If you want to keep your peace and be in a happy mood, give whatever you are doing the time it takes to make it complete." Hobday points out that no native language she knows of contains words either for "late" or for "work." Work is a "divisive word," for it cuts us off from our play and our heart's passion. Hobday's father used to say, "Try many things. When you find what you love, do that. Then figure out how to make a living with it."

—Matthew Fox, *Reinventing Work*

When pushing too hard, there is no way to be in flow. You have outrun the Universe and it needs time to catch up with you.

Here are some productive activities that will keep your mind busy while the intuitive process meets you:

➤ *Slow down.* Whatever you're doing, keep doing it—slower. Keep going at a much slower pace. While this may sound ridiculous to you, especially if you're a boss, think about how you and your business might benefit, for just a moment. When deals are approached slower, important details are handled effectively and not overlooked. Processes are done carefully with fewer mistakes.

➤ *Reduce the risk.* Some stockbrokers and traders start doing paper trades after a few bad calls. This keeps them in the game, yet without the risk. At some point, they're back in sync with the market and can resume. Adapt this philosophy to what you're doing. Take yourself out of risky play, yet keep playing. Do what you can do to get back in rhythm.

➤ *Add some fun.* Break the tension by laughing at yourself, at an old joke, or funny story. Remember Lucy in the candy factory or stomping grapes to make wine. Find something funny about what's happening right now and share it with someone.

➤ *Do something surprisingly wonderful.* Do something for someone that will delight and surprise him or her. Catch someone off-guard with flowers, a note, a toy, a word of encouragement, or a compliment. Make a phone call and say "hello" and thank them for a good shared memory. Get out of your "stuckness" by doing something completely different and unexpected.

➤ *Do something physical.* Take a drive, a walk, a swim, anything to get your body moving.

➤ *Get a massage.* Enough said!

➤ *Take a nap, have a dream.* Dreams are often a way intuitive information is accessed.

The Five-Minute Intuitive Catch-up

This workout can be completed with your eyes open or closed. Squeeze and release your scalp as if it were an arm or leg muscle being stretched. Squeeze and release your neck muscles in the same way. As you inhale, notice the flow of energy in and around your brain and neck. Shake it out.

Pushing too hard, comes from grasping for answers. If the answers are out there to be grasped, you will never find them in time. There is too much space to explore. It's like looking for pennies on the beach. You know they're there, but who wants to look through all that sand?

It's better to attract the answers to you by becoming a magnet for them. Become a magnet by focusing on the present moment. The present moment is where the power is. That is the only place where true action can happen. The past is already done, the future isn't here yet, the present is all there is. Focus there for power. If there's an answer, it is in the present moment. Look there to find it.

Yes, Virginia, There Are Angels

Sometimes when we are stuck, "angels" help us in unexpected ways. By *angels* I don't mean winged visitors from heaven (although I don't rule out the possibility!). What I mean is angels in the form of people who happened into our lives with the right information or support. They often then just disappear, like the Lone Ranger. You can't make an angel appear; you can only be prepared to receive the gift when it occurs. It is also a blessing to be the angel for someone else. To reach out a hand and help someone over the abyss they face is no effort. It is a gift.

Tried & True

Ace inventor Dan Gold was stuck on a design problem. He needed one particular part of something he was working on, and he couldn't find it anywhere. Then he had a dream: "I was out in the wheat fields some place. I ran into this guy. We were chitchatting about who-knows-what. His final words were 'What you're looking for is in Kansas.'" Puzzled, Gold wondered if it had anything to do with motors, because that was the part he needed for his new invention. Knowing one person in Kansas, he called him and asked if he would look in the Yellow Pages for a machine shop in Kansas City. There was one listing. Gold called and discovered that it had the part he was looking for.

Failure Happens—It's Not Personal

The worst possible response to hitting the wall is the one that happens most often; taking it as a sign of failure and of personal ineptness. Nothing could be further from the truth. Remember, the Universe won't change to suit you, yet you can get in sync with the universal plan. That message may sometimes have a bite to it, especially when it's in a different direction from the one we are moving in.

History is filled with those who hit the wall but kept following their path. Imagine how many setbacks British feminist Emmeline Pankhurst experienced while lobbying for nearly 15 years for the Representation of the People Act. It finally passed in 1918, giving women the right to vote. Niccolo Machiavelli lost his civil service job in Florence, was imprisoned and tortured, and over the next 13 years in exile wrote *The Prince* and *The Art of War*.

Practical Wisdom

If you follow your bliss, you put yourself on a kind of track that has been there the whole while, waiting for you, and the life you ought to be living is the one you are living.

—Joseph Campbell

> **Tried & True**
>
> Tolstoy had his first bicycle lesson at age 67.
>
> At age 51, Confucius left private life to enter government office. Unpopular, he lost office and gained fame only later through books written about him by his disciples.
>
> At 57, Anna Sewell, a disabled author long dependent on horses for transportation, published *Black Beauty*.
>
> James Counsilman swam the English Channel at age 58.
>
> Leadbelly sang his first official concert at the age of 49, after being "discovered" in prison by a visiting folk-music historian.
>
> —Jeremy Baker, *Tolstoy's Bicycle*

Let Go of "Why"

When I began to write this chapter, I hit the wall. It was no longer fun, my neck was tight, and I had no ideas. After struggling for a while and indulging in a bit of negative self-talk I realized what was happening. I was fully experiencing what I was writing about. I made an appointment for a manicure and a massage, took the afternoon off and ignored the deadlines hanging heavy over my head. While breathing into the pain of having my tight shoulders released, I got the vision for this chapter. I realized that it needed to be an inspiration. Something to keep you, the reader going through your own walls, and to provide some role models of imperfect, successful people. Real people.

Get Beyond the Image of Success

If you're at all like me, you've read all or most of the books on building prosperity. They're all great books and help keep the mind focused on success. The one problem with all of them, in my opinion, is that they don't make room for failure and loss. They don't honor the fact that the pain of falling down and losing everything has equal value and deserves equal respect to making the big sale, or investment, or whatever brings success.

> **Practical Wisdom**
>
> Pursuing "why" something went wrong has been the downfall of many. Instead of pursuing the "why," move on to another "what."

Our culture likes to ignore those who are experiencing the downside of success—those who have run out of luck and hit hard times. Yet these are the times that strengthen the vision, muster the strength, and build the skills necessary to truly succeed. We either want to fix the problem for them by telling them what to do or by giving them money, or shy away from the whole thing and stop talking to them.

The next time a friend of yours shares that things are not going so well, keep in mind the following questions and travel down the path with your friend for a little while:

➤ *What is that like?* Be interested in your friend's journey and experience.

➤ *What are you learning?* Rather than seeing him or her as a victim, see him or her as a learner.

➤ *What are you doing now?* Listen to your friend's plan rather than telling him or her what to do.

> **Practical Wisdom**
>
> Do your work, then step back.
> The only path to serenity…
> He who clings to his work
> will create nothing that endures.
> If you want to accord with the Tao,
> just do your job, then let go.
>
> —Lao Tzu

These are good questions to ask yourself whether you're down or up. Stay in touch with what you're experiencing and learning all the time. The flip side of the cultural disdain for failure is its glorification of success. Just because money is being made doesn't mean that everything is beautiful. New challenges and responsibilities come into play that make life interesting and a continual learning experience.

Just the other day a dear friend of mine who has been marketing her stress management audio tape successfully for years, called to ask for help. She was stuck and had no where to turn. She wanted to come over and get my advice on what to do. She did, and we explored together what was going on and managed to lift the burden she was under and discover the next steps of her path. She probably could have worked it out by herself. I've never known anyone who worked harder than she does. Yet, working together made it fun and meaningful for both of us and reinforced our friendship. The moment of despair she experienced enabled her to seek another, more fruitful way for her to proceed.

Intuition Still Loves You

When all else has failed, it may be the perfect opportunity for an intuitive message. Sometimes, after things have crashed, there is less of a barrier between our conscious mind and the intuitive mind. About 20 years ago, I knew that my life was going to be about intuitive work, yet I didn't believe that it could support me financially. Three big business failures hit me one after the other. Everything I tried to do failed miserably. After the third failure I let go. At the time, I had children who were six years old and six months old, was newly married, and was completely broke.

221

It was June and a friend (one of those angels I was talking about) let us stay on Fire Island during the week for a couple of days. I remember very clearly sitting on the beach and asking myself what I should do now. A clear internal voice said: "Teach your classes." I spoke back to the voice complaining that it was June, nobody was in town, I needed money now! The voice just said "Do what you really want to do." That was it. I decided to devote myself to the intuitive work. I figured that if that failed, I would know that this voice is full of it, yet if I never let go to it, I would regret it for the rest of my life.

Back in New York City, after a few phone calls, it turned out that there were several people interested in working with me. And the rest, as they say, is history.

Here's a workout that lets you talk directly to your intuition:

1. Imagine yourself in some wonderful place that you'd love to let go in and just be.

2. Imagine that everything you have worked toward in your life is gone. You're starting over with a fresh slate.

3. Allow yourself to feel the emptiness and openness of the moment.

4. Invite your intuition to be with you and ask "What now?"

5. Listen, allow, feel. Write down your answer.

> **Practical Wisdom**
>
> When things have stopped, projects failed, opportunities faded, don't rush into something new. Give yourself the gift of p-a-u-s-e. Let your creative voice have a say in what moves you to action.

The freedom of letting everything go and starting over, even if only mentally and emotionally, can be rejuvenating. Look at what you would do and compare it to your present life. What elements from your vision do you want to add to what you're doing now? What part of what you're doing now are you ready to let go of?

Take Yourself Out of the Game

Earlier in the chapter I said that there was no way to avoid the wall, and anyone who said there was is lying. Well, that is still true, yet there's a way to experience the wall less as a complete stoppage and more as a natural transition.

My daughter called from college one day to tell me she had decided to drop physics as a co-major. At the time, she was majoring in both math and physics and had been enjoying both subjects. In her own words she described what happened: "During my morning exercise routine I felt something shift. All of a sudden I knew that I was finished with physics. I no longer needed to study it. Even though I was completely prepared for the week's work, I dropped the class and changed my major that day."

"Wow!" I thought after she shared this with me. She is really in tune with her life path and allowed that transition so easily. When young people are encouraged to trust themselves and given the tools to explore their interests, their life path naturally unfolds. Not without transitions, changes, and learnings, but with joy and acceptance.

For those of us conditioned to struggle, there's still hope. Take yourself out of the game periodically for rejuvenating breaks. Make it part of your plan to give time-outs, periods of reflection, vacations from life. It doesn't have to be a four-week stay in Monaco. It can be a 15-minute walk every day.

15 Power Minutes

Fifteen minutes every day is more effective than an hour once a week. The daily routine is important and trains your intuition to provide inspiration during those 15 minutes. Put together your own routine for 15 power minutes using the following guidelines:

Practical Wisdom

A new beginning can happen in the midst of chaos and despair with one simple act. Wherever you are—begin now.

➤ The only purpose is to be with yourself—do it alone.

➤ Actively let go of normal life thoughts—use inspiring music, reading material, or beautiful scenery.

➤ Stay conscious—napping doesn't count for these power minutes.

➤ Draw, play a musical instrument, do woodworking, or sing.

➤ Having a focus question is okay—it's also okay to not have a focus question.

Longer periods of personal retreat are also a great way to give yourself the opportunity to make shifts and avoid the extreme pain of dramatic slams into walls.

Keep Getting Better

In the intuitive world, there is no success or failure. Each event opens other opportunities and the flow keeps going. Nature functions in a very intuitive and creative way. If there is no room to grow in one direction, it finds another. A plant hits a wall, but it grows up the wall, through it, or around it. The wall is just an event that triggers new direction.

In the analytic world, we make distinctions. Some events are good and desirable, others are bad and to be avoided. One allows for continuous movement and growth, the other for focused direction and goal achievement. They work together to form our world.

One way to keep getting better is to learn from success and failure. Any time some event either pleases or displeases, pause. Allow your intuition to help you get better by reflecting with the following questions.

Practical Wisdom

Out of more than 600 songs written by Irving Berlin, no more than 50 were hits. The Beatles were turned down by every record company in England before they made it. *Chicken Soup for the Soul* was rejected by 33 publishers before it was picked up by a small, unknown publishing house.

After a success, ask yourself:

➤ What worked? What didn't?

➤ When did I know what to do?

➤ How did I get to that point?

➤ What is repeatable about this? What is non-repeatable?

After a failure, ask yourself:

➤ What worked? What didn't?

➤ What warnings did I not pay attention to?

➤ What am I learning from this?

➤ If my intuition could speak to me about this, what would it say now?

Success and failure are two sides of one coin. They go together, flowing in and around, like ocean tides moving stuff in and out to keep the ocean clean. Rejection and avoidance of one prevents the other. Those who succeed big have failed big.

The Least You Need to Know

➤ Accept that you will hit a wall—or several—during your quest.

➤ Use the down time as an opportunity to reflect, recombine, and create.

➤ Forcing forward when things stop working could be hazardous.

➤ Allow for intuitive "angels" to help along the way.

➤ Allow for ups and downs in your plan—they're equally valuable.

➤ Drop out voluntarily and regenerate at regular intervals.

Part 4

Getting Over Fear, Greed, and Self-Doubt

When I asked the lawyer what he was going to charge us, he said, "Let's not worry about that right now," and something in the pit of my stomach went very sour. At the same time my courage to speak disappeared: No one else in the room seemed upset by his response. Was I the only one? My fear kept me from speaking up, and my greed for wanting everything to work out overrode my screaming intuition.

Imagine the worst, and that's what happened at the end of this story.

There will be times when, although you know what to do intuitively, your personal gremlins will prevent you from taking action. Part 4 walks you through intuition workouts that will help you manage your fear, neutralize your greed, and heal your self-doubt. You'll also learn to accept your intuitive power and keep a handy list of safety tips for flying over troubled waters.

Chapter 16

Managing Fear

In This Chapter

➤ Learn the critical difference between fear and anxiety

➤ Discover your safety zone

➤ Stop the damage done by overthinking

➤ Discover the difference between risk and danger

➤ Stimulate your curiosity muscle

➤ Learn to make friends with change

"I don't want to do it. I refuse to do this; you can't make me." These are familiar words from children when asked to do something new and different. Many children resist change and new activities. Parents need to evaluate whether what they're hearing from their children comes from nervousness and apprehension of the unknown or what might be real fear. As adults, we also can react negatively and nervously to new situations. An inability to flow into something new creates strong resistance to change and make it difficult to know the difference between appropriate fear and rigidity.

This chapter takes you on a journey through the minefield of things that block the intuitive process. Once fear, desire, and greed have been turned into assets, you'll find your safe place to stand, flex your curiosity muscle, and actually learn to love change.

Fear Is Not the Enemy

You have experienced the difference between fear and anxiety. Remember a time when you encountered a dangerous situation. How did you feel? What did your body do? What did your mind do?

Remember a time when you were anticipating something new and challenging. "I don't want to do this; this is going to be terrible," you might have said to yourself, building up the anxiety and anticipation of something terrible occurring.

Tried & True

As she locked her car, a figure standing in the shadows caught her eye. A thought crossed her mind: "Maybe I should put the luggage in the trunk...nah, I won't be long." Arriving back at the car, she discovered broken glass and no luggage. There might have been no real connection between the person standing in the shadows and the thief who stole her luggage, but her intuition used the image as a warning, a way to communicate the impending danger.

Think back into your past and remember people with whom you felt immediately safe and secure, from the first time you were in their presence. They might have been a teacher, relative, friend's parent, or perfect stranger. Contrast that feeling with meeting someone you immediately didn't trust or feel safe with.

Practical Wisdom

If you feel unsafe after walking into a room, upon meeting someone, or upon hearing a request—get out. Do whatever you need to do to get to a feeling of safety.

Think now of a time when you were anticipating something you wanted to do but were nervous about doing at the same time. The first-time experience of amusement park rides, for example. There might have been anticipation, excitement, nervousness, and fear all rolled up into one experience.

As human beings, we are wired for safety and wired for growth. We have an internal mechanism that is programmed to protect. Of course, there are situations where there's no way out, accidents and terrible things happen that are beyond anyone's control. Young adults and children are seduced into harmful situations by manipulative adults. These kinds of situations can be used to help validate intuitive knowing in the future. It's not useful to use these experiences as fuel for self-doubt and self-recrimination. Yet in our day-to-day lives, there are many instances where the danger signal is flashing but goes ignored.

Many have been trained to either fight or avoid their fear, thus disabling their intuitive safety mechanism. Fear is not the enemy—it's the key to safety. Getting comfortable with the feeling of fear will enable you to use it effectively.

Caution: I Brake for Intuition

In the intuitive world view, we are each, individually, part of a larger whole. The larger whole wants to survive and create as well as do the individual parts.

Imagine for a moment that some good friends of yours went on a road trip. After they left, you received a call from their mechanic saying that the brakes hadn't been fixed correctly and were very dangerous. You'd do what you needed to do to contact them and let them know. Your friends, on the other hand, wouldn't suspect that anything is wrong. When you showed up they'd be shocked and surprised, but they'd respond to the information you gave them.

Intuition works the same way. We are part of a larger network of information. You may not know that something you're about to do is dangerous, but another part of the network

Practical Wisdom

When you accept the survival signal as a welcome message and quickly evaluate the environment or situation, fear stops in an instant. Thus, trusting intuition is the exact opposite of living in fear. In fact, the role of fear in your life lessens as your mind and body come to know that you will listen to the quiet wind chime, and have no need for Klaxons.

—Gavin De Becker, *The Gift of Fear*

does. It sends a warning message to you to watch out! Because this all happens on an intuitive level, many won't believe or listen to the message.

Tried & True

Ben Mancini, president of a private bank in Beverly Hills, was asked to make a large loan to a businessman with impeccable credentials, credit history, and a sound business deal in front of him. But something didn't feel right to Mancini. He stalled on the deal and finally told his board that he wasn't going to approve the loan, to their extreme confusion and displeasure. The businessman ended up defrauding two other banks out of millions of dollars.

How might your lifestyle change if you knew that you'd be warned, without a doubt, whenever you got close to something dangerous, and, at the same time, you'd be guided toward a fulfilling and successful life? Your job would be to do to the best of your ability what is in front of you and to respond to the information and signals received from "intuition central."

Nothing To Fear but Fear Itself

A friend was sitting in a restaurant and glanced over to notice a couple getting up and leaving the restaurant. He knew intuitively, without a doubt, that they were leaving without paying their bill. Two other times in his life he had experienced a similar clarity of intuitive knowing and not acted on it; this time, though, he was determined to do something. He walked over to the waitress and asked if those people had paid their bill. She looked, noticed they were gone, and shrieked, "No! They left without paying!" The manager ran after the couple, and they were apprehended.

The feeling my friend had was an intuitive fear signal—a sharp sensation of knowing. Many people think that intuition is a part of our subconscious mind that gathers all the little bits of information, puts it together into a picture, and spits out information to our conscious mind. Others feel that intuition comes from "guardian angels" who are here to guide us out of danger to safety. Still others feel that intuition is the voice of God directing and instructing us. All may be correct. They're all good descriptions of the process. The point is that right now it doesn't matter where it comes from but only that it works and can be trusted.

Practical Wisdom

Whenever you say to yourself, "I knew I should (or shouldn't) have done that," know that your intuition is working and asking for your attention.

Even though fear is something most people think about in personal terms, fear plays a significant role in guiding successful business opportunities. What is said "no" to, what isn't chosen, is often as significant as what is said "yes" to in the world of business.

A credit manager for a large chemical company was asked to determine whether a new customer was credit worthy. The customer passed all the normal standards and was ready to be approved to receive a large order of chemicals on credit. Somehow the credit manager didn't feel good about this customer. Every time he spoke to the person on the phone, he got an uncomfortable feeling. On a Friday afternoon, the customer called to ask for the release of the product saying that he was writing an initial check and sending it that day. The credit manager felt sick to his stomach. Intuitively, he knew that the guy was lying, but there was nothing he could do about it. The company's analytic standards for good credit had been satisfied. As you can guess, the check wasn't in the mail, and the company spent much time and money collecting.

There is a range of intuitive knowing about danger. Like a spectrum of color or sound, the signals become louder and more overt if the more subtle signals are ignored. Here is a list of the spectrum of intuitive warning signals:

➤ Loss of energy, the door closes, there's no flow

➤ Concern about what is going on

➤ Pit in the stomach, sour feeling

➤ Automatic urge to back off or move away physically

➤ Creepy, shivery feeling

➤ Events seem to move in slow motion

➤ Heightened alertness or attention to detail

➤ Urge to act—perhaps out of character

➤ Total physical and mental awareness riveted on the situation at hand

This spectrum isn't necessarily linear. In any particular situation, you may jump to complete alertness, or you may not experience an uncomfortable feeling. Your individual signals may vary, but there's a pattern and you have experienced it.

Anxiety

Anxiety is the anticipation of pain. Imagining and projecting that some event in the future will be painful isn't intuition—it's hell. Living with a feeling that at any moment something could go wrong is debilitating and humiliating. It prevents creativity and slows emotional maturity. Depending on the frequency and severity, it may need to be addressed professionally.

If one is always afraid of a particular activity, such as traveling in an airplane, it's not intuition, it's a phobia. Some phobias can be lived with, while others present barriers to living your dream and need to be addressed.

Anxiety can be recognized as a continuous loop of fearful self-talk. The following sections suggest ways to help manage your anxiety.

Managing Your Anxiety

The debilitating side of fear is anxiety. When caught in a cycle of anxious, fearful feelings, try walking yourself through the following F-E-A-R workout:

➤ F is for Face the fear and name it. Call it fear—don't run away from it. Fear is a feeling, not a fact. Someone might be asked to speak to a group of people about a subject she's an expert on. That person may keep putting off the speaking engagement because of too many other commitments. The truth is that she wants to speak, but is afraid. The whole situation feels uncomfortable, so it is just avoided, not acknowledged.

231

➤ E is for Evaluate the fear. We are not as afraid of events as we are afraid of feelings. Identify the feelings that are behind the fear (failure, humiliation, inadequacy, or rejection). For example, if someone is anxious about speaking in front of a large group of people, he may be afraid of feeling foolish, humiliated, or stupid. Those are the feelings to identify.

➤ A is for Align yourself as the one in charge of both your intuition and your fear. Someone may have something important to say and want to be in front of a group, but she has anxiety. Acknowledge both of those feelings. On the one hand, the challenge is wanted, on the other hand, it's scary. Both can be true at the same time.

➤ R is for Respect both. Imagine yourself driving a carriage pulled by two powerful horses. You are in charge of steering them toward where you want to go. Respect their strength and remain in charge. Find a way to follow your intuition—your desire and at the same time take care of your fear. Someone might begin by speaking in front of small groups, getting some coaching, and joining Toastmasters, thus taking care of their fear by not overshooting their abilities, and moving forward with attaining their goal.

Intuitions About Others

In a recent seminar a woman shared that she was married to a fireman. Often she would get a tight feeling in her chest and think about him during times that he was out. She didn't know how to trust this feeling, what it was telling her, or whether it was general anxiety. I recommended that she take a deep breath every time she felt that feeling and let go. If it comes back three times, I told her, follow up with imagining a connection from her heart to her husband's heart to acknowledge their love and deep relationship. If there's something she can do to help or assist, she will know it then, if not, send him love and go on with her day.

Sometimes we receive intuitive information about others and there's nothing that can be done directly. Reinforcing the heart connection is the best approach to dealing with these feelings. Sometimes there's something that can be done, though—in which case do it.

Listen to Your Fear

Here's a workout to help you listen to your fear:

1. Take a relaxing, deep breath.

2. Invite your fear to meet you. Allow an image of fear to emerge in your imagination.

3. Say hello to the image. Have a conversation with the image of your fear.

4. Ask about an early experience in your life where fear played an important role.

5. Ask about current situations and any warning signals you have ignored.

6. Discuss ways in which you can develop a reliable working relationship with fear.

7. Thank this image of fear for becoming your friend and for being a part of your life.

Teach Your Children Well

A newspaper article recently discussed how a mother felt uncomfortable about letting her daughter stay overnight at a friend's home. Instead of talking to the daughter directly, she just said no when permission was asked. While the mother's feeling is important, a great opportunity to teach her daughter to pay attention to her own intuitive signals was lost.

I would have recommended that the mother say no to overnight stays, but yes to day-time play dates. Then, casually ask her daughter if she was comfortable and felt safe at her friend's house. The daughter has good intuition, the younger the better, as long as it has not been confused by too many cultural instructions.

Tried & True

As a consultant to the CEOs of several successful companies, including Commodore International, Bally Manufacturing, and Wendy's, Greenberg has always insisted on receiving equity as well as a fee. He gets this mainly for making good judgment calls that help to bolster his clients' stock. "Most people sense instinctively when things are wrong," he says. "Or at least they have 20/20 hindsight about their mistakes. I sense when things are right."

—Roy Rowan, interviewing Steven Greenberg, Chairman, Anametrics, Inc.
in *The Intuitive Manager*

Train Yourself To Find Safety

Just as danger can be sensed, so, too, can safety. Sometimes in this world of fast-paced business, finding a safe haven and a sense of safety seems impossible. The only safety is the safety of being away from it all, isolated on a tropical beach, where no one can reach you. The urge toward safety is as strong as the urge away from danger, and it has been equally miseducated. There is a spectrum of safety, just as there's a spectrum of fear. Look at the following list and see how many of these experiences you have tasted. Does it make sense to you to go forward with projects and people that feel safe, as opposed to those that feel dangerous?

➤ Feeling the flow—the open door
➤ Able to breathe freely
➤ Curious
➤ Comfortable
➤ Interest engaged
➤ Move closer—get involved
➤ Needs addressed
➤ Willing to risk vulnerability
➤ Vulnerability respected
➤ Trusting

You should note the difference between risk and danger. Risk is what you're willing to do for a specific goal. Risk is chosen; you're walking into something with eyes wide open. Something becomes dangerous when safety is harder to get to.

Philippe Petit walks a tightrope. He does it across buildings 103 stories high, across deep ravines, and over rushing rivers. For him, it's a risk he is willing to take. For most of us, it would be dangerous. He knows how to find safety through balance and skill. Most of us, attempting to walk a tightrope as he does, do not. If you were hiking through the wilderness and came upon a gorge that needed to be crossed by walking over a fallen tree, that would be dangerous. You'd have to weigh the need against the danger and determine whether you're willing to take the risk or not.

Don't Use Your Head

Known in the business world as "analysis paralysis," the glut of data pouring into modern lives is overwhelming and can bury intuitive knowing under a pile of paper. Looking for analytic confirmation of an intuitive sense is one thing. Looking for guarantees is another. If analytic thinking is used to alleviate fear, it will never work. If someone is afraid of failure, that will just be validated by the numbers he comes up with. You can make success or failure a self-fulfilling prophecy.

Using analytic skills as a backup to intuitive knowing works. Analytic data can provide the external evidence to validate the internal, intuitive evidence. Analysis becomes a barrier when it's given more value than other kinds of information. In this modern world, most have been deeply trained to trust the analytic and distrust the intuitive and non-analytic information. It takes discipline to recognize the analytic bias at work.

Analysis used as a safety net can diminish personal responsibility. If something doesn't work out, the numbers can be blamed. "It looked like it should have worked," sounds much better than, "Oops, we went out on a limb on that one, and it didn't work."

Analytic techniques are powerful. They can provide alternative perspectives and validation for ideas in an effective way. They can also be used to avoid personal commitment to a project and plan.

Practical Wisdom

As a group [lawyers] are the most intelligent entrepreneurs in the country. Too intelligent. They can always find a reason for not doing a particular deal. That's why lawyers don't start outside businesses. They will serve as advisors or become investors. But they never take that intuitive leap themselves.

—Steven Greenberg, Chairman, Anametrics, Inc., in Roy Rowan, *The Intuitive Manager*

The achievement of goals can be looked at as the focused application of human energy—the full spectrum of human energy, including physical, emotional, mental, and spiritual. When these forces are working together toward a common goal, there is involvement and attention toward specific outcomes. When reliance and responsibility are placed on outside forces, such as external validation, the human energy involvement is reduced.

If someone says "Do it this way," less energy is applied toward creating its success. More human energy is applied toward creating success when there is personal involvement. What do you want from the people who work with and for you? What kind of environment do you create?

Here is a simple tool for getting past analysis paralysis:

1. At any moment in the course of accomplishing a goal, ask yourself or your teammates, "What action can be taken now without further investigation?"
2. Take that action.
3. Evaluate. Ask the team, "What do we know now?"
4. Ask again, "What action can be taken now without further investigation?"
5. Repeat the process.

235

This looks time-consuming, but it can be done one-on-one in short amounts of time. The progress made greatly outruns a more analytic approach of laying out the whole plan up front before taking action.

Curiosity Won't Kill This Cat

When faced with a new situation, person, or opportunity there are two main responses. One is to open to the newness, explore it, and welcome it. The other is to shut it out, don't let it in, and close down in self-protection.

Most children at young ages greet everything in life with curiosity and openness. They're constantly learning from and taking in data from their environment. Newness and differentness are mostly welcomed. A grasshopper jumps in front of them and they're curious about it. At some point in development, children learn to shut down. Instead of being curious about new things, they react with fear. Newness and differentness become frightening.

To be successful in this world, with a constant influx of new and different things, unlearning the fear response and relearning curiosity is essential. It can only happen with an inner sense of safety, which comes from trusting that the intuitive warning system will kick in when there is danger.

Think of this in very basic terms. If you want to create a new business or business venture, you aren't going to be able to do it all yourself. You will need to find others who can do the parts you aren't good at. That will require individuals different from you. If those who are different from you trigger a fear reaction, your project is doomed. If you pick a team that mirrors yourself, the project is doomed. If you pick people who are different from you with a curiosity about who they are and how they do what they do so well, your project has a chance to succeed.

Try the following workout to awaken your curiosity:

1. Think of something or someone new in your life with an unsure comfort level.

2. Take a piece of paper, lay it sideways, and write the thing or person in the center.

3. Around the word in the center draw four lines in different directions. At the end of each line write one word that describes an attribute or quality of the word in the middle.

4. For each of the new words write how that quality might benefit you, your project, and how it might interfere with the project.

5. For each of the preceding thoughts, write how you might manage the qualities to channel it toward achieving your goal.

6. Notice how something that might scare you has now become something you can be curious about; something that evokes your creativity.

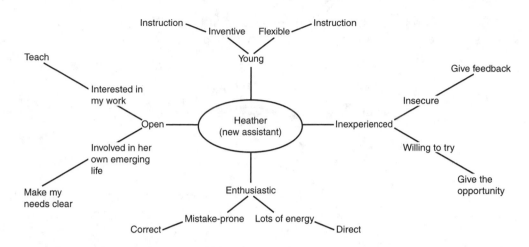

Work out the qualities of teammates.

Here is another one to try, too:

1. Imagine two doors in your heart. One door opens to curiosity and openness, the other to fear and defensiveness.

2. Think of someone you love. Think especially of a moment in your relationship when this love was unconditional. Remember some of the things this person did that seemed just delightful to you, that if they were done by anyone else, they would have been disturbing. Feel how the doors in your heart are responding to this person and to what this person does.

3. Think of something that's changing in your life that creates fear. Open the curiosity door to it and take a few moments to allow the change into your life without fear or defensiveness.

4. Write down some new ideas about how you can work with the change in a constructive way.

Remember that you're still in charge of choices here. You can be open to something new without having to say yes to it. It may not be what you need, but you won't know that if you don't give it a chance. Curiosity opens the choices.

Fall in Love with Change

You know it's true no matter how much it hurts to admit it: Change is here to stay.

But to fall in love with change? Isn't that asking too much?

Remember the doors in the heart? The only response is either fear or curiosity. As The Borg say in Star Trek, "Resistance is futile." So you might as well be curious about something as essential as change.

Loving change and submitting to it are two different things. Loving change means to actively engage, expect, anticipate, and play with it.

"Before you leave the store, could I interest you in an upgrade?"

It has been said that people:

➤ Love to buy, but hate to be sold

➤ Love to learn, but hate to be taught

➤ Love to change, but hate to be told what to do

Falling in love with change demands that we live in the middle of a huge paradox: We need to take the reins of our life and direct the flow while actively relating to the surrounding influences, new and old. If we remain too focused on directing, the help, support, and new input is missed. If we remain too open to all the newness in the environment, progress toward the goal will be slowed considerably.

Catch the Intuitive Wave

Modern science has long passed thinking of events as cause and effect, linear or rational. In their book *Breakpoint and Beyond*, George Land and Beth Jarmon summarize the current scientific world view and its relationship to practical life:

"Neutrons, electrons, and protons carry a wave that is as real, concrete, and important as the object itself. It is real because the future carried in the wave is going to happen. If you do not know that a wave is part of matter, you will miss the opportunity to use its possibilities. This was a major discovery in unlocking the secret of the atomic and subatomic world. Only with this knowledge and the use of the wave reality could the amazing break-throughs of modern science and technology have happened."

You may ask, "So what? How can I use this information in my own life, with my family, or to help my organization?" As part of nature, you also exist in two simultaneous states: being and becoming. As a human being, your invisible—and real—wave state consists of all your thoughts. You carry your future around with you, right now, in your mind. Your thoughts make up your wave potential. Your invisible wave state carries within it the probable future states of your life. Your wave of potential, the wave of your children, your organization's wave, are the most significant factors in creating the emerging future.

Practical Wisdom

We say that people innately resist change. But the resistance we experience from others is not to change itself. It is to the particular process of change that believes in imposition rather than creation. It is the resistance of a living system to being treated as a non-living thing. It is an assertion of the system's right to create itself. It is life insisting on its primary responsibility to create itself.

—Margaret J. Wheatley and Myron Kellner-Rogers, *A Simpler Way*

Extraordinarily successful people intuit this wave reality and use it.

You carry with you the wave of future change. What your life is about right now is helping to create the changes we are all experiencing. Think of your present moment as the handle of a long whip. As that handle is moved with intent and power, the rest of the whip responds with a snap! The snap is contained in the initial movement—it just takes a few moments to happen.

Putting Fear and Change Together

When we remain unaware of and uninvolved in stepping into the power we possess in any moment, negative fear and anxiety take over and change becomes a source of helplessness.

Recognizing that we have the power to know the difference between safety and danger and that we actually are the change that's happening empowers us to take charge, be open to new experiences, meet different people and experiences with curiosity, and engage in continuous creativity.

The Least You Need to Know

➤ Fear is your protective friend—not your enemy.

➤ You are part of an intuitive network designed to support and protect while you remain growing and changing.

➤ Anxiety is debilitating—manage it.

➤ Children are capable of learning to distinguish real, protective fear from anxiety.

➤ If you think too much about something, it will never get done or get done too late.

➤ Choose curiosity over fear when encountering someone or something different and get used to change.

Chapter 17

The Sky's the Limit

In This Chapter

➤ Discover limits you never knew you had

➤ Learn to use the cycle of limit/no limit and back again

➤ Discover the limitation of greed

➤ Learn to live in an unlimited world

➤ Transform limitations into gas stations

➤ Stop being limited by your own imagination

Coco Chanel, a French clothes designer, lived from 1884 to 1971. She trusted her vision and revolutionized women's fashion by doing what came naturally to her while ignoring the limits that bound the rest of the world. In Paris around the turn of the century, women were wearing corsets, frills, and tight, high-collared dresses that allowed very little movement or physical freedom. To Coco, this was ridiculous. Using common fabrics such as wool jersey, at the time used only for undergarments, she fashioned comfortable, elegant clothes in which women could actually live and function.

Through fashion, Chanel made it possible for women to join the world of work and practicality. Of course, she faced the limitations of her background as an orphan raised in poverty and lacking in business or social connections. She transcended these limits, however, her vision and vitality motivating her to do what seemed natural to her: make beautiful clothes that function.

She also had "limits" in the sense of the powerful, useful boundaries that molded her success. Each garment, each design had to fit perfectly. She worked hard to design what she had in mind, not giving in to settling for something merely "good enough."

The beginning of World War II, in 1938, caused her to pause and close her factory, creating another kind of limit. However, in 1954, at the age of 70, she began again when she saw women's fashion heading toward "rustling petticoats, draped fabrics, and cinched waists."

In this chapter, you will explore what is limiting you and go beyond it. I'll share with you tools and techniques to help you break through those limits and live like Chanel in a world where there are no limitations, only powerful boundaries you will learn to use to your advantage.

Yin, Yang, and the Lava Lamp of Life

In China more than 2,500 years ago, the complementary concepts of yin and yang helped clarify the way things worked in the world. In this view, everything is considered a combination of the two forces in varying degrees. Receptivity, openness, softness, and dark are qualities of yin. Strength, directness, hardness, and light are qualities of yang. Parallels can be drawn between yin and yang and the concepts of no and yes, open and closed. It is not a concept of good and bad—there is no judgement—just a recognition of a state of being.

Studying yin and yang, one discovers that they continually blend and flow into each other. Once there's too much yin, it becomes yang. Once there's too much yang, it becomes yin. For the western mind, it's easier to understand this concept by using "opening" and "closing." Opening to something is a yang characteristic. Opening is active, involving, and engaging. Yet if one remains open for too long, with no hint of closing, it becomes yin, receptive, no longer active.

For example, someone may be open to new opportunities and actively pursue them in a yang manner. The opportunities may keep coming and this person keeps saying yes to the opportunities and becomes overwhelmed with the possibilities. At that point, the person becomes inactive. Nothing can be accomplished because too many "yeses" have occurred without enough "nos." Yin takes over and closes down the operation.

Most are familiar with the following image that represents the constant flow from yin to yang and back again. Notice that each element contains a dot of the opposite. This maintains a proper balance and keeps one element from dominating the other.

Yin Yang.

Life is constantly flowing between yes and no, opening and closing, yin and yang. Understanding this concept and applying it to your life will result in success. It will also help you work with and anticipate the shifts and jolts of change.

Yin and yang describe the world of limitation within which most people live. Looking at the circle that surrounds the movement of yin and yang takes you to the world of no limits.

Imagine that you're a colorful bubble in a lava lamp. When the heat is on, you move away from the heat, only to hit the bottom of the glass and travel back up. This is classic yin and yang motion. You may understand the movement, you may even anticipate what will happen next due to your powers of perception, but you're still controlled by the limits of the system.

Step outside of the lamp to become an observer of the lamp and all of a sudden you have freedom. No longer limited by the system, you can play with it. You might adjust the heat, change the colors, redesign the lamp altogether, or walk away from the whole thing.

Coco Chanel lived on the circle. She wasn't limited by the fashion dictates of her time; rather, she saw beyond it and played with it. Those in her time who couldn't understand what she was doing and tried to stop her lived within the lava lamp, unable to get beyond the limits of the system they were in. Imagine living in the lava lamp and watching someone outside play with the heat or change the color. You'd scream: "You can't do that!" From your perspective, you're right—but your perspective is limited.

We all live and work in lava lamps we don't see. It's time to get outside the lamp and live outside the edge of the circle, working with the yin and yang as well as the whole.

Understanding will help you maneuver within a system; transcendence allows you to create a new system. Understanding comes from information; transcendence comes from grace.

Take It to the Limit

To discover the lava lamp you are living in and move beyond it is simple, but not easy. Anything that you think is limiting you is, in reality, not. It's that simple. The perception of a problem is a signal that you have reached the edge of the yin/yang symbol, where the yin is just about to move into yang. You're just about to flip into the opposite mode, unless you move backwards into less of what you have been doing.

Sixth Sense

Transcendence describes the act of going above and beyond the current reality. It refers to the ability to "crossover" or "ascend" to a higher place.

Grace is the profound experience of a personal shift in awareness. It can be accompanied by an insight regarding a current dilemma or a release of tension and anxiety around a specific situation. "Grace" cannot be controlled or created—it can only be cultivated and allowed. It's occurrence is not based on skill, desire or need. It is a gift.

That's right, I said "less" of what you're doing. Remember the rule about yin/yang. Too much of one leads to the other. For example, take people who are runners. They run and run and run. They run so much that their shins begin to hurt. If they keep running (doing more of what they're doing), they'll surely injure themselves to the point that they need to stop running altogether and experience the "opposite" of running. If they run less, they'll move back into the yang state. Running less will keep the runner in the same "lava lamp." Even if they keep running, they'll end up having to stop running for a while and, after their recovery, begin the cycle all over again. Nothing learned, nothing changed.

Practical Wisdom

The opposite of a truth is not necessarily a falsehood. It is often an even greater truth.

—Neils Bohr, Nobel Prize-winning physicist

If the runners looked at the pain as a signal that it may be time to shift running styles, change to a new shoe, or get some advice on stretching and strengthening exercises, the runners would shift from their current state and grow into something new. Their view of running would have to change and the old restrictions of how much running their legs can take would disappear.

The following workout is designed to help you find and transcend your limitations:

1. Write down something that you think is limiting you from having what you want. State it in a clear and precise way such as: The big bad wolf is preventing me from visiting my grandmother.

2. Now write down the opposite, such as: The big bad wolf is helping me visit my grandmother. The opposite statement takes what is viewed as the block in the first sentence, and turns it into the solution. Write it down, even though it feels totally untrue.

3. Think about how both statements are true. In this case, the big bad wolf makes it scary to visit my grandmother, but at the same time, knowing that the wolf is there motivates me to go see her to make sure she is all right. I may ask a hunter to help me.

There—I just shifted the problem into solving itself. Once both statements are viewed at the same time, the mind shifts into seeing the whole, and we are blasted out of the lava lamp into seeing the lamp from the outside.

Looking simultaneously at both the yin and the yang of the situation shifts the perception of the problem, which is what's blocking the solution in the first place.

You may be thinking that this is a great trick, but what does it have to do with intuitive thinking? Good question.

Intuition is the natural flow of ideas, solutions, creativity, and energy in every moment. This particular section is addressing what gets in the way of intuitive knowing. One of the main blocks to intuitive flow is mental rigidity. If I stay stuck in the thought that the big bad wolf is preventing me from visiting my grandmother, I will have to solve the problem from a limited perspective. As soon as I allow the opposite to be true, the obvious, intuitive answer emerged.

Let's try that last workout on something closer to home:

1. My ability to do what I want is limited by the fact that I don't have enough money in my life.

2. My ability to do what I want is increased by the fact that I don't have enough money in my life.

3. If I had all the money I wanted, it would encourage me to do nothing, so the fact that I don't have enough money motivates me to do things I want in creative ways that create the flow of money into my life.

The preceding scenario was actually true for me about 15 years ago. It was one of the first realizations I had that not having money was what I needed at the time. It kept me in the game. At this point, I will continue to do what I do no matter what. I love it and do it even though the financial pressure no longer exists.

Do the workout for yourself and see what you come up with. It may take a little while to get from Step 2 to Step 3. You have to shift your perspective to the whole. Your level of attachment to the yin or yang of your situation will slow down your shift to the whole.

Tried & True

"If ever in life there is a clairvoyant experience, I had one that day. I saw a radiant and hopeful image of how the world ought to be. It opened up a portal for me that suggested that there might be a whole range of possibilities and experiences that I had not explored. It was night and day—literally. I saw a line and I thought: This is dark, and this is light. And I need to go where the light is."

Bill Strickland walked into a high school ceramics classroom a lost 16-year-old black kid, bored by school and weighed down by life. He emerged a man with a vision, with a craft and a way to make sense of this world. Thirty-five years later he is a leader in social entrepreneurism, training children and adults to find themselves and new skills through the arts.

—*Fast Company*, September 1998

Greed Kills

Greed fits the limitation scenario we just explored. It's such a potent limit for those seeking financial success that it deserves some discussion of its own.

Everyone reading this book wants to make more money and to make it using more of who they are. There's nothing wrong with that. Money is energy just as food is energy. Both provide nourishment and personal satisfaction. Food can be high art, provide opportunities to deepen relationships, heal illnesses, nourish vitality. Food can also diminish energy, become an obsession, create illness, and damage relationships.

Money is very similar. It is potent energy, necessary for modern life and can support a full, abundant life. It can also become an obsession that drains and destroys.

The yin/yang cycle of money keeps the economy going and within that, helps keep our lives going. There are ways to manage and transcend the money cycle. Begin with a balance between making money and spending money. If more money is spent, the cycle moves toward the opposite, which is having no money to spend. If more money is saved, it moves toward the opposite where it will have to be spent, possibly in taxes or by those who inherit it.

This cycle can be managed and a full, happy life can be lived within it. This cycle can also be extreme—going from one end of the spectrum to the other.

Practical Wisdom

People are often more comfortable with an understood problem than with a new solution.

Greed is the feeling of never having enough. The feeling—if believed and given in to—limits the flow of money. The overpowering feeling of needing more creates an extreme state of yang, which flips over into yin. The result is that no matter how much money is acquired, the pockets feel empty and the lifestyle reflects emptiness.

Several years ago, one of my husband's clients got involved with a stock that had just split and was selling for $10 per share. It went up to $80 and my husband advised her to at least take out her cost basis. She didn't. The stock then went up to $150 and split three for one and began selling for $50 per share. It went down from there and she finally sold it for $20 per share. At that point, she did nothing with the funds. She made loads of money. At each point in the game, she could not let go of the possibility of making more. By the time she sold it, it had gone down and she ended up feeling disappointed because she hadn't sold it at its high point!

Had she done what her adviser suggested, she would have sold at least a portion, and put it into AT&T, before it split, in the 1980s. Had she done that, she and her descendants would have been several hundreds of thousands of dollars richer.

This woman wasn't a "bad" person, but her feelings of fear and greed prevented her from flowing with the moment and focusing on the immediate sense of loss rather than the overall gain, which was tremendous.

The universe is constantly expanding and has an abundant, flowing, ever-creating nature. Money flows in a similar way. There is natural expansion and abundant flow when the creative process is allowed to function fully.

Admittedly, there's a fine line between holding the vision of an abundant life and slipping into greed. Greed is like a cancer. Cancer begins as a normal cell, then mutates into a cell that knows no boundaries and consumes all the healthy cells in its environment. Greed might begin as a healthy desire for abundance. It can mutate into a desire that knows no boundaries and consumes the thoughts and feelings of your life until nothing else is left. These are symptoms of the "greed disease." When any of these symptoms are noticed, discipline yourself to counteract the disease and take preventive measures before it takes over your life.

You know that greed is growing in you when:

➤ Your main source of pleasure is buying something new.

➤ More than 25 percent of your time is spent worrying or thinking about money.

➤ There's no time for anything other than work.

➤ You have to do most things yourself because no one else does it right.

➤ You spend far too much time feeling disappointed—in others and events.

➤ When you do something non-work related, you're still thinking about work.

➤ The only thing that stops you from working is exhaustion.

➤ There is no more joy.

Preventive and curative measures you can take when one or more of the preceding symptoms are present:

➤ Remember something you loved to do as a child and begin doing it again as a hobby.

➤ Take an afternoon off, during the week, and do something fun (retail therapy doesn't count!). See a show, visit a museum, play a sport, take a walk, anything fun.

➤ Have a non-networking lunch with a friend.

➤ Volunteer regularly.

➤ Join a workaholic anonymous group.

We're back to the yin/yang of money. Greed focuses on overaccumulation. Until its opposite is embraced (under-accumulation or the non-pursuit of money), there will be no peace. Each life requires a balance of pursuit and non-pursuit of money. To ignore the fact that money is important in this world is, in my opinion, to hide from an uncomfortable truth.

The cycle of acquiring and spending money is transcended by looking at the whole. Transcending the cycle means looking at the purpose behind the flow of money.

Having a purpose, a plan, a vision for living puts the money cycle in perspective. The money will flow up and flow down, flow in and flow out. The fluctuations in the flow will not disturb those who are focused on their purpose or those pursuing a mission.

Tap Your Power of Unlimited Thinking

Here are some examples of folks wearing their limits on their respective sleeves:

➤ "Airplanes are interesting toys but of no military value."
—Marechal Ferdinand Foch, Professor of Strategy, Ecole Superieure de Guerre

➤ "Everything that can be invented has been invented."
—Charles H. Duell, Commissioner, U.S. Office of Patents, 1899

➤ "Drill for oil? You mean drill into the ground to try and find oil? You're crazy."
—Drillers whom Edwin L. Drake tried to enlist to his project to drill for oil in 1859

➤ "The bomb will never go off. I speak as an expert in explosives."
—Admiral William Leahy, U.S. Atomic Bomb Project

➤ "You want to have consistent and uniform muscle development across all of your muscles? It can't be done. It's just a fact of life. You just have to accept inconsistent muscle development as an unalterable condition of weight training."
—Response to Arthur Jones, who solved the "unsolvable" problem by inventing Nautilus weight training equipment

➤ "I'm glad it will be Clark Gable who's falling on his face and not Gary Cooper."
—Gary Cooper on his decision not to take the leading role in *Gone With The Wind*

Need I go on? There are many, many more famous and not-so-famous limited thinkers always ready to say "This will never work."

In all of these examples, power was asserted in a limited way. Each of these individuals closed the door on something and established a sense of power in the moment.

Unlimited power feels more vulnerable the moment it contacts something new, yet results in creating tremendous power by blending what is known with what is unknown and allowing the intuitive process to unfold.

Each of these opportunities was taken up by others who were willing to explore and create without knowing when, where, or if it would work. That's vulnerable and that's the power of unlimited thinking.

Limited thinking is a byproduct of analytic intelligence. Unlimited thinking a byproduct of intuitive intelligence. Analytic intelligence is based on what has happened in the past, while intuitive intelligence is based on what can happen in the future.

Everyone has both types of intelligence. They can work either together or against each other. Many have been trained to have the habit of thinking analytically, while ignoring or discounting intuition. Even after a great idea or intuitive insight occurs, the analytic intelligence kicks in and says "That's stupid" or "No one will believe that."

Working together, the intuitive intelligence sets the direction, envisions the future, and allows for new ideas and input along the way. Analytic intelligence looks at the problems and barriers that occur along the way, discovers ways around them, gathers data and information, and seeks to understand and form models for what is occurring.

Bill Strickland, CEO and founder of the Manchester Craftsmen's Guild, a fantastic social entrepreneurial enterprise in Pittsburgh, Pennsylvania, said it precisely: "You start with the perception that the world is an unlimited opportunity. Then the question becomes, 'How are we going to rebuild the planet?'"

Tapping into unlimited thinking is easy because it's a part of who you are. It doesn't even take more time to think in an unlimited way. The barriers are habitual thinking and lack of willingness. If you picked up this book, you have the willingness and habits can be broken once observed.

Unlimited thinking requires staying focused on the whole and continually looking for the new whole that gets created when two opposite or opposing ideas come together.

Take a Pit Stop

Any barrier that emerges is seen by the intuitive mind as a "gas station." Each barrier is an opportunity to refuel, check the vital signs of the project, realign to the vision, and accept in new ideas and opportunities. The barrier becomes the next opportunity. It's an opportunity to strengthen and build the force of the vision by blending with the wisdom and insight contained in the barrier.

You can wait until you run out of gas completely and then struggle to get to the nearest gas station, or you can read the intuitive signals that will indicate when it's time for a break, a refill, or a new opportunity. Either way, the magic works. One way uses more frustrating energy than the other.

The next time you hit a barrier, do the following:

➤ Redefine it as a gas station and begin to look for how it might enhance and support your project.

➤ Pause to assess the impact of the barrier.

➤ Don't resist the direction the barrier is moving you in.

➤ Continue to move toward your goal at the same time.

Here is how it worked for one person:

1. Stuck with not enough money to attend an important conference, essential to furthering her career dream, this woman could not see a way out.

2. The impact of the barrier is frustration as well as a resolve to get to the conference.

3. She stops and pauses with the two opposing forces of wanting something she can't afford—looking at the situation as a "gas station" that somewhere has an opportunity for her.

4. The idea of "asking others for help" occurs to her and is at first dismissed as personally unacceptable. Upon reflection, she realizes that people who ask for help often get it, whereas those who don't ask are certain to not get it. When she asks for help, friends are more than willing to loan her the money for attending the conference—plus, she gets an infusion of support and new contacts for expanding her business.

5. The "barrier" of no money was transformed into an opportunity to "ask for help" which shifted her outlook on her business and increased her communication skills.

Tried & True

Bill Strickland's journey of creating successful, continuously creative, and growing entrepreneurial programs directed toward social change provides an example of limitation-busting. Peter Benzing, a retired vice president of Bayer Corporation, met Bill Strickland while looking for ways to educate the Pittsburgh work force to meet Bayer's needs for chemical technicians. Bill's program was training youth and adults in job skills, but nothing that technically demanding. Bayer traditionally hired college graduates for lab technicians, whereas most of Bill's students barely completed high school. Rather than seeing barriers and problems, they both saw opportunity and a chance to work together to create something new.

Both of their programs changed and were renewed by the interaction. Within 12 months, Bill's programs began graduating workers who could compete with college graduates for jobs at Bayer and other highly technical positions.

Cultures have spent centuries fighting, trying hopelessly to destroy each other, when world views clashed. Much destruction has occurred, but nothing, no idea or world view has been destroyed. Dominated, perhaps; diminished, yes; but destroyed, never.

Unlimited thinking is a more creative and sustainable way of meeting a new idea, an enemy, or a different way of life. There is more power in having a greater number of options than there is in having only one way to respond.

Tried & True

You'd think an astute business person is one who deals only in the facts, or at least the facts as he or she sees them. But the most astute business people are those who have done just the opposite. Fact, 1980: Chrysler Corporation may soon be out of the car business. Fact, 1993: Chrysler Corporation is still alive. If Lee Iacocca had accepted the fact that Chrysler could make only second-rate cars and was perpetually a government bailout candidate, Chrysler most likely would still be there. Yet in Iacocca's vision he saw an even more powerful truth. And then he acted to make it happen: He led the Chrysler Corporation from losses to profit.

—Allen Fahden, *Innovation on Demand*

The following points of view will help keep you in unlimited mind:

➤ See different points of view as diverse pieces of the same puzzle. Look for the whole puzzle they both fit within.

➤ Look beyond the immediate moment to possible results. Ask yourself, "What would the world look like if they did work out?"

➤ Wait until your initial emotional reaction has subsided before responding. Strong emotion, whether elation or negation, can interfere with intuitive knowing and limit your thinking.

➤ Ask, "What would Albert Einstein (or any other genius you relate to) do with this?"

➤ Ask, "What would a 5-year-old do with this?"

➤ Say, "That's an ugly seed, I wonder what it'll grow into?" Use your imagination to grow something that's in a pre-growth stage. Have you ever seen a Dahlia root? They're ugly and bear no visual relation to the beautiful flowers they produce. If we judged flowers by their seeds, bulbs, and roots, no one would garden.

➤ Say, "I don't like this; I wonder who would?" This project, idea, or thought might not be something in line with your vision, but it might fit perfectly with another.

Managing in a World Without Limits

The world of unlimited possibilities is a pretty open space. Without a structure or focus, it's easy to get lost in the openness. The linear approach to life can be summarized as follows:

➤ Work first—focus on tasks and responsibilities.

➤ Play, if there's time.

➤ Create when possible.

Work, tasks, and responsibilities provide the structure that is accomplished and rewarded. Those who accomplish the most, take on the largest responsibilities, and work the longest get the praise and rewards in this culture. Whether what they accomplish is beneficial to others is often secondary. Certainly, the need to be productive and busy doing something has become an obsession.

Your Intuitive Management Plan

The intuitive approach to life is more interactive. Tasks and responsibilities are accomplished within the realm of all possibilities. It's a circular process where everything happens at the same time. Feedback, creativity, and new ideas are constantly incorporated into the task at hand.

Structure and discipline are essential for success in this system too, but the discipline centers around taking time to listen, deeply. In this system, listening deeply is rewarded by being at the right place at the right time and connecting with new opportunities in spontaneous and unusual ways.

Shifting the daily focus from a task orientation to a listening orientation is a fun thing to do. See it as taking a vacation without leaving your job. Tasks will still be accomplished but with less effort. At first it may seem extremely uncomfortable. Try it for two weeks and then evaluate.

Here is an outline for a two-week, stay-where-you-are vacation. It is an opportunity for you to try-out living in the world of intuition.

Sixth Sense

When a stringed instrument is tuned, it's strings are made to resonate at a certain frequency, which is harmonious to the other strings. When you *attune* and spend time attuning, you are putting yourself in harmony with both your own vision and long-term goals as well as with universal forces which will support you in their fulfillment.

> ➤ *Discipline.* The discipline around which this system works is the discipline of listening and attuning to the realm of all possibilities. Whether or not you're an experienced meditator isn't important. For these two weeks, you will begin your day with 20 minutes of personal attuning time. Take another 10 minutes in the middle of the day, and a final 20 minutes at the end of the day. These periods can be spent journal writing, meditating, reading "holy scripture" of your choice, praying, breathing, visualizing, using one of the workouts in this book, or walking slowly. This is the core structure of your time. These moments are essential for the next two weeks.

> ➤ *Responsibility.* Your responsibility during these two weeks is to take care of what needs to be taken care of in your life and to respond to the insights, synchronicities, and intuitions that occur. Pay less attention to your "to do" list and more attention to what is needed in each moment. In other words, practice being present to what is happening now rather than preparing for what might happen in the future.

> ➤ *Accountability.* You are the only one who will know whether or not you are fulfilling your commitments. Be honest with yourself. There is no punishment. This is an opportunity to experience a different system of self-management, one based on your relationship to the larger whole. Keep a journal recording your experiences, feelings, responses, intuitions, and synchronicities.

➤ Results. At the end of the two weeks, review what happened, including the following:

➤ How you felt

➤ What got accomplished and what didn't get accomplished

➤ How you'd improve the discipline

➤ What you'll keep doing

To Infinity—and Beyond!

Many books have discussed and outlined the value of visualizing specific goals in order to realize them. This does work and it's important to learn to use the particular power that individuals have.

Something that might hinder the visualizing process for success is that it's based on your imagination. Your imagination is limited to what you can imagine for yourself. Think about the goals you had in high school. What if your life had been limited to fulfilling those goals? I don't know about you, but the thought of a lifetime term of prom queen and cheerleader are not my idea of a full life anymore. I am extremely grateful that those dreams did not happen.

Intuitive intelligence connects you, your individual gifts, and desires to the larger whole. Tapping intuitive intelligence allows for visions that go way beyond the limits of your personal imagination. Letting intuitive intelligence provide opportunities expands the possibilities of your life in ways you can't imagine. Personal imaginations can be limited by too many shoulds and shouldn'ts.

The Least You Need to Know

➤ Moving from yin to yang, no to yes, closed to open and back again is what makes the world go around.

➤ Stepping outside the cycle of yin and yang releases the hold of limitations.

➤ Greed limits by focusing on narrow goals that are fear-based.

➤ Barriers and difficulties feed and strengthen your project.

➤ Practice living in the world of unlimited possibilities by taking three intuitive pauses every day for two weeks.

➤ Don't be limited by your imagination.

Chapter 18

Dealing with Self-Judgment

In This Chapter

➤ Stop being so hard on yourself

➤ Discover how much you really know

➤ Learn the difference between making a good judgment and being judgmental

➤ Learn to toot your intuitive horn

➤ Be your own intuitive coach

"We were struggling for a year and a half to find a perfect model to use in our videotape program, 'SyberVision Muscle Memory Program for Gold.' Then I thought of Al Geiberger, who is recognized by golfers as having perfect golf form. He also set the record—59—on the PGA Tour for the lowest eighteen-hole score in Memphis in 1978. But almost as soon as I thought of him, I thought, 'Well heck, I'm not really qualified to call somebody like him.' Then Gold Digest ran a three-month special series on Al Geiberger, which I read. I thought, 'I would really like to call him and invite him to be a model, but he doesn't know who I am. He'd probably hang up on me, or, you know, I'm insignificant,' Then I said to myself, 'Come on!' And I kicked myself in the rear end. I said, 'I am significant, and I know from my past experience that all I have to do is create a mental blueprint of whom I want to choose and the events out there will make that happen.' So I called him."

That's Steve DeVore, Founder and CEO, SyberVision Systems, Inc., talking. Michael Ray and Rochelle Myers include this excellent example of how self-judgment can hinder intuition in their book *Creativity in Business*.

In this chapter, you'll face the demon of self-judgment and learn tools to defuse the power it has over you and your life. Self-judgment runs deep and is reinforced through continuous media images projecting perfect people with perfect lives to compare ourselves to. At the end of this chapter, you'll learn to speak your intuitive truth more clearly to others and to coach yourself.

Don't Let Intuition Scare You

A client of many years ago shared the story of when she was seven or eight years old and she "knew" without a doubt that the train her brother was scheduled to take back to college was going to crash. She also "knew" that no one would believe her so she locked herself in the bathroom. Her family banged on the door, screamed and yelled at her, and couldn't understand what was happening. When she finally emerged, they raced to the train station only to miss the train he was scheduled to take. Disappointed and angry, everyone waited for the next train.

That night, at around midnight, her father was listening to the radio and heard that the train his son was scheduled to be on crashed. He went into his daughter's room and told her that he now knew why she had done what she did. The incident terrified her, and she mistrusted her intuition for most of her life.

I remember having a clear, open intuition as a child. I anticipated events, sensed appropriate decisions for myself, and felt solidly connected to some deep truth. I never spoke about it and never shared it with anyone. Sometime around second grade I must have awakened to the fact that nobody else seemed to do anything similar—or at least they didn't talk about it. My feeling was that it was wrong. Another kind of knowing was valued and rewarded in school. It didn't take long for me to completely forget about my intuitive self for many years. Even now there are times when self-judgment and self-criticism get in the way of knowing what I know.

I often wonder what the world would look like if children were encouraged to trust themselves, were given more opportunities to discover what they already know, and helped to bring that knowing into the world in creative ways.

You are connected to a vast network of intuitive information. You don't need to have all the answers beforehand, they appear as needed. When merchandise is ordered from a catalog, it appears at your front door in a day or two. The intuitive network functions in a similar way. Information is ordered, and it arrives as soon as possible. The amount of intuitive information available is unlimited. The limiting factor is our willingness to believe it, use it, and act on it.

Tried & True

Intuition is an important source of power for all of us. Nevertheless, we have trouble observing ourselves use experience in this way, and we definitely have trouble explaining the basis of our judgments when someone else asks us to defend them.... Research by Wilson and Schooler (1991) shows that people do worse at some decision tasks when they are asked to perform analyses of the reasons for their preferences or to evaluate all the attributes of the choices.

—Gary Klein, *Sources of Power*

Many years ago I was waiting for my newly met significant other (who is now my husband) to call when he returned from a two-week trip. He had said he would call around 4 or 5 p.m. and it was already 7 p.m. I was getting anxious and wondered what was going on. Taking a moment to breathe deeply and release the feeling of anxiousness, I suddenly "knew" without a doubt that he would call at 9 p.m.

When he called at precisely 9 p.m., it blew my mind. I was so frightened I closed the door on intuitive knowing for several months. Sometimes it's scary to know what we know and what we can know.

How Much Power Do You Really Want?

Discovering that I had information available that was beyond what I could gather logically and rationally meant that I could no longer wallow in self-pity, blaming others, or being victimized by circumstances—although I still give it a try now and then for nostalgic reasons! There was no doubt that at any moment I could know exactly what I needed to know to take appropriate action, even if that action was to do nothing. All the energy expended wanting things to be different than they were, for events to hurry up, and to find my place in the world, became an obvious waste. All that was needed was to keep doing what was in front of me to do and know that any information and help necessary to keep doing what I was doing would appear or could be gathered when appropriate.

To be active and involved in your life is not only important but essential. To take on the personal sense of responsibility for it all to happen by next week is crazy and locks out the role of the helpful Universe. Allowing intuitive wisdom to flow in and participate with your life releases an internal tension and tightness associated with having to "be good enough." Your "good-enoughness" comes not from knowing all the answers in advance but from trusting the answers to emerge as necessary. Living in your intuitive flow allows the breath of life to breathe through you.

Tried & True

Two days before Judy W. was to be interviewed for a PBS Television program, an old article stored for years on the shelf, dropped onto the floor. It was on the same subject as the upcoming interview and helped Judy tremendously as she had just returned home from the hospital after receiving bypass surgery.

How We Deny Our Intuition

How many times have you said to yourself: "I knew I shouldn't have (or should have) done that!"? This classic statement validates that we do indeed have intuition and that we often choose not to listen to it. There are three main ways intuitive information gets shut off:

➤ We don't trust the information. A feeling, hunch, or sense is experienced and immediately its possible validity is denied. Phrases like "This couldn't be" or "No Way!" may be spoken out loud or internally, stopping the flow of information. Sometimes the information is taken to other people to get their opinions. When they say "Couldn't be" or "No way" their conviction overrides any chance that we might have trusted what was heard.

The information is not trusted because it conflicts deeply with the current track of action or with the status quo. Sometimes we are just too lazy to make the phone call or complete the task that's being intuitively nudged, so it's ignored.

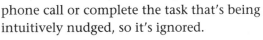

Yellow Light

If you hear yourself say "I can make this work" or "I can live with this," you're going in the opposite direction of your intuition.

➤ We don't trust ourselves to take the action. Sometimes an intuition is heard and the first response is "That's a great idea, but I could never do it" or "I don't have the skill to do that." Many people have shared with me how they had an idea for a new business and dismissed it as too hard, too complicated, or too obvious, only to see someone else profit from it within a year or two.

➤ We don't want the consequences. When it comes to intuitions that are closer to home, the information can be heard, yet the consequences seem way too risky. The potential emotional pain or conflict inhibits any action. Instead of acknowledging the emotional response, most people deny the information. It's easy to rationalize intuitive information away because it's so nonanalytic and usually without concrete evidence. Even with concrete evidence, it's easy to deny that there's anything at all that needs to change.

This Way Through the Minefield

Even with all of the denial discussed previously, intuitive information is still always available and ready to be accessed. Here are some tools to pick your way through the minefield and navigate through issues that involve lots of self-judgment, self-criticism, and insecurity.

Practical Wisdom

In our fear-frozen minds, we sometimes think we have no other choice. That's seldom, if ever, true. It's merely a sign of our fear that has paralyzed us.

—Spencer Johnson, *Yes or No*

Phrases To Phorget

Information that doesn't fit within the current context is hard to take, whether intuitive or not. Add the element of nonanalytic, subjective, intuitive information and it's easy to dismiss. Here are some of the key phrases that we use to dismiss intuitive information. They're heard often enough to be familiar. Perhaps you say these phrases to yourself, to someone else, or someone says them to you:

Discounting	"This is just an accident or coincidence; it's not important."
Denying	"I don't know, see, or understand what you're talking about."
Deflecting	"Let's get back to the real issue" or "Enough daydreaming, back to basics."
Demeaning	"This is really stupid."
Disbelieving	"This can't be true."

Self-judgment is a minefield. The mechanism for blasting intuitions and ideas is hidden underground and can explode unexpectedly. When these phrases are said to you, whether internally or externally, or you find yourself saying them to someone else—pause. Take a moment to say to yourself: "Wait a minute. What just happened and what feelings, images, or hunches were just blasted away?"

Practical Wisdom

What concerns me is not the way things are, but rather the way people think things are.

—Epictetus

259

Tried & True

In their book *Creativity in Business*, Michael Ray and Rochelle Myers describe how many business people use physical exercise to break the habit of self-judgment. One executive says, "I found that when I am running, swimming, or cycling, only rarely do I find myself passing judgment on either myself or others. I now realize that the quitting of my judgmental mind chatter is one of the reasons I exercise. I previously exercised just for the sake of quiet concentration, but now I know that I must do it to silence my judgmental mind."

Don't Jump to Conclusions

The analytic mind automatically jumps to the end result. One of the skills of the analytic mind is to anticipate results. The problem occurs when dealing with emotionally charged questions. I'm not just talking relationships here. Business, money, and career changes all have high potential for emotional charge.

Here's a good example, Bobby was looking for a new job. He was a lawyer with many skills and much experience in the world of entrepreneurial endeavors, socially involved projects, and non-profit agencies. He was looking for an opportunity to use his skills in a job that would be in alignment with his overall life values and provide an income to support him and his family.

One day on the subway, he noticed a man reading a book that was interesting to him. On a whim, he asked the man about it, and they started a conversation. It turned out that the man on the train was looking to hire lawyers for a government job. The job was somewhat aligned to Bobby's ultimate goals, but was clearly bureaucratic and low-paying. The need Bobby was feeling to find a job seduced him into thinking that this may be something he should consider.

Bobby's analytic mind was jumping to conclusions all over the place. "This is it. I should take this job. It will solve my current problems." The only problem was, it really didn't fit. Bobby was overqualified for this job. It was the last gasp of his self-doubt and self-judgment that was urging him to take the job.

Luckily for him, his wife saw what was happening and nixed the job right away. Once she spoke the truth about the job and gave him permission to let it go, Bobby felt complete relief. Soon after that, real opportunities emerged.

Tried & True

Brainstorming sessions held at many organizations to stimulate open-minded thinking give new ideas a chance. Keeping creative juices flowing requires a free flow of ideas. The corporate world often snuffs out a new idea before it can evolve into the answer to an "unsolvable problem."

Stay in the Moment

Whenever you feel yourself on the downward spiral of negative, self-critical thinking, bring yourself back to the present moment. The present moment contains no criticism. In the present moment, it's possible to see, feel, and sense what is happening.

Get to the present moment by asking yourself the following:

Yellow Light

Good detectives will never jump to conclusions because doing so limits their ability to see the evidence. Once a mind is made up—it stops observing.

➤ Where am I right now? Do a quick reality check. Remind yourself of the date, place, and time. This simple reminder will bring your mind back from the past or future projects where the criticism is taking place.

➤ What's going on? Review what is actually happening right around you. This will help keep you focused in the present moment.

➤ What do I really know? Get back to reality. What do you really know and what are the conclusions you're drawing from what you know. Also, allow the deeper, intuitive knowing to come to the surface.

➤ What are my choices? Check your choices. Remind yourself that a choice always frees you from the tyranny of self-judgment.

Take Your Sweet Time

Move slowly when there's uncertainty. Take your time. Uncertainty is often an intuitive signal for "it's not time yet, but soon." The intuitive wisdom might be to keep alert and ready to move when the time is right.

Being Judgmental Is Not Good Judgment

There's a skill called "good judgment." This is very different from being judgmental. Good judgment is a process of combining analytic data, observation, and intuitive knowing, which results in the ability to take action without complete certainty.

Practical Wisdom

Good judgment comes from experience. Experience comes from bad judgment.

Doctors do it all the time. They are asked to work with incomplete data and make conclusions based on their observations of symptoms and the knowledge gained from laboratory tests. In medicine, as in many fields, absolutely conclusive evidence is a luxury not often available. Judgments need to be made in order to move forward with a healing process.

Although similar in sound, making a good judgment and being judgmental couldn't be further apart in meaning. Making a good judgment allows for new information to be added at any time. Being judgmental implies making a snap judgment and sticking with it, even after evidence is offered that refutes the initial judgment.

Being judgmental involves assessments of value, often measuring one thing better or worse than something else. Making judgments involves making the best choice at the time, given the information available and the surrounding circumstances. There may be other choices and more effective choices as time goes on. The ability to make good judgments balances the need for timely action and limited information. Intuition plays a major role in making good judgments.

Practical Wisdom

The process of nurturing new ideas is a skill worth learning.

Spit It Out

A young advertising executive was in a high-powered client meeting supporting the presentation of new advertising ideas. During the course of the meeting she had several ideas stimulated by the conversations. Instead of sharing them with the group, however, she judged their merit by saying to herself: "Why hasn't anyone else thought of these? They seem obvious to me, but I'm the youngest person here. How can my ideas be any good? Someone must have thought of them before and rejected them. I'd better keep my mouth shut if I don't want to look foolish."

Later on in the meeting someone else stated the ideas she had had but not shared. They were received quite favorably, with accolades and credit going to the one who shared them.

Cat Got Your Tongue?

Sound familiar? This kind of thing happens often. Intuitive ideas and inspiration happen spontaneously—in the moment—on a need-to-know basis. The kind of second-guessing that went on in the preceding story comes from a fear of making mistakes and appearing foolish.

Intuitive ideas seem obvious to those who have them. It seems unlikely that everyone else hasn't had the same idea.

If the idea occurs to you, it's up to you to do something with it. Share it, write it down, or act on it. Not all ideas that occur are worth pursuing, but deciding which ones to pursue and which to let go requires first that the ideas come out of you and into a more concrete form.

Speak Intuition

A way to share your intuitive ideas without feeling foolish is to acknowledge the intuitive source of the idea. Don't state it as truth or something you've given years of thought to. Preface the ideas with phrases like this:

➤ "It just occurred to me…"

➤ "I don't know for sure but I have a sense that…"

➤ "That last idea triggered something else…"

➤ "This is a wild idea, let's see where it might take us…"

➤ "My intuitive sense is…"

➤ "My gut feel is…"

Having a few phrases like these help buffer the flow of new ideas. Once the idea is out on the table, it can grow or feed other ideas. It's never wasted.

The feeling of excitement and internal pressure that takes place when something wants to be spoken can be experienced as anxiety. It's the intuitive flow pushing the idea through you out to the group. If you resist it, it will find another door, perhaps another person, to go through. It is said that nothing is as powerful as an idea whose time has come.

Practical Wisdom

Don't get so hung up on whether or not you'll fail. Most people consider success and failure as opposites, but they're actually both products of the same process. An activity that produces a hit may also produce a miss. (Take baseball, for example. The batter does the same thing every time he or she comes up to bat and sometimes hits and sometimes misses.) It's the same with creative thinking; the same energy that generates good creative ideas also produces errors.

—Roger von Oech, *A Whack on the Side of the Head*

Practical Wisdom

When in doubt, ask a dumb question.

Practical Wisdom

Success is doing what seems obvious to you, regardless of whether others agree with you.

If you allow it, more ideas will flow and the group will have an opportunity to come into sync. A group comes into sync when it allows intuitive wisdom to create in the moment through those present. All of the self-judgment, criticism, and extreme devotion to an agenda and timetable clog up the flow and create creative constipation.

The more individuals are willing to share their spontaneous ideas, the greater the chance the group will flow into creative sync. This snowballing effect is powerful and the creative joy of it is wonderful to behold. Seeing a group of "doubters" recapture the intuition, creativity, and joy of their childhood is an image that makes me smile.

Going To Visit Dr. Feelgood

Self-judgment, as I've said before, is a sneaky devil. It can creep up when least expected. It can take many forms that make it seem so logical, while at the same time it's shutting the door on new possibilities and creative energy.

Watch for feelings and self-talk that negates, denies, criticizes, or minimizes. Avoid phrases like "You didn't want to do that anyway," "That would have been a waste of your time," or "You can't do that very well." Phrases of that sort bury energy. Here are three ways to support positive self-esteem and subvert self-judgment.

Practical Wisdom

The world is not fixed but is in constant flux; accordingly, the future is not fixed, and so can be shaped. Humans possess significant tacit knowledge—we know more than we can say. The question to be resolved: How to remove the blocks and tap into that knowledge in order to create the kind of future we all want?

—Joe Jaworski, *Synchronicity*

Keep a Journal

Write in a journal every day for a set amount of time or number of pages. (Read Julia Cameron's book *The Artist's Way* for more on this.) Consistently writing, regardless of how you're feeling, regardless of whether what you write is coherent or not, and regardless of whether you ever read it again or not, will prime your creative and intuitive pump.

Writing gets the garbage of self-judgment out of your mind and onto the paper where it won't be able to infect you. Don't take what you write too seriously, at least not at first. Let it just be a brain dump of everything that naturally comes out. It's like opening an attic that has had stuff crammed in it for the past 50 or so years. The first thing that has to happen is to let everything fall out. Then you can go back and sort through what is worth saving and what needs to be tossed. More will be added to your journal writing in Chapter 24.

Go to the Head of the Class

Take up a new hobby or craft, or just learn something new. Pick something that you think you might enjoy or something you've always wanted to try and yet something you don't need to excel in. Take the class and be willing to be awkward and willing to try.

Learning something new will allow you to be in "Beginner's Mind" where you don't have to be perfect. The gift of imperfection will spill over into the rest of your life eroding the power of your internal judge.

Join the Club

Join an organization, club, or support group focused on something you're interested in. Give yourself the opportunity to learn new things, share what you know, and develop relationships in a non-pressured, low-expectation environment.

Self-judgment loves to compare you against others. Are you better or worse? The truth is you can always find someone who has more than you and you can always find someone who has less. There is always one more thing to have or do, and always something that needs fixing or improving.

Don't Expect Miracles

One of the more important comparisons to watch out for is comparing yourself to some ideal image. If you feel from reading this book that you should be able to hear your intuitive voice without any fear or doubt, forget it.

Aim for identifying intuitive intelligence working in your life and begin to give it more room. The room will still have other things in it that you'll find a way to work with.

Think of self-criticism as dirt that gets tracked into your room, or clutter that builds up. Yes, it needs to be dealt with, but it isn't part of the essential structure and design of your room.

Yellow Light

Constantly comparing ourselves against others is a mental illness that zaps creativity and individual achievement. Buddha talked 2,500 years ago about this constant comparing and evaluating of self as the last illusion to go before enlightenment.

The Power of Criticism...

There is a yin/yang element to criticism and judgment. One can become overly sensitive to being nice and non-critical to the point where it becomes its opposite—over-protective. The truth is that the world isn't always a nice place. People say and do things that offend, criticize, and hurt, either intentionally or unintentionally. To not learn from that is a missed opportunity and stunts growth. To take it too personally is equally a missed opportunity and also slows growth.

Practical Wisdom

Self-respect means coming from your power, not your weakness.

—Sanaya Roman, *Living with Joy*

Yellow Light

If you think it, it's true.

The point of personal power is where self-confidence and self-reflection create a whole. Too much self-confidence flips into arrogance where mistakes can't be acknowledged and learned from. Conversely, too much self-reflection flips into noninvolvement and the inability to act on what is known.

Positive criticism or "atta-boys" should also be examined. You can enjoy praise, but keep it in perspective. Becoming co-dependent for approval can give power to people that lead with a roller-coaster ride of praise and withheld praise that is both draining and counter-intuitive.

Intuitive intelligence is the point where the needs of the individual meet the needs of the whole. Both are equally represented. Living intuitively means living with a foot in the world of the whole and a foot in the world of your needs and desires. Your personal focus gives the whole something to flow through. Self-criticism and self-judgment clog up the connection, as do criticism and judgment of others.

... And How To Tame It

When a criticism is noticed, either from yourself or from someone else, try the following:

1. *Catch and identify.* For example, you may catch yourself doing or saying something and realize: "I think I'm a spendthrift" or "I think I'm too generous" or "He thinks I don't know what I'm talking about" or "She thinks I have no taste." This is difficult to do. Most often criticisms are either ignored or absorbed. To catch it and articulate it puts you in the power seat. Often it requires separating what was said from how it was said.

2. *Look and learn.* Decide whether it's true in this particular situation or not. Ask yourself: "How might this be true right now?" or "Is there something in what I'm hearing that I can learn from?" If the criticism stings, it's most likely because it has some truth to it. It may not be packaged neatly, and it's probably not all true.

3. *Remember.* Whether it is all true or partially true, it's only true for a moment. It doesn't describe your essential self, only some of your behavior. You aren't stuck in cement, you can change if you choose to.

4. *Acknowledge.* Acknowledge, out loud, the truth in what they're saying and learn from it. Whatever is not true, let go.

Meet Your Intuition Coach

Your job, as your own intuition coach, is to do the following:

➤ Remind yourself that you have an intuitive voice to listen to.

➤ Catch and defuse self-criticism before it becomes destructive.

➤ Cheer yourself on and manage your anxiety when you decide to take a less traveled road.

Here's a workout that'll show you how to meet your intuition coach. Make yourself comfortable for about 15 minutes so you can meet and establish a relationship with your coach. Then do the following:

1. Close your eyes and take a few deep breaths.

2. Imagine yourself in a wonderful room, designed to create a feeling of peace.

3. Take a seat in the most comfortable chair.

4. Invite in your intuition coach. Allow your mind to open with no preconceived image, and allow whatever images, sense, or feeling to come into the room with you.

5. The image may be extremely clear or fuzzy. Possibly it's a feeling with no image. It may also be someone you know, someone you've never seen, or something completely different, like an animal or spiritual force. Accept whatever comes, without trying to change it.

6. Say hello to your coach. Welcome your coach to your room.

7. Ask if there's anything your coach would like to say to you. Is there anything important for you to pay attention to right now? Listen to what your coach has to say to you and ask any more questions that occur to you.

8. Thank your coach, and establish a way to stay in contact—perhaps through the image of this room or through a particular feeling. Often, all you need to do is to remember your coach's presence and, boom, you are back in touch.

9. Take a few relaxing breaths and open your eyes. Record what happened in your journal.

After you do this workout for a few weeks or a few months, you'll have established a strong relationship with your intuition coach. You'll remember and hear your intuitive voice, catch self-criticism before it becomes toxic, and feel your internal guidance as you blaze the trails of your life.

The Least You Need to Know

➤ Self-criticism blocks the intuitive flow of ideas.

➤ Watch for judgmental thoughts and phrases.

➤ Take it slow, and don't jump to conclusions.

➤ Speak up!

➤ Write in a journal. Learn something new. Join a club.

➤ Draw strength from criticism.

Stepping into Intuitive Power

Chuck Norris, in his book *The Secret Power Within*, describes an exchange he observed between Carlos Machados, a world-class jujitsu master, and his landlord:

> "You and I have talked about how we can apply the Zen philosophy to our lives, and this is a case in point. My landlord came here determined to raise the rent. He began the discussion with me by anticipating a confrontation, which didn't occur. As you well know, that initial element of surprise is the basic premise of jujitsu. When you are attacked, you give way just enough to unbalance your opponent, and then turn the attack to your advantage by using skill or strategy.

> "Most people fear an attack by somebody bigger or stronger than they are, but if you allow yourself to be intimidated and fearful, then your opponent has gained even more power. But if your attitude is that no matter how strong or powerful the attacker is—and in this case my landlord was convinced he had the upper hand—you are better prepared, because you have trained and you have knowledge he does not possess; at that point he's vulnerable."

Stepping into intuitive power means making a commitment to living your life based on intuitive principles, and, has many parallels with the philosophy of martial arts. This chapter will help you live more comfortably with the intuitive muscles you've been building it through the workouts in this book. You'll be invited to stop making excuses for both your successes and your failures. Additional respect will be paid to the skill of listening to intuitive warnings, and you'll learn to follow the energy of success.

Practice Being Powerful

The preceding story illustrates two things about intuition: knowing and anticipation. The story continues:

> "When I had him off-balance, I brought him down with a surprise move. I had done some research and learned that recent laws had been passed that require new tenants to have a certain number of parking spaces for each five hundred square feet they occupy. There are no parking spaces available for the building. Since I have been here such a long time, I don't come under the law, but a new tenant would.

> "My research into the new law was the move that took him off balance and sent him out of here thinking he was lucky to have me remain and deciding not to ask for an increase in rent."

Any surprise or change can feel like an enemy attack. Just as the plan is working, something happens that disturbs the even flow. For those uninitiated in the martial or intuitive arts, the surprise causes a reaction and there may be an impulse to change direction and start all over.

The confident intuitive knows that whatever happens is new information that will become part of the mix. The power, in the face of change, comes from within. The intuitive can be confident that if it's important to move, change, or shift strategies, the impulse and the knowing of what to do will come from within, not from without. That is true power.

Tried & True

Cristina Sanchez is Spain's top woman bullfighter, one of an elite few women who have succeeded in the male-dominated sport. She says, "Bullfighting is as much about intuition and mental power as strength.... It's a question of measuring the intelligence of man against the strength of the bull."

At any moment, confident and competent intuitives have information no one else has. They know what is the right action for them. In the preceding story, Carlos knew his internal strength. He wasn't about to engage in an argument or try to "fight" the landlord. Carlos used the power of non-resistance and listened carefully and attentively to everything the landlord said, then acted with confidence, addressing the concerns of the landlord.

The other power point of intuition illustrated by this story happened before the interchange took place. How did Carlos pick-up the needed information about parking spaces beforehand? For some reason, Carlos was inspired to research the new law regarding the number of parking spaces required for rental space. That is a perfect use of intuitive knowing.

Often, an article in a newspaper, magazine story, or TV sound bite will grab your attention for no apparent reason. It will make an impression that stays or perhaps inspires deeper research. A situation will soon emerge where that information is exactly what is needed. Trusting the anticipatory nature of intuition is key to stepping into its power.

Two Power Tools

These two intuitive elements—intuitive knowing and intuitive preparation through anticipation—are powerful tools for wielding intuitive power:

1. Be confident of intuitive knowing. This whole book has been a preparation for this tool. Step into intuitive power by knowing what you know and responding to it. This doesn't happen overnight. Pick two or three intuition workouts shared in this book and practice them every day, tracking your results. A daily practice of 10 minutes will build confidence in your intuitive knowing.

2. Be open to and go with intuitive anticipations. Practice by intuitively scanning reading material. When a headline catches your eye, read it.

Practical Wisdom

Only intuition can protect you from the most dangerous individual of all—the articulate incompetent.

—Robert Bernstein

A seminar participant shared a dramatic story of intuitive anticipation. When going to the grocery store, she grabbed her big, thick down parka and put it on. The weather at the time was quite warm, and the jacket was totally unnecessary. In the car on the way

Practical Wisdom

Just trust yourself. Then you will know how to live.

—Goethe

to the store, she wondered why she was wearing this jacket, but kept it on anyway.

She wore it in the store, feeling a little foolish. On her way out of the store and back to her car, she was mugged. Several young men attacked her, pushed her onto the ground, hit her a few times and took her purse. At the hospital, the doctor told her that the thick coat she was wearing saved her from serious injury.

This is a dramatic story of intuitive anticipation, which happens quite frequently. Even more frequent is the anticipation of useful information.

Let the Power Happen

Intuitive power is not the power of strength. As in the martial arts, it's the power of non-resistance. If asked to point at the power of intuition and prove it, it disappears. Its power appears in action, not in abstraction. It will not be controlled or regimented.

Practical Wisdom

Most business people would not mess up half as much if they just took a few minutes to close the door and do nothing for a little while.

—Businessman interviewed by Kate Ludeman for *Executive Female*

Any attempt to line up intuitive knowing in an ordered fashion only weakens it and will ultimately fail.

However, like harnessing the power of the wind, understanding and molding your life around intuitive principles puts you in line to benefit from its power.

The Stages of Intuitive Development

Through reading this book, you have furthered your travels on the intuitive path. The following stages are cyclical in nature and tend to come around a few times throughout a lifetime. See if you can identify places in your own life that are resonant with these stages.

Use these stages to gain a greater perspective and respect for the cycle of intuitive knowing. They are:

1. Beginning/Awakening
2. Learning and Searching
3. Using
4. Mastering Skill
5. Failure/Betrayal
6. Letting Go

7. Integrating

8. Effortlessness

Beginning/Awakening

Often we awaken or reawaken to the power of intuition when an intense event triggers clear intuitive knowing. Without a doubt, something is known intuitively that is validated concretely later on. It may be something involving a choice, a loved one, or an event. The gift of knowing stimulates a need for more. There has got to be a way to know in this way more often. Thus, the search is on and the cycle has begun.

Practical Wisdom

If you have a problem accepting intuition, a good first step is to at least not fight it. Give it some room to grow each day. As time passes, it will grow and become part of the skill set that brings you personal and professional success and happiness.

Learning and Searching

Reading on the subject, taking classes, speaking with friends and colleagues: all of these activities stimulate the search for more information and greater skill. Trying out techniques, learning skills, and developing a daily routine stimulate intuitive skill. The discovery is that there is something there that can be developed and improved. When people attend workshops on developing intuition, they often leave feeling powerfully connected to a source of knowing that has been there all along, yet had been set aside. The ease with which they begin to use their intuition is astounding.

Using

Applying techniques, such as the ones in this book and many others, actually works. Intuitive information seems harnessed. It can be focused for specific purposes and used to achieve goals. It's a powerful tool for success.

Mastering Skill

Confidence, strength, and success mark mastery of intuitive skill. It's there as a solid tool. When needed, it's called upon to work its magic. There is no doubt of its existence, and the feeling it gives is invincibility.

Failure/Betrayal

It doesn't work. Either you walk into a dangerous situation unwarned or something that intuitively felt right turns rotten. This is an important stage, worthy of a little more discussion because it's often avoided or hidden. The feeling is one of complete "not knowing." After incredible confidence and success, it's like someone turned out the lights and shut the door. Nothing.

Up to this point, you've been developing your intuitive skill with good intentions, and with a natural need to use it for personal gain, for the success of your goals, and with particular results in mind. Intuition is often first developed as an extension of will-power and ego.

Creating a structure for intuitive knowing isn't bad, but it is limited. To go further, the structure needs to be released. It's like an eggshell that gives the chicken embryo developing within it nourishment and protection. It's necessary for the development of the embryo. And when the embryo outgrows the shell, the only way through it is to destroy the shell.

In Western culture, failure is bad. It's often met with shame and personal disgrace. The danger of the shame and disgrace is that it can stop the process rather than strengthen it, which is its true purpose. What has failed is not intuition; what has failed is the interpretation and attachment to results.

A friend of mine recently shared how he had truly trusted his intuition and done all the visualizations, affirmations, and meditations to help guide him through a particularly stressful and challenging career change. Everything seemed to have failed. Nothing was happening, and he felt that everything he had learned about the intuitive process must be wrong. The only thing left to do was to go back to "making something happen," but that didn't feel quite right either.

Tried & True

Statistics show that most pilot-related accidents occur in the novice and expert stages in careers. Limited experience and too much experience can equate to disaster. Keep learning and keep your eyes open.

When I pointed out to him that he was in the betrayal phase, something in him lit up in recognition. He intuitively understood what I was talking about and was able to let go. When he let go of his feelings of betrayal, the next phase began.

Letting Go

The only thing to do after you've hit the betrayal phase is to let go. In the case of the newly hatched chick, all it can do is vulnerably and humbly relate to new surroundings. After being in complete comfort, protection, and security, the new world is insecure, vulnerable, and completely unknown.

In the world of intuition, what is being "let go" of is the structure that has helped to mold and shape intuitive knowing. The shift is from "your way" to the "high way." What is meant by the "highway" is the realm where intuitive knowing connects you as an individual with the greater whole. The shift in intuitive information will be substantial, and it will be experienced in a different way.

Remember learning to drive? At first, it's all about rules, coordination, and practice. Once you gain a certain level of competency, you feel a sense of freedom and power. At some point, something will happen that shocks and jolts you, and we pray that it's not fatal. As a new driver you need to learn that you aren't invincible. There are always circumstances and events beyond your control that require humility, respect, and, above all, constant attention.

Letting go is acknowledging that there will always be more to learn and more to respect. Intuition is about more than personal gain and glory; it's about being in a harmonious relationship with yourself and the larger environment you live in. True success is only possible when you feel in sync with your life.

Integrating

Letting go leads naturally into integrating a more refined form of intuition. Rather than a tool to be used, it becomes part of your nature. Thinking automatically incorporates intuition and intuition automatically incorporates analytic thinking. You can't act without it feeling right. An ignored intuitive sense creates such discomfort; it can't be ignored for very long.

Effortlessness

Decisions are no longer made. Something is either right or not. If it's not right, more information is gathered until it appears clearly the right course of action, or else it is released. Planning for long-range goals is appropriate, but short-term planning becomes less important. Opportunities appear as needed and the events of life unfold effortlessly. Projects require attention and effort is put into the work at hand, but the struggle to make something happen no longer exists.

Practical Wisdom

If a man does not keep pace with his companions, perhaps it is because he hears a different drummer. Let him step to the music which he hears, however measured or far away.

—Henry David Thoreau

Getting What You Want Is Scary, Too

As the old saying goes, "There are two tragedies in life: getting what you want and not getting what you want." Forty percent of those who win the lottery go bankrupt within three years. Many reach their financial goals and feel empty and miserable inside. They have money, but no life.

Stepping into intuitive power requires looking closely at what you want, why you want it, and what you're going to feel once you get it. Chapters 5 and 6 helped you look at what you want and why you want it, this chapter focuses on how you're going to feel once you get it.

If having what you want is always a dream about something far away, it will most likely not happen. If it does, the feeling of actually having what you want, which was such a distant dream, will feel very uncomfortable and you'll most likely lose or misuse it.

Yellow Light

You take yourself wherever you go. No matter how much money you make, you will be the one to spend it. Focus on self-improvement, self-reflection, and helping others achieve their goals. Your wealth will then be able to grow from a solid foundation.

Live As If You Have What You Want

Wanting is all about emotional feelings. What is wanted is a new feeling. It is the feelings that flow through your consciousness that determine your perspective on life—feeling secure, abundant, loved, useful, confident, smart, competent, and so on.

The opposite is also true. What you don't like about your life right now is how it's making you feel, not the thing or event that is happening.

Feelings come and go. They're as transient as the food we eat. Food is real, and it's important. It also comes and goes very quickly. To hang on to food that is getting old would be dangerous and foolish. Hanging onto feelings is equally dangerous.

Enjoy and savor the feelings of your life just as you enjoy the food. Some is bitter, some is sweet, but all of it passes. Move toward what you want to feel, get used to it, and keep tasting it.

Practical Wisdom

Try thinking: "What would an abundant person do in this situation?" or "What would someone who has already achieved great success do?"

No More Excuses!

"I just didn't have time to do it right." "My car needed gas, that's why I'm late." "The road was slippery from the rain; that's why I swerved off the road." Every time you make an excuse for why something did or didn't work you lose energy. Even if there's is a really good reason why something didn't happen, it interferes with your flow.

> ### Practical Wisdom
>
> It's what you learn after you know it all that counts.
>
> —John Wooden,
> UCLA basketball coach

> ### Tried & True
>
> A Marine recruit is taught to respond "no excuse, sir" to any question about a failure to perform perfectly. The drill instructor can accept the answer or ask for the "reason" for not meeting the required standard of performance. Be your own drill instructor at times. Try it. Remember there are no excuses.

What? Is the Universe out to get you? Are there forces of evil looking to thwart your every move? No. If you've learned anything from this book, you've learned that you're part of the flow and that the Universe wants you to succeed. Using excuses puts the fate of your life in the hands of some random force that at any moment might come in and snatch away your chance for success.

Hold Your Tongue

Try the following workout to eliminate excuses and watch your intuitive power grow: Spend the next month eliminating excuses from your vocabulary. Whatever happens or doesn't happen, don't make up an excuse. Even if it's a really good one that seems to be true—don't use it. For example, if you're late, acknowledge your lateness without an excuse. "I know I'm late; sorry." That's it. Don't make up or use whatever happened as an excuse. Similarly, if a project fails, acknowledge what happened without an excuse: "It didn't work out the way we/I had wanted it to."

Two things begin to happen as excuses are eliminated:

1. The reality of what happened has a chance to sink in. The feelings of those involved, including you, have an opportunity to be experienced and released.

Practical Wisdom

"There are no excuses for failure. Zen masters believe that peace of mind comes from having done the best you could with your life and not worrying about what you didn't do or don't have. To me, the saddest words I hear are apologies for failure, such as "couldabeen," "shouldabeen," or "mightabeen." Too many youngsters who fail in school or in other endeavors fall back on such apologies, when the truth is, they didn't try hard enough."

—Chuck Norris, *The Secret Power Within*

When there is an excuse, it immediately negates any feelings anyone may have about what happened. All the feelings are shoved aside, after all, there was a good reason for whatever happened. When an excuse is accepted, no more is done to discover what happened and what can be done next time to make it better.

2. The power to live on purpose becomes clearly available. Once the illusion of excuses is dispelled, the true place of responsibility opens up. It's up to you to move toward what you want and away from what you don't want. No excuses.

Relying on excuses assumes that success is determined by fate or destiny. One can act, yet some external force can come in and change the whole thing. It becomes a matter of luck.

Life Rolls On

You don't have to look very far to see individuals, families, and businesses devastated by weather conditions such as floods, hurricanes, and earthquakes. There is no denying the power of natural forces and our inherent helplessness over them.

Tragic accidents and brutal crimes change lives forever. Some things happen that are unforeseeable and unstoppable. Two of the very real feelings that flow through every life are pain and loss.

Yellow Light

Watch for intuitive warning signals such as: feelings of unease, hairs vibrating on the back of your neck, the click of a safety belt being unhooked, shivers, chills, a cold wind passing through you, a warning flash or any other way you experience a sinking feeling of potential danger.

But still there is hopefulness. Out of every tragic situation, it's up to those who are left to keep going and to determine what they're going to do with what is available. Eliminating excuses doesn't deny that tragedies happen, and it doesn't use the tragedy as an excuse for self-destructive behavior.

Watch for Warning Lights

One seminar participant described the warning as "a penalty flag on the field." It was time to stop the play, wherever it was, and look around. Something just happened that disturbed the integrity of the deal.

Another described it as "I felt like I had just stepped off the shore into very deep water. I could no longer touch the ground. I knew that from now on I had to watch what happened very carefully for I was now vulnerable."

At some point in your life, you received an intuitive warning—a sense that something wasn't right before you could pinpoint the actual fact of what wasn't right. Learn from that experience, whether heeded or not, to identify the subtle way your intuition warns you.

Tried & True

I think the one lesson I learned is that there is no substitute for paying attention.

—Diane Sawyer

Eliminating excuses doesn't mean to ignore intuitive warnings. Taking more responsibility for what happens in your life will increase the strength of intuitive warning signals.

Good Vibrations

Charlie Warner of Warner Brothers once said the following of Robert Pittman, inventor of MTV, who then worked for Charlie, "He knows how to win whereas most business people know how not to lose."

Chuck Norris tells his martial arts students, "Always remember that your success begins inside you: If you can't see it first, no one else ever will."

Success has energy. It has a vibration and feeling that goes with it. If you've been doing some of the workouts in Chapter 13 on picking stocks, you've most likely discovered that you can begin to sense the energy of the stock as positive or negative.

This workout will help you reinforce the sense you already have about the energy of success and failure:

1. Remember a time of success. It doesn't have to be something that everyone else recognized, although it might be. It could be an experience where you succeeded at something that was important to you. If you can't remember a time of success, imagine one. What do you think it would feel like to be successful?

2. Extract the essence of success from this moment. Translate the essence into words, into a feeling, color, sound, sense, or an image.

3. Put the essence of success aside.

4. Now remember a time of failure. Large or small, it doesn't matter. If you can't remember a time of failure, imagine what it would feel like.

5. Extract the essence of failure from this moment. Translate the essence into words, into a feeling, color, sound, sense, or an image.

6. Now, bring the two images together. Hold them in front of you. See and feel the difference between them. Put them aside for now.

7. Think of a situation you might get involved with. Extract the energy from the situation. Translate the essence into words, feelings, color, sound, sense, or images.

8. Compare this essence with the essences of success and failure. Where does it fit? Which energy does it most closely match?

9. Allow this workout to trigger what you may know intuitively about this situation or your reasons for getting involved.

10. Take notes on your results.

No Pain, No Gain

From the intuitive, holistic world view, the universe wants you to be successful. Every major event of your life has prepared you for what you're doing today and what you'll do tomorrow. Positive and painful experiences provide opportunities, information, and wisdom to help you succeed at being truly who you are.

From the analytic world view where everything and everyone is separate, the Universe is neutral at best, and most likely cruel. We are all on our own and need to provide for ourselves. Help or support is unlikely and, if it happens, it's a one-time occurrence. It's okay to take from others because if they had a chance, they would take from you.

Practical Wisdom

In life as in the dance, grace glides on blistered feet.

—Alice Abrams

Both worlds exist. Both worlds need to be contended with. If you choose to live in the intuitive world, you'll also use analytic tools to determine the details and gather external evidence, yet your overall life plan and major decisions will be made intuitively. Your core philosophy will be based on the principle that you are connected to everything and everything is connected to you.

If you choose to live in the analytic world, the intuitive world will intrude occasionally, providing synchronistic coincidences when possible. When it happens, it will seem extremely unusual and you may rationalize it away, or perhaps not even acknowledge that it happened. Your core philosophy will be based on the principle that you are alone in this world and need to fend for yourself.

Both worlds are true. It is how you put them together that helps determine the course your life will take. I combine the two by acknowledging that I am responsible for my life, for the choices I make—at the same time, what I do sends ripples into the world, which effect everything in subtle ways. I can make a positive difference or not, based on how I act, what I say, and who I am in the world. We, as a group, are constantly creating the future world we live in by what we decide today. I am also connected to an incredible source of support, guidance, and information, which enables me to live successfully in relationship to all that is happening around me while making a positive impact myself.

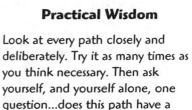

Practical Wisdom

Look at every path closely and deliberately. Try it as many times as you think necessary. Then ask yourself, and yourself alone, one question...does this path have a heart? If it does, the path is good; if it doesn't, it is of no use.

—Carlos Castaneda,
The Teachings of Don Juan

"Stepping into intuitive power" means choosing to live fully in the intuitive world. To live on the foundation that we are all connected, all of equal value, and all with unique gifts. As our gifts unfold we help others to discover and use their gifts. How it all happens is a mystery. There is pain, change, and loss—but also joy, guidance, and miracles.

Judith, a friend of mine, worked for many years as a high-powered marketing consultant in Hollywood. Working on a tight deadline to design a new project, she struggled and struggled for the right ideas, to no avail. Her frustration mounted to such an extent that she finally slammed her hand on the desk and said "Alright! If there is an idea out there I need it now!"

At that point she "let go" to her exhaustion, and suddenly new ideas started flowing. The whole project unfolded before her eyes, and she could barely keep up with writing it down.

Judith opened to the energy of success in that moment. She tapped into the intuitive world and experienced how much information, creativity, and vitality was available just for the asking. Success comes not from frustration and tightness but from flow and ease. Sometimes the desires to "make it happen" and "do it myself" interfere with intuitive flow. Acknowledging that answers, ideas, and information are available just for the asking is the gift, and the mystery, of living intuitively.

How often has something similar happened in your life? Doesn't it make sense to stop making excuses, follow the flow of your life, open up to your intuition, and let the pieces come together?

The Least You Need to Know

➤ Intuitive power is built on trusting what you know and anticipating what you need.

➤ Get to know the eight stages of intuitive development: awakening, learning, manipulating, mastery, betrayal, letting go, integration, and effortlessness.

➤ Get comfortable having the "feeling" of what you want before what you want arrives.

➤ Excuses hamper your ability to take responsibility and pursue goals.

➤ Choose success by getting familiar with the energy of success.

➤ You can choose to live in the intuitive world.

Chapter 20

When in Doubt...

In This Chapter

➤ Learn where solutions come from

➤ Discover the power of doing nothing

➤ Use the power of what "you'd never do"

➤ Learn how having fun and being outrageous actually solves problems

➤ The solution you seek just may be in your closet

➤ Learn the power of play

➤ Learn to keep an "unsolved issue" file in your mind

Fred Bauer holds about 40 patents and is the founder and chief executive of Gentex Corporation, based in Zeeland, Michigan. Next to his office is a playroom filled with a collection of plastics, glues, wires, and a 20,000-volt transformer. When he gets stuck, he goes and plays in his room, taking his mind completely off of the situation at hand. He returns to his desk with a clear head and a better chance of solving the problem at hand.

Bauer also rewards anyone in the company who comes up with innovative ideas by immediately writing bonus checks. He recently wrote a $12,000 check for an employee who secured a big contract and a $5,000 to another who finished a project ahead of time.

According to a recent article in *Investors Business Daily*, such extensive support of innovation is paying off for Zeeland. Their profits are up by an annual average of

34 percent over the past five years; return on equity in 1997 was more than 23 percent; and sales in 1997 jumped more than 25 percent from the year before, reaching $186.3 million.

Thomas A. Edison is one of Bauer's heroes. Edison kept a similar collection of play stuff and spent many hours of undirected tinkering in his lab when searching for a new solution.

In this chapter, you'll learn the importance of getting into a completely different mindscape to solve problems. To keep working on a situation in the same old way when it's going nowhere is a total waste of time. Once you understand the nature of being "stuck" and how to get "unstuck," you'll save yourself, your company, your employer, your friends, and your family a tremendous amount of time and money. Most importantly, you'll eliminate loads of frustration and replace it with joy—all while becoming a star problem solver.

Where Solutions Come From

In the world of intuition there are no problems, only pieces of the puzzle that haven't been noticed yet. When something isn't working, only three things can be done: change perspective, wait, or do something completely different.

Practical Wisdom

To do things the same way and to expect a different result is not logical.

In the world of intuition, when something gets stuck, it's most likely an issue of timing. The appropriate time for something to occur is not now. Often, important information or resources that will create a better solution are on their way.

If you aren't in the world of intuition, answers don't appear because the mind gets stuck on one channel or one perspective. In that case, the answer may be available and the timing may be right, but it can't be seen. The first thing to do in this case is to reconnect to the world of intuition.

Bridging the Intuitive Gap

The world of intuition is not far away. It is right with you. This distance is in memory, not miles. Once you become familiar with, and have a relationship to intuitive awareness, all that's necessary will be to remember.

Until your relationship to the intuitive world is established, bridges need to be built between the everyday, analytic mind and the intuitive mind. Once the bridges establish a connection, the bridges are no longer necessary.

There are three main bridges to the intuitive world:

➤ Breath, which builds a bridge to your gut feel

➤ Imagination, which builds a bridge to your intuitive mind

➤ Sensing, which builds a bridge to the unconditional love in your intuitive heart

Practical Wisdom

Archimedes discovered the law of special gravity in his bathtub. We often remember something when we stop trying to remember it.

These bridges can be used when stuck or stumped with a situation or problem, whether at home or at work. Developing these bridges will ease the use of intuition during times of stress. Use them all for a few days. It may be that one works more effectively for you. If that is true, use that one exclusively. If you like using more than one, that's okay, too.

Every Breath You Take

Close your eyes and take a few deep, slow, complete breaths. Feel your breath making a passageway from the back of your skull all the way down to your gut. When you inhale, feel the air moving from the back of your throat down to your gut, and feel your gut filling up with air. Your "gut" is where your physical intuition lives and may be in a different location for different people.

Let your breath guide the pathway to your gut. Keep breathing in this way until the passageway is complete and open. Take a few more breaths to guide the intuitive information from your gut to your mind. When you open your eyes, go to your issue or problem and take another look at it. What new solutions are available to you now?

Just My 'Magination

Take a few relaxing breaths and close your eyes. Imagine a bridge being created from your everyday mind to your intuitive mind. Allow your imagination to sense where the bridge begins and where it ends. Notice the shape, size, and design of the bridge as well as what it's made of. Take a few moments to enjoy the creation of the bridge—make it something that is beautiful, as well as functional. It may take more than one session to complete the bridge, depending on the time you have available. Taking your time to build the bridge is completely acceptable. It's more important to enjoy your bridge than to complete it quickly.

Once the bridge is complete, imagine yourself walking from one side to the other. On the other side, you are in the world of the intuitive mind. Let go to the images, thoughts, and feelings that occur while on the intuitive side of the bridge. Whenever you're ready, walk back across the bridge. Open your eyes and write down any thoughts or impressions. Go to your issue and see if there are any new approaches that come to mind.

All You Need Is Love

Sensing combines the use of breath and imagination to focus on the sensing capacity of the metaphorical heart. The heart is a doorway to deeper wisdom and insight. Take a few relaxing breaths and close your eyes. Focus your breathing right in the center of your chest.

Imagine that there's a cavity inside your chest that expands as you inhale and contracts as you exhale. This cavity contains complete peace and is filled with unconditional love. Place your awareness in the center of this cavity. You might imagine that you're sitting in a comfortable chair or couch, soaking in the peace and unconditional love available in this cavity.

If you have any difficulty imagining unconditional love, remember a moment in your life when you felt completely loved. Regardless of how lasting or fleeting the experience of unconditional love in your life, you can extract the essence of the feeling and use it here in this cavity right now. The feeling of unconditional love is universal and doesn't need to be attached to a particular event or person to be experienced.

Once you have spent a few moments soaking up the unconditional love, leave the cavity and come back to your waking consciousness. Write down any thoughts or feelings you may have. Go to your problem and take another look at it. See if you have any new insights or approaches that now seem viable.

The Power of Befuddlement

Knowing what to do all the time thwarts the intuitive process. Discovering new pathways and opportunities is almost always a by-product of necessity. If you know what to do (even if flawed), you won't be open to another way. Being clueless, and having the self-confidence to admit it, opens the doors to creativity.

In the world of intuition, solutions and new answers come from the wisdom of the collective whole, which individual intuition is plugged into. When a wall or barrier is reached, it's more like a shift in the current. Imagine floating down a river on a raft with a fairly fast current. All of a sudden, the river flows into a huge lake and the current slows. It may feel like all movement has stopped, but it hasn't. It has shifted relative to what it was.

With intuition, it's very similar. You may be flowing with a particular project at a fairly fast pace. All of a sudden it seems like things have stopped. If the focus stays on keeping the speed going, the new terrain will

Practical Wisdom

If Nantucket Nectars disappeared tomorrow and we tried to set up something similar to replace it, I'm not sure we could do it. We know too much now, and we'd probably be too careful.

—Tom First, co-founder of Nantucket Nectars, in Ron Lieber's *Upstart Start-ups!*

not be taken into account. Valuable information and opportunities may be lost.

To function effectively in the world of intuition, the following new skills are necessary to support the discovery process:

➤ Waiting productively

➤ Managing impatience

➤ Keeping an open intuitive channel

Practical Wisdom

Stop to ask yourself: "If I were clueless, what would I do next?"

Procrastination by Any Other Name

Waiting is one of the most difficult things any human can do—at least the humans in modern Western culture. As stated before, the intuitive world sometimes needs a little bit of time to pull the pieces of the puzzle together. To rush it only creates an inferior result. Waiting allows for a complete picture.

When in doubt…ask yourself: "Is it possible to wait?"

There are many things done to make waiting productive. Often gathering more information, doing research, and playing with numbers is a way to wait productively in a business environment. Waiting in this way, however, becomes unproductive when the research, information, and numbers are expected to produce an answer.

The answer or moment of action will emerge and be experienced intuitively. The rest may stimulate or provide back-up, but it can't substitute for "sensing" the time to act.

My husband and I had done one of the intuition workouts from Chapter 13 on picking stocks. We agreed on which stock to sell and which to buy. He went to work and got involved in another project. Suddenly, he felt an internal urge to do the stock transaction, pronto! He did, and the stock sold started to drop dramatically over the next several weeks while the stock bought began to go up.

Managed Impatience

The sister skill of waiting productively is managing impatience. The urge to accomplish and complete something is a powerful force. Like a river pulled downhill, a force at least as strong as gravity compels movement toward completion.

You may be asking, "What is the difference between knowing when to take action and the need to complete something?" A very good question. The Eskimos have dozens of names for snow because their lives depend on sensing subtle differences in the accumulations on the ground. Becoming a skilled intuitive requires sensing subtle differences in feeling states, as well as physical cues.

The call to financial action described previously by my husband came out of a field of openness. His mind was on something else. The message to "ACT NOW" came seemingly from nowhere as a clear, direct message.

He might have ignored it or put it off years ago, but with the experience he has had in having these feelings, he knew to stop what he was doing and take care of it right now. He gets the same feeling about making phone calls and visits.

The pull toward completion is more of a value system, paradigm, or field within which action takes place. One always feels that completing something is good. It's a constant. Like a tank on its way over the hill, the purpose is clearly to get over the hill, no stopping and smelling the flowers along the way. Pulls that focus solely on results are apt to miss many of the intuitive points of interest along the way.

Managing impatience blends the pull toward results with the new, intuitive information in the moment. You want to keep moving with the current toward completion, but it's important to read the signs and signals of the terrain, the water, the rocks, and the weather along the way. It will make your trip more enjoyable and perhaps safer.

I love the image of a well-trained hunting dog. She will run directly toward the target, but at the first call of her master she will stop and listen. While moving toward your goals, keep an ear toward the voice of your intuition. When you get a whistle, stop and pay attention.

Are there unproductive ways to manage impatience? You bet! Pushing too hard, trying to make something happen before its time, and talking yourself into something you don't yet feel is right.

Keep the Channel Open

When nothing is going on, when the way to your success seems jammed with traffic, keep an open intuitive channel. The "bridge" workouts will be invaluable at this point to help keep the channel open.

When things are clogged on the action plane, they're still open on the intuitive plane. Feeling this buildup will only increase anxiety and the chances of taking ill-fated or inappropriate action. Just at the moment when your best friend slams the car door on your fingers is not the best time to say how you really feel about him. Wait until the pain has healed, and the channel to your friendship is clearly open.

Having an open connection to the intuitive plane is like having a terrible day and then remembering that there will be someone at home who loves you no matter what. It might be your dog, cat, fish, or lover. This can make the worst days bearable.

The intuitive plane connects you to the long-term view of life. You may not feel it at the moment, but you're still moving. On the intuitive plane, it is clear.

Keep the channel open by consistently building bridges between your daily mind and your intuitive mind. Eventually, they will integrate.

Confusion...

I wish I had a nickel for every time someone has said, "I'm so confused, I just don't know what to do." Most of the time when that phrase, or a variation of it is spoken, the person saying it knows exactly what to do, he just doesn't like what he knows.

Confusion is static created to disperse or diffuse intuitive knowing. It's disempowering and promotes helplessness. It's much more powerful to acknowledge that you don't know what you're going to do. You aren't ready to act yet. That's not confusion. That is clear. It's also more powerful to acknowledge that you have an intuition about what to do, but are not emotionally ready to do it.

During the course of a five-day seminar on developing intuitive skill, one participant just wasn't getting anywhere. After each exercise she kept saying, "Nothing happened; I have no intuition." We spent some time talking over her current situation, and it became clear that she did indeed have an intuitive sense that it was time for her to move from her home of more than 20 years.

When she acknowledged that thought, she knew it was right for her, but wasn't ready to follow through with it. It was still very uncomfortable and scary to think about, to say nothing of the logistics and the overwhelming thought of having to deal with it. It was easier for her to just say, "I don't know anything. I'm confused."

Once she admitted that she knew the move was important, she could determine her own schedule for getting it done, a weight lifted. Somehow in her mind the act of acknowledging the need for a move meant that she would have to start taking action immediately, so she mentally blocked the information and preferred to stay confused.

How is that for an example of how powerful we truly are? Not only do we know what to do, we know how to keep the information away from our conscious minds.

...and How To Beat It

Help yourself step out of confusion and into "knowing what you know" with the following workout:

1. Write down what it is that you feel confused about.

2. Write down five actions you'd never take in this situation.

3. For each of the five actions you'd never take, imagine someone who would. Imagine someone (either an imaginary person or someone you've never met) who would be perfectly comfortable taking this action.

4. Now imagine that each of these imaginary people is a mentor to you. Each has an important message. Spend a few moments listening to what each has to tell you and write it down.

For example, a manager was confused about what to do with a problem employee. His workout went like this:

1. What can I do to get Mr. X to do what he is supposed to do?
2. One thing I'd never do is murder him.
3. An assassin would have no trouble murdering him.
4. The assassin said to me, "In order to do my job, I need to be precise and detached."

The manager realized that being precise and detached were two things he wasn't being with this employee. Perhaps if he were more precise with his goals and instructions, and he was detached from the way in which this employee got the job done, things would go more smoothly.

The Light Side: Hanging Out with Doubt

The rest of this chapter shares some fun things to do when you find yourself in doubt. Doubt is not to be avoided or ignored. Having a doubt about something just might be an intuitive warning signal. Having a doubt about whether to proceed with something also may be a reflection of your lack of self-confidence. Recognizing the difference between doubt and self-doubt may take some practice.

Try the following workout to explore your relationship with doubt:

1. Remember a time when doubting something turned out to be a mistake or missed opportunity for you. For example, one person related how he had briefly met someone and felt completely comfortable with her. He had a chance to follow-up and doubted that she would be interested. He did not take his opportunity, and regretted it.

2. Remember a time when doubting something turned out to help you. Another person had been told that the business had been awarded to someone else, but felt the decision was still up in the air. He made the call and made the sale.

3. Remember a time when you were filled with doubt about your ability to do something, and you did it anyway. Filled with doubt about her ability to learn to ski, my mother, at 50 years of age, gave it a shot anyway, and learned to love skiing.

4. Remember a time when doubt saved your life, or close to it. A petite, female parole officer's territory was a dangerous section of the South Bronx. She survived by always responding to any feelings of doubt. If a certain hallway felt "unsafe" in any way, she came back later.

5. Reflect on all these memories and highlight the essence of the feelings and their differences.

Do Squat

When in doubt...hang out! Take no action. (Well, maybe do a workout from this book...)

Be Wacky

When in doubt, do something outrageous and unexpected. If the doubt is coming from a lack of self-confidence, this will cure it. Do something with the idea that if nothing results, you'll survive it and, who knows, perhaps something unexpected will happen as a result of your willingness to be outrageous.

A friend of mine who was scheduled to present a program at a conference also wanted to make a general announcement to the whole audience about a non-profit project she was starting. The head organizer only met people with appointments and kept his schedule very tight and protected.

My friend decided that the only way to meet with him was by storm. She walked into his office, bearing gifts, and surprised him with her boldness. What she wanted him to do was to give her a five-minute spot to talk about her project. He ended up giving her 15 minutes and it generated enough interest to get her project going.

Tired & True

This was the tack that David and Tom Gardner took when they named their online personal finance site the Motley Fool. "We knew what we wanted to do," David recalls, noting that most personal finance guides at the time were dry, boring, and lacked any sort of edge or attitude. "We just didn't have a name for it. And then we thought of the fool. It's actually a great position to come from because there's no pretension whatsoever about it."

—Ron Lieber, *Upstart Start-ups!*

Clean Your Closets

One of the most magical ways to start off in doubt and end up with clarity is to clean out your closets, attic, garage, kitchen drawer (you know, the one drawer that everything goes into), or glove compartment.

First, the act of sorting, throwing away what you don't need, and organizing what you do, puts you in an altered state that can access instant clarity. The mindless work can help shift the focus completely away from what you're in doubt about—that in itself can jiggle open your intuitive channel—and allow for instant enlightenment.

Second, you put things in this place because some part of you knew it was valuable, but didn't know how or where to use it at the time of discovery. Going through it now may uncover just the needed information, stimulation, and inspiration.

Make Play Dates with Yourself

Some people tap their intuitive mind more easily while being physically active. Katherine Sarafian works an extremely high-pressure job at Pixar, the computer animation company that created the film *Toy Story*. A *Fast Company* article recounted Ms. Sarafian's secret for preventing burnout: hard play. "She goes from an improv class to a volleyball game. She plays in a highly competitive basketball league two nights a week, takes an amateur drawing class, and performs from time to time with the Pixar Singers, an a cappella group."

Sarafian has a regular routine of high energy fun that keeps her mind clear and present. For some her schedule looks insane, but for her it works. If you're an action person, action will be what relaxes you. Get out of the mindset that everyone benefits from yoga or meditation. Regular, high-energy activities may be just the thing to keep your mind open and clear for intuitive impressions.

Tried & True

Many runners say their best ideas come to them during their time on the road.

Keep an Open File

Never give up on an idea. Always keep an "open file" in your mind. Some projects and plans may need to be put on the shelf for a while to age or on the back burner to cook, but never put them in the trash.

Putting an idea in the trash, even mentally, closes a door on allowing the idea to be a "gathering place." An open idea file allows ideas to attract bits of information, ideas, and images that may eventually cluster with other ideas to form something ready to pop!

Keep an actual physical file somewhere where stray ideas and thoughts can be slipped in for later perusing.

Keep an open mental file. Watch out if you hear yourself thinking "That idea is dead" or "This will never amount to anything." Rephrase it and say to yourself, "I don't know what to do about that idea—I'll put it in the open mental file."

Have Doubt, Will Travel

Doubt is here to stay. It's an important mental state. It can create the pause that prevents jumping into something dangerous or prevent throwing something out before its value is determined. Respect the power of doubt and allow it to empower you!

The Least You Need to Know

➤ Solutions come from shifting perspective, not from working harder.

➤ Staying connected to the realm of intuition allows for new perspectives.

➤ Intuitive bridges can be built to your gut, mind, and heart.

➤ Not knowing what to do has power.

➤ Being in doubt is more powerful than being confused.

Part 5

Enjoying Your Intuition's Fruition

Manawa is a Hawaiian term meaning now is the moment of power. *This part shows you how to savor the fruits of your intuitive labors while avoiding the dangers that will accompany your newfound success. The air's a little thinner up here, and the stakes are higher; you need a new set of skills to keep your money tree healthy and avoid pitfalls like self-sabotage and friends who might resent your new path.*

We'll work on integrating your intuitive ability so that it becomes a natural part of the way you do things. You'll discover the ultimate investment strategy of tithing, the power of gratefulness, and a whole new reason to celebrate yourself, your achievements, and your newfound intuitive powers.

Stormy Weather: Keep Choosing Success

Meteorologists tell us that when a cold front meets a warm front it creates intense rain, wind, thunder, and lightning storms. That's pretty powerful. When you think about it, a cold front is just cold air, and a warm front is just warm air. Two elements with no real physical substance meet and create a force with tremendous physical power.

The same thing happens when spiritual energy meets material energy. That's what this whole book, and specifically this chapter, are about. Spiritual energy combines the overall intention of soul with the more immediate intention of personality. The result of this energetic combo is the creation of an individual life that ripples through and interacts with everything around it. Through this interaction, dreams and intentions are made manifest.

For many people, the stormy nature of intuition is enough to make them run for cover once they've had a few successes, without completing the full mission of their life. Granted, understanding how intuition works isn't easy: Just when you thought you had it made, it moves you toward new skills and new directions. But never fear! In this chapter, you'll learn to manage and compound on your success wisely, rain or shine.

You'll also learn to deal with friends who might resent your success and to recognize the signs of self-sabotage before it's too late.

The Eye of the Storm

If you have been following the program in this book, you're on your way to achieving your dreams (if you aren't there already). That's just the beginning. Achieving your intention puts you squarely in the center of a hurricane. It's now up to you to manage the results and consequences of your actions.

When the power of your intention meets and co-creates with physical reality, your lifelong dreams are achieved. More importantly, your real work can begin.

Think of it as spiritual growing up. Learning to focus intention and manifest it is like completing formal education. Now you can apply all that you've learned and share it with others.

Similar to growing through adolescence, there is urgency and excited energy that motivates the process. Just as a teenager may feel a big "Is that all there is?" after achieving their social and scholarly goals, a spiritual crisis can occur when you achieve your dream.

When intention finally becomes a physical reality, there is a complete change of dynamics. After being part of the hurricane, suddenly, you're in the center.

Thus the paradox: the most dangerous moment in your life is the moment of success. Vulnerability to disaster is the highest when material goals are achieved. Two destructive directions emerge from the peak of success: complacency and emptiness.

Complacency

Once goals, material or otherwise, are achieved, it's tempting to get lazy. After all, you have accomplished a tremendous amount, have financial security, are comfortable in a lifestyle, and have gained the recognition of your peers. With a certain amount of maintenance, the security can be kept up for the rest of your life. This will lead to your next challenge.

Intending the Unattainable

A huge void is created after your goals are achieved and self-destructive behavior can result. A wave of emptiness is a natural occurrence. It requires a set of tools different from those used to create the initial success.

The following workout is designed to help you articulate the larger, unattainable intention inherent in the goals you have set. Having an unattainable intention will minimize the risk of dropping into complacency and emptiness. It opens the path to making the most of your life. Here we go:

1. Write out your current life goals.

2. Rewrite the goal to reflect what it would be to have another person truly receive your accomplished goal. For example, if your goal is to live an abundant life and have $1 million in the bank, the rewrite might be: "To help and guide one other person to live an abundant life and have enough money to secure his or her life." This is actually a very attainable goal after you have achieved yours.

3. Rewrite your goal again to reflect what it would be to have the whole world truly receive your accomplished goal. For example, the rewrite might be: "To work to guide everyone in the world to have the opportunity to live an abundant life." This goal is unattainable, but will keep you busy and continue to supply you with creative juice.

Just as giving birth is the beginning of a lifelong endeavor, achieving goals is the beginning of manifesting who you really are in the world. You've created the opportunity, now live it.

How many entrepreneurs blow it at this point? Too many to count. How many movie stars and musicians self-destruct just at the point of making it? Even more. How many artists lose touch with their creative spirit after they have achieved notoriety? And those are just the ones who are visible through the media. It isn't easy managing creative energy over the long haul.

I heard a great rap/hip-hop song last night on the radio with a lyric that describes the dilemma perfectly because he felt he was not selling out but buying in. The singer of the song was extremely cynical about the possibility of remaining true to the creative muse once the "buy in" had occurred.

This is an ancient dilemma: Can creativity exist without struggle? What happens after you've made it? Is there life in the happily-ever-after phase?

Enough philosophizing; let's get back to reality. You have made it. What will it take to stay with

Practical Wisdom

Being pregnant is most often a blissful experience. There is an inner glow accompanied with special attention from others. It does nothing to prepare you for the actual birth and the jolt to your life that's coming with the baby. Different, unrelated skills are required for each stage.

Any parent knows this. Having children is one of the most blessed, mysterious events humans can have, and at the same time it's one of the most intense.

299

In his recent concession speech, President de Klerk of South Africa praised his rival, Nelson Mandela, as follows: "Mr. Mandela has walked a long road and now stands at the top of the hill. A traveler would sit down and admire the view, but a man of destiny knows that beyond his hill lies another and another. The journey is never complete."

—Julian Gresser, *Piloting Through Chaos*

the new creative flow and manifest who you really are in the world? Let's take a look.

Manifesting Success

Keep choosing success by choosing to stay in the game of growth and change, wherever it takes you. The moment you attach to a particular phase, you're doomed to failure. In choosing success, you have become part of the cycle of creative life—giving birth to something new and then allowing it to, in turn, give birth to something else. In the process, everyone is changed.

Understanding the manifestation process will help you move with the changes. There are three stages to manifesting:

➤ Seeding

➤ Growing

➤ Harvesting

Each phase has a gift and a challenge.

Seeding

The seeding phase encompasses setting the intention and establishing a magnetic pull between where you are to where you want to be. If you have gotten this far in the book, you have already established your seeds. To get to this phase requires awakening to the possibility of changing your life. A creative spark has been ignited where the possibility of wanting something and actually being able to get it is real.

Tried & True

Nothing is a waste of time if you use the experience wisely.

—Rodin

There is tremendous growth in this stage. The magnetic pull is felt, activity is generated, and ongoing attention and involvement in the creative process is experienced.

The gift of seeding is the burst of excitement and vitality new life brings. The challenge of seeding is persevering in the face of unknowing and unsureness.

Growing

Growing involves change and transformation. In a plant, the growing phase revolves around photosynthesis and the absorption of nutrients in their continual pursuit of building new structures, nurturing, and expanding.

In a personal sense, this phase requires learning new skills, adapting to changing environments, and actually becoming what was programmed in the seed. Allow the creative process to flow through your life and continually stretch to fulfill your intention.

Here you realize that the purpose of having goals is to walk the path. The goals are real and remain stable, but what's important is the growing that's going on.

The gift of growing is power. Seeing the results of intention and transformation generates power. The challenge of growing is finding stability in continual chaos.

Harvesting

At some point, the goal of the growing is met and a completely new process begins. Instead of building new structures, the plant begins to reproduce itself. The chemistry and the focus shifts. Instead of continual growth, flowers, and fruit are created.

In your life this phase is the danger zone spoken of earlier in this chapter. When your goal is complete, it's time to harvest it. Receive the gifts of what you have worked for and pass it on to someone else. Crystallize what you have accomplished and acknowledge its beauty, then let go. The next round of growth and manifestation is about to begin.

Unlike plants, your next seed may or may not resemble the one before. Humans have an ability to hybridize in new and unusual ways. At the least, it will be a different version of what has gone on before, and at the most it will be completely new.

The gift of harvesting is connecting with the larger cycle of life. Having gone through one phase of the cycle successfully, a connection with the larger whole is established. Once a tree reaches a certain stage of maturity, the forest can recognize it as one of its own.

> **Practical Wisdom**
>
> Trees grow and mature gracefully and naturally. At some point, a tree will slow down its quantitative growth and change to qualitative growth. It switches its internal relationships and starts suddenly to bear fruit. It enters into a new relationship with its neighbors, becoming an integrated part of a complex and interdependent ecosystem.

The harvest phase requires:

➤ Patting yourself on the back

➤ Paying yourself

➤ Passing it on

Some of you may be thinking that this sounds easy. Accomplishing, receiving, and sharing are blessings that you look forward to doing. While this is true, look again at your own experience. Whoever said "It is better to give than to receive," meant to say "It is easier to give than to receive, especially from yourself."

1. Pat yourself on the back. To breathe in requires breathing out first. To begin something new requires acknowledging what has been completed in the past. In the world of intuition, accomplishing something means that you've successfully brought something from the world of ideas into the world of physical reality. You've actually created something new. That's not a simple thing to do; it requires all the things we've talked about in this book, especially intention, action, and perseverance.

Take a moment to write down the things you have brought from the realm of ideas into the world of physical reality. It may be a new recipe for brownies, a new racing record, a screenplay, or a skyscraper. Don't judge your accomplishments; write them down.

2. Pay yourself. This means more than just giving yourself a treat. It means allowing the thing you accomplished to truly change you. You aren't the same person you were before you did what you did. Breathe in to being the new you. Honor who you have become.

Look at the accomplishments you wrote in Step 1 and list how you have changed as a result. See them as personal rewards for what you have done. Are you happy with the changes? Are you moving toward who you want to be?

3. Pass it on. The true sign that you have become the new you is that you can share your accomplishment freely with others. It's one of life's paradoxes: You don't really have something unless you can give it away.

Practical Wisdom

"If it hadn't been for you, this would never have happened." This phrase is used to point out some negative behavior. It's equally true and more productive to point out to yourself the opposite—that the wonderful things in your life would not be possible without you. You're the "TV set" that allows for your unique creativity to happen. It's your ability to receive and be open to translating the signal that has allowed your life to happen so fully.

Ask yourself "How have I already shared what I have learned?" and "Who else can I share it with?"

Now you have truly acknowledged and integrated the new you. If you were a stalk of wheat, you would have created seeds, distributed some for next year's crop, and provided some to be ground into flour.

You are open for the next phase. It may be continuing to do what you have been doing at a deeper, more expansive level, or it may be moving on to something else. Your field is now clear for the next seeding.

Watch the Success Seed Grow

The following "harvest time" workout is a gift. Give it to yourself after completing or accomplishing anything. It builds on the workout in Chapter 10 that instructed you to plant an imaginary seed and watch it grow:

1. Imagine yourself in front of an open field. Notice the season, the weather, and the surroundings.

2. Imagine yourself holding a seed. Feel the texture and size of the seed. Sense its weight. This seed represents what you have recently accomplished.

3. Plant the seed in the field and watch what happens.

4. Watch and feel what it grows into. See it mature. Notice what it produces.

5. This growing thing could be a plant or something else. Go with whatever happens, accepting what your imagination gives you.

6. Ask the following questions and wait for an answer. Pause after asking each question and allow the answer to emerge from the experience. If there is no answer, that's fine. Go on to the next questions: If this image could communicate, what would it say? What has this image learned? What would it like to share? What is its gift to you? How can others get involved with what you have created?

7. When you're finished, thank your intuition for providing this insight. Allow the image to fade away.

8. Open your eyes and write the experience in your intuition journal.

I've Fallen and I Can't Get Up: Self-Sabotage

Self-sabotage can come in many forms. Here are a few examples; their repeated occurrence most likely means that you're in deep yogurt:

➤ You keep ending up broke

➤ You make stupid decisions

➤ You keep following what others tell you to do, and it never works

➤ You spend more time straightening out your desk than doing what needs to be done

These are just the symptoms; the real disease is below the surface. If the real issues are not addressed, you may find yourself sent to jail, without passing go and collecting $200, have to go back three spaces, or end up taking a chance card and losing all your money.

To avoid these disasters, pay attention to the following three culprits behind self-sabotage:

➤ You aren't ready for success

➤ You love the excitement of "almost" too much

➤ You've forgotten why you came to the party

Tried & True

Sabotage comes from the French word *sabot*, meaning "shoe or boot," and derives its meaning of deliberate delay or obstruction of work from some use of sabots for this purpose. One story is of workers throwing their wooden shoes into factory machinery to cause damaging delays.

—William and Mary Morris, *Morris Dictionary of Word and Phrase Origins*

Not Ready for Prime Time?

It may be very simple: you don't have the emotional, mental, or spiritual maturity to handle success. Imagine being thrown into the ring with a sumo wrestler without any training. You don't need to be psychic to imagine what would happen. It would be stupid to get into the ring if you didn't know what you were doing.

The same is true with success, although it takes a different kind of muscle. As discussed before, success has a certain stormy quality that needs to be managed. If you aren't ready to manage it, it's best to admit it to yourself, and go build the skill and vitality you need to handle success.

Why do so many folks who win the lottery become bankrupt within three years? Because they lack the maturity to handle that kind of money.

Go back to Part 3 of this book to review the material on building wealth. Perhaps you missed something the first time around, and you can pick it up now. Reset your financial and career intentions and proceed.

Don't beat yourself up. Congratulate yourself on realizing that you aren't ready, then do what you need to do to get ready.

Addicted to Excitement?

When young children learn to walk, they begin by pulling themselves up on anything that can possibly stabilize them. It becomes an obsession. They can get very cranky and demanding when the adults around won't constantly hold their hands and help them practice standing and walking. Just about every moment of every day is spent practicing. All of a sudden they get it. They can do it. At that moment there is incredible elation and personal satisfaction. Then, it's like they've been walking for 10 years. No big deal.

The excitement builds as you get close to achieving your financial and career goals. Just like the young child learning to walk, it can become an obsession. After the goals are realized, it's like, "Oh, okay, so I'm there. Now what?"

Rather than adjust to the new reality of goal realization, some people get overly attached to the feeling of excitement and stay in the state of "almost there" for too long. It's more enticing. There is the energy of pursuit, which can be more thrilling for some than the self-satisfaction that comes with achievement.

If you think this description fits you, try to do the previous "harvesting" workout at least once a week for a couple of months. You need to get used to harvesting what you have created.

Also, take your next paycheck and don't spend a penny of it. Let it sit in your bank account for two weeks. When the two weeks are up, don't binge and spend it all. Begin a regular savings program. You need to build your wealth tolerance. Build your achievement tolerance as well by doing the "pat yourself on the back" workout earlier in this chapter.

Lost Your Way?

If you achieve your goals, but then immediately sink into self-destructive behavior, you have most likely lost your way. You've lost touch with the original, more spiritual reason you did what you did. Somewhere along the way you became attached to the material goal and lost sight of the intangible, more long-term goal.

Repeat the workout described earlier in this chapter in the "Intending the Unattainable" section. If it doesn't work the first time, do it once a week for a while. You need to get back in touch with your original motivation. Go back to Part 2 and redo the workouts in Chapter 5. Reset your life intention. Review the large steps you've taken from there, and see if you can discover where you got lost.

Here is a sample life review, extremely simplified, in which the original intention is to be happy and to make others happy:

Step 1   Make myself happy.

Step 2   What will make me happy is having a certain amount of financial stability and work that I love.

Step 3   I like this—having lots of stuff is fun. Maybe more stuff will make me happier.

Step 4   Emptiness, bad decisions, self-sabotage.

The place where this lifeline got lost was in focusing on the accumulation and forgetting about personal happiness and happiness for others. Everything was going just fine until the original intention got lost in one of the steps.

Tried & True

Looking back at these years, it's difficult for me to understand how I could have maintained such a fragmented existence for so long without caving in to its incoherence and lack of central commitment. Life was an absolute blur—I was popping from one activity to another without a moment's hesitation to reflect and consider my overall life direction.

At the time, I considered this to be a great life, but in fact, I really didn't know life at all. Mine was a Disney World sort of life—inauthentic, narrow, utterly predictable, and largely devoid of any real meaning.

The end to this illusion would come to me, as it has for so many, by means of a personal crisis.

—Joe Jaworsky, *Synchronicity*

Managing the Success Backlash

One of the challenges of getting what you want happens when your friends don't get what they want. A split between where you are and where they are occurs. It's a painful thing to watch.

In the movie *Rounders*, Matt Damon plays a character whose best friend from high school gets out of jail just as Matt starts law school. They have lots of wonderful history together but are just no longer on the same page.

If you are reaching your goals but your loved ones aren't, there's no inherent reason why the relationship has to dissolve. On the other hand, some relationships in our lives are important for short periods of time and then end; whereas others might continue over the years.

Keep in mind the following three principles of intuitive relationships as your life unfolds. They will provide the best groundwork for addressing all the relationship issues that occur as you grow:

➤ *Equal value:* Everyone has equal value. No one is worth more or less, including yourself. Value is not based on money, achievement, fame, skill, creativity, or history. It isn't even based on being human. In the larger scheme of things, everything has equal value and an equal right to live its life.

➤ *Unique gifts:* Everyone has unique gifts. While there is equal value, each individual brings unique qualities, talents, and abilities to the table. Sharing and combining talents and gifts to realize mutual goals and dreams is what this world is all about.

➤ *All connected:* We are all connected. This point has been covered by talking about the great web we are all connected to. As you change and your friends and family change, just remember that you're still connected no matter what happens. Whether you stay in physical contact or stop seeing each other, you're still connected.

Practical Wisdom

Each man had only one genuine vocation—to find the way to himself.... His task was to discover his own destiny—not an arbitrary one—and live it out wholly and resolutely within himself. Everything else was only a would-be existence, an attempt at evasion, a flight back to the ideals of the masses, conformity, and fear of one's own inwardness.

—Herman Hesse, *Damian*

The Least You Need to Know

➤ Your life-long work begins after you get what you want.

➤ The most dangerous moment of your life is the moment of success.

➤ Linking your life to unattainable goals will keep your creative juices flowing.

➤ Don't forget to pay yourself when you've accomplished something great.

➤ After accomplishing comes sharing. You never really own something until you give it away.

➤ If your life stops working, you're probably sabotaging yourself.

Chapter 22

Masters of the Universe

In This Chapter

➤ Master your intuition

➤ Learn about the relationship of God to intuition

➤ Develop a daily spiritual practice

➤ Learn the value of oracles

➤ Discover the benefits of developing an intuitive support group

➤ How to work with a professional intuitive

"I began meditation with two problems to solve. The team effort took too long. There was no doubt that we had to solve that problem. I also noticed something else, of which my colleagues on the teams were not aware. The ideas the teams created weren't very great. People also weren't getting very many ideas. The ideas they got weren't very creative or unusual."

At the time Michael Munn, Head Astrophysicist for Lockheed, wrote this passage for his book *Beyond Business As Usual*, he'd been using intuition to solve his own problems for years. Now he was going to introduce it to his team so they could solve problems together.

When it has become unthinkable for you to approach a complex issue or make a decision without using and trusting your intuition, you have become an intuitive master. It has become such an integral part of who you are and what you do that ignoring it would be unthinkable.

This chapter helps you attain intuitive mastery, which is an intimate relationship with your intuition. We'll explore the question of God and His/Her relationship to intuition and spiritual reality, and helpful tools such as oracles and support groups will be discussed. Finally, we'll attack the issue of working with intuitive professionals, both individually and in corporate settings.

Meet Your Intuition

In the preceding story, Michael Munn naturally relied on his intuition, through meditation, to provide insight on a challenging problem. Knowing that the usual solutions wouldn't work, he needed something new. With his years of experience in using intuition, he was confident that an answer would come, and it did.

You too, can start relying on your intuitive skill to solve deep and complex issues, to provide insight, and be a part of your daily guidance. Intuition is already a part of you. This next workout, an extension of the "Intuition Coach" workout in Chapter 18, merely confirms it and gives you an opportunity to experience your intuition as an integral part of who you are:

1. Make yourself comfortable and give this workout about 20 minutes of uninterrupted time.

2. Take a few relaxing breaths.

3. Close your eyes and begin to imagine yourself in a wonderful outdoor environment. It may be someplace you have been before or it may be a fantasy place you're making up right now. Imagine the weather, the surroundings, the smells, and the colors. Feel what it would feel like to truly be there right now.

4. Imagine that you can reach out and touch something that's here. Feel its texture and temperature. See its color. Smell it.

5. Find some place in this environment where you can feel completely comfortable.

6. Now, invite your intuition to come and meet you. Allow the image, sense, or feeling to emerge from the environment. It may be someone you know, an animal, an abstract image or feeling of spirit. Let the image be whatever it is, even if it seems impossible to you.

7. Ask your intuition if it has anything it would like to communicate to you. Be open to hearing what your intuition has to tell you. It may communicate through telepathy, movement, or some other form of communication. Be open to receiving the communication in any form.

8. If you have a question about something in your life, or a concern you'd like some help with, present it to your intuition now. Receive the guidance your intuition has for you.

9. Now, make room for your intuition inside of you. Allow your intuition to become a part of you. Let it merge and find a home inside of you.

10. Your intuition may be part of your whole body or it may find one spot where it's most comfortable.

11. Take a few moments to allow this transition to take place, making sure that you're comfortable having your intuition inside of you and that your intuition is equally comfortable.

12. Now that your intuition is inside of you, practice your communication system. If your intuition needs to warn you or give you unasked for information, how will that happen? What will your intuition do to signal you? Try it out right now.

13. Now, what if you want to ask your intuition a question, or get information, how will you do that? Practice it now.

14. Take a few moments to get comfortable with this new, intimate relationship. Realize that you will always have the guidance and insight you need; all you have to do is remember the presence of your intuition and use the signals.

15. Thank your intuition. Take a few deep breaths. Open your eyes and write your experience in your journal.

Tried & True

I was thinking of you the other day when I was driving along this very curvy highway. Suddenly, a feeling of anxiety came over me and I slowed down considerably. As I drove over the next hill, a very bad car accident had just happened, probably when I had the feeling.

—Al, local video store owner

The results of this workout are as varied as those who have used it. Some discover their intuition as a dear pet, either dead or alive. Others discover a mentor, a parent, or a friend. One person had a cartoon figure and someone else had a butterfly. Beings of light, angels have often appeared in the role of intuition. Be open to meeting an image of your own intuition. As stated in Chapter 5, "Whoever comes is the right people."

Tried & True

A smart CEO asks, "Does this person have the kind of character it takes to get the job done?"... More often than not, a person with character will make better decisions, especially a person with integrity, intuition, and insight.

Integrity, because people who have integrity won't fool themselves about a situation. They'll cut through the nonsense and get to the true core of things quickly.

Intuition, because people who have learned to trust their intuition won't look to others to make their tough decisions. They can depend on themselves and the CEO, in turn, can depend on them.

And insight, because if people are unaware that they can unknowingly sabotage their own results, my company will eventually pay the price for it.

When you find top people with these character traits, you hire them and pay them well, because they will pay for themselves many times over.

—Frank, a CEO quoted by Spencer Johnson, *Yes or No*

Oh, God

I've successfully trained thousands of people to use their intuition without ever using the word God. At the same time, however, I've noticed that those who are able to fully trust their intuition have or develop a sense of a larger spiritual presence in their lives.

Yellow Light

Don't expect your intuition to make sense. Let it run with the images and feelings without the restraint of needing to "make sense." Later on, your analytic, logical mind will do that.

Many of you reading this book are looking to build lives that are abundant spiritually and emotionally as well as financially. The concept of God may be too loaded with old, paternalistic images for some of you, but the realization that you're part of something larger is very real.

For some with strong, yet broad spiritual beliefs, intuition is the voice of God. For others, it's the guidance of angels, nature spirits, and spiritual guides. Scientifically-minded individuals believe that intuition is a natural power of the mind we are just beginning to uncover. For others, it's biochemistry. I agree with everyone.

Just as a seed has all of the information it needs to grow into a full, complete tree, each of you has all of the information you need to become fully who you are and to live a successful and fulfilled life. That information is locked inside of you. Perhaps it's part of your DNA. However it's coded, it's the essence of your uniqueness—it is your soul. The only way that information can be known is through your intuition. Your internal voice and signals let you know whether you're on track with your coding or not.

A seed may fall on rocky ground and struggle to grow a few feet tall. It has done the best it can with the available resources. You too are growing within a time, a culture, a family, and an environment. With the help of intuitive guidance, much can be overcome and transformed. A fuller expression of who you are is possible through tapping the power of your intuitive programming. Discovering your uniqueness and deciding to live it unlocks tremendous power.

This Is Your Life

Here's a workout that delves into your personal and spiritual history to help you discover your uniqueness:

1. On a piece of paper, draw a large "V" and then add one more line in the middle. At the bottom of the "V" draw a circle.

2. Each line you have drawn represents a part of your "essential" history: the evolution of your essence. One line represents your father, another your mother, and the third one Intuition (or the Whole). If you don't know one of your parents, make it up: Imagine what they might be, knowing yourself. Adoptive parents are valid sources of history, too. If you have step-parents, use them also. Use as many lines as you need to pour into the circle.

Practical Wisdom

People are shopping around, not only for the right job but for the right atmosphere. They now regard the old rules of the business world as dishonest, boring, and outdated. This new generation in the workplace is saying "I want a society and a job that values me more than the Gross National Product. I want work that engages the heart as well as the mind and the body, that fosters friendship, and that nourishes the earth. I want to work for a company that contributes to the community.

—Anita Roddick, founder of The Body Shop

Practical Wisdom

...a great and strong wind rent the mountains, and broke in pieces the rocks before the Lord, but the Lord was not in the wind; and after the wind an earthquake, but the Lord was not in the earthquake; and after the earthquake a fire, but the Lord was not in the fire; and after the fire a still small voice.

—1 Kings 19, verses 11 and 12

3. Write on one line qualities you have inherited and learned from your father, on another those from your mother. Continue with all your parental figures.

4. On the third line, go back to the image of your intuition from the "Meet Your Intuition" workout. Write the qualities of your intuition that you also share.

5. In the circle, write words and phrases that describe what your life seems to be asking of you. What your dreams, thoughts, and the demands and responsibilities of your life seem to be asking of you. What role do you keep playing in your life? What roles have the most vitality and satisfaction for you?

6. Now draw two lines from the bottom of the circle to the bottom of the page (like legs that carry the rest of the picture).

7. On these lines, write your daily activities.

8. Look at the whole picture. You may want to enhance it with color and sketches that fill it in. New ideas and thoughts for each area may need to be added.

9. Are you using your resources? What is the life path you're walking? Is your life involved with healing something from your parents and helping to transform it for others? Are you continuing a tradition in new ways? Are you a clean slate? What are you passing on? Spend sometime with these questions and write in your journal reflecting on your human and spiritual history.

You'll want to spend some time with this workout, going back to it periodically to review and gain more insight into who you are. Make it a long term goal to discover who you are.

I also use the preceding workout with corporate groups to help them discover new solutions to challenges. The top lines outline the "parents" of the current problem and the original need or desire that started the ball rolling in the first place. The circle contains the current environment, what is working and what isn't, and the legs at the bottom—what is actually happening now.

Work out your spiritual and personal history.

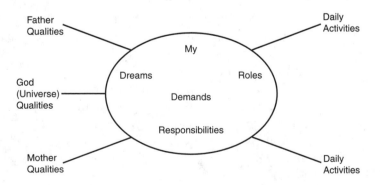

Tried & True

I awoke one day with the clear thought: "Maybe I could make some money helping someone to write a book." I have no idea why this thought came to me, or how I thought I could do this since I had virtually no experience. Nevertheless, I called my friend Candice, since she was the only person I knew who was connected to books and writing and told her, "If you hear of anyone who needs help writing, let me know." Before the end of that day, she called me back. She had "just happened" to hear about a doctor who was looking for a ghostwriter.

—Carol Adrienne, *The Purpose of Your Life*

Back to the Future

This next workout can be used in conjunction with the preceding one to help you gain a sense of your unique essence through a meditative experience; or it can stand on its own:

1. Take a few relaxing breaths and close your eyes.

2. Imagine yourself as the connecting link between two powerful forces: the past and the future. Allow the past to be behind you or on one side of you, and the future to be in front of you or on the other side. Take a few moments to sense the presence of these two forces. Feel yourself allowing the past to flow through you to the future.

3. Focus first on the past. Let yourself imagine a field of energy flowing into you from the past. Notice how it feels. Does it have color? Texture? Movement? Magnetic pull?

4. Focus now on the future. Imagine the energy you're flowing into. Does it have color? Texture? Movement? Magnetic pull?

5. Focus on you. How does it feel to be in the middle of these forces? How are you handling it? Does one dominate? Are you the leader here? Is there a way for you to feel in the flow and in charge at the same time?

6. When you're ready, open your eyes and draw a picture of the images. Write your experiences in your journal.

Both of these workouts give you a deep sense of yourself within a larger context. The second one can also be used to help solve particular problems. Place a problem situation in the field of the past and the desired resolution in the future. You, as the connecting link, represent the solution. Watch how you do it. This can also be done with a team as the center link.

The Pause That Refreshes

Intuitive mastery requires daily moments when you tune yourself to the cosmic channel, rituals that inject a deep pause into the doingness of your life, allowing you to remember the larger whole of which you are a part. These moments can be as short as 10 minutes or as long as an hour. It depends on your schedule.

Tried & True

Learning any martial art involves the step-by-step memorization and perfection of movements and techniques, but all the technical skills in the world can't create a great martial artist and, in fact, will mean nothing if they are not applied to a mind receptive to their use. The sword master could have taught the student lessons in how to hold the sword, various techniques of footwork, parries, and thrusts, but those lessons would have been empty and meaningless.

Instead, he taught him the frame of mind necessary to a great swordsman, the frame of mind in which the swordsman is completely attuned to his surroundings, ready at any moment to respond. The other lessons could come later, for the student had learned something of what can be called the Zen of swordsmanship.

—Chuck Norris, *The Secret Power Within*

When faced with any difficult problem, seemingly insurmountable odds, turning points, or tragedy, a daily spiritual routine is key to getting through it with guidance, direction, and grace. Here are some elements you can use to develop such a routine:

➤ *Ritual:* A ritual is a spiritual habit that creates a mood and sets a tone for contemplation. Lighting candles, incense, ringing a bell, anything that reminds you that you are entering a sacred moment.

➤ *Prayer:* Have a conversation with God. Ask and listen. Unburden yourself and allow God to fill you up.

➤ *Meditation:* There are many forms of meditation, all effective. The purpose is to get you out of your daily active mind and into your receptive, intuitive mind.

➤ *Walking:* Walk in a way that keeps you present to the moment, appreciating the surroundings, listening to your inner voice. Or, use walking as a meditation, focusing on each step and nothing else.

➤ *Writing:* Daily journal writing supports creativity and intuitive development.

➤ *Drawing:* Painting and drawing get you out of your daily focus and into an altered state.

➤ *Intuition workouts:* Any of the intuition workouts will tune you in.

➤ *Reading:* Read silently or aloud, sacred and inspirational books. There are also many "daily" reading books containing short, spiritually focused material that can help remind you of your intuitive voice.

Practical Wisdom

Design a spiritual practice that requires just you. At those moments when you think you can't go on, that the pressures are getting to you, you can always turn to your spiritual practice and just breathe, pray, walk, sing, or remember a loving time in your life.

You can put together a specific daily routine that's done at exactly the same, every day. You can vary it and use different elements. You may be able to spend five minutes one day and 20 minutes another. Work with your schedule, but do something every day. Here is how a few folks I know have creatively put a daily practice together:

Example 1: Working Mom. She lights a candle while she puts on her makeup in the morning. It's the only time she has to herself. Lighting the candle reminds her that she is preparing both her soul and her body for the day. As she puts on her makeup she is also tuning in her intuition.

Example 2: Lunch and lives. A woman eats her lunch by a beautiful water fountain and reads spiritually inspiring books. A man joins a weekly meditation group that started at work. Another man spends half his lunch hour sitting in a church near work and meditating.

Example 3: Wall St. prayer. Right off the train near Wall St. NYC, is Trinity Church. This man has joined a prayer group that meets once a week, the other days he visits the church on his own before work to pray and center himself.

Example 4: Baby's nap time. While the baby is sleeping, this new mother sketches portraits of the baby, the dog, whatever. Sketching puts her in touch with herself and a new perspective.

Example 5: Early riser. Up early every morning, this person meditates for 30 minutes every day.

Example 6: Cosmic commuter. Reading spiritually inspiring books on the way home, this person takes a cosmic break between work and home.

Example 7: Evening prayer. Writing down all that she is grateful for, this person writes her evening prayers.

These are just a few of the possibilities. Let them inspire you to come up with your own. The point is, there is no excuse for not doing it. The busiest day has time for a 10 minute spiritual break.

The Oracle Next Door

Oracles are tools for divination. We know humans have used oracles since the beginning of written history, and suspect that they're much older than that. They work on the principle of synchronicity: Ask the Universe a question, and you get immediate feedback in the form of an answer or deeper reflection. Your intuition uses the answer to clarify what you knew in the first place but couldn't quite see.

Traditionally oracles are people or shrines, but they can also exist in the form of literature or cards. Many such oracles are available on the market today; I happen to collect them. The following are four of my favorites. Some will really grab your attention whereas others won't fit. Experiment and have fun. The ones I use are listed in Appendix B.

Sphericles

Developed by Christine Roess and Joann Black, two high-powered business women, the Sphericles oracle consists of a book and a bag of 33 numbered marbles. The marbles correspond to a specific "reflections" which are clearly explained and easily applied to modern situations both business and personal. Sphericles is a great tool because it's written in business-friendly language. It contains 33 "reflections" that are clearly explained and easily applied to modern situations, both business and personal.

I'm going to ask the Sphericles a question right here, right now, and share it with you to give you an idea of what they can do:

1. First, I formulate a request: "Please comment on the purpose of this book and provide ideas to make it even more effective."

2. I take the little red velvet bag filled with 33 plastic marbles, each with a different number. I shake up the bag, reach in and pull out a number. The marble I selected was number 12.

3. I then look up the number in *Sphericles* for my answer. Each answer consists of a poem or quote, then a "teaching" followed by suggested "action." I just read Sphericle #12 and I swear to you that I did not cheat. This is truly the one that came up and it's perfect. I share it here verbatim:

12: Imagination

There are no mistakes and it's never boring
on the edge of the imagination,
which is only pure spirit out having a bit of fun.
—Hugh Romney, AKA Wavy Gravy

Teaching: When you were a child, you were the ruler of an incredible universe. You could create anything, from being a banana to being the prince or princess of a distant galaxy.

The Imagination Sphericle is daring you to open up to a powerful fountain of possibility, accomplishment, and joy. Imagination is made welcome when you let your intuitive mind run free and your dreams flow.

Let go of your limiting beliefs with regard to the work issue at hand. To be truly imaginative requires a willingness to not know and a boldness when ready answers are insufficient to handle the challenges.

This Sphericle is counseling you to rely on your imaginative power in this situation. Throw your analytical mind to the wind and entertain fantasies your "sensible self" would never allow you to think.

Action: Pick a challenge or opportunity in your work and set aside time to capture your "beyond your wildest imagination" ideas, preferably with one of your more free thinking colleagues or friends.

Practical Wisdom

Given the need for a profit and certain clear ethical restraints and guidelines, why not allow people to realize these goals according to their own inner images of what is right, good and true?. . . Why not have faith in the complexity that arises from their interacting individual images, their imaginations?

—David Whyte, *The Heart Aroused*

Hmm…I guess that says it all.

Crop Circle Cards

One of the newer oracles I've played with, Crop Circle Cards, are quickly becoming a big favorite. I thought they were pretty weird at first, even for me, but I was quite intrigued by how they looked. Cariel Quinly, who has spent years studying the "crop circle phenomenon," took 63 of the designs and made them into cards, each representing a different quality or reflection on a question. There's a bit of spiritual, otherworldly language used with the cards that you sometimes need to read between.

Here's what happened when I put the cards to a very relevant test via the following steps:

1. Ask a question. I asked, "What can I say about this deck of cards that will most clearly explain to the readers of this book how they might benefit from using the Crop Circle Cards?"

2. Shuffle. I shuffled the cards, fanned them out, and picked one: number 15.

3. Refer to the book. I looked up the number 15 in the little book that goes with the cards and read this:

   Shadow * Integration

   I am shadow, conflict, and separation. I keep the dual 3-D world occupied. You must integrate me if you are to enter higher dimensions. I magnify your inner fears and dark side issues in order to force you to take responsibility, resolve conflicting relationships, and transmute the energy towards life instead of death.

   At this time, you're taking responsibility for your life. You may be deciding whether to remain with or leave a situation. You may separate or divorce. You no longer have to repeat an old pattern. You have transmuted and/or integrated a big part of self and are ready to move on. You're connecting to a higher love-light frequency in relationship. Congratulations!

4. Reflect. At first I wondered what the heck this had to do with anything; and then I got it. This book is about making money using intuition, right? It's about using a "higher dimension" of self in the real world. It's about making clear decisions regarding how you live your life and encouraging you to live it with your whole self, to choose "life instead of death." One of the reasons I wrote this book is because I believe it to be important to use intuitive and spiritual skills in practical ways—what the cards refer to as the "3D world."

Tarot Cards

There are literally hundreds of tarot decks on the market. The only way is to use intuition and trial and error in picking one that's right for you. I like the Crowley Tarot deck, used with *The Tarot Handbook* by Angeles Arrien. The images on the cards are rich, and Angeles has a broad, multicultural way of interpreting the cards.

Let's have some fun:

1. Ask a question. For this one, I decided to ask a totally off-the-wall question: "What will be the flavor and mood of the U.S. stock market at the time when this book is released to the public?"

2. Shuffle and select. I shuffle the cards and pick one; it turns out to be the Ten of Wands. As Arrien's book explains:

The Ten of Wands is oppression. On this card the two Tibetan dorjes, or the sacred spiritual power objects, are dulled or grayed-over, to symbolize the state of oppressing oneself, either through holding back, editing, or rehearsing oneself or not fully expressing oneself—mentally, emotionally, spiritually, or physically... Saturn is the planet of discipline and knowing one's limits and boundaries, as well as being able to set limits and boundaries. There may be a tendency to limit oneself or one's vision, which is represented by the astrological sign of Sagittarius.

3. Reflect. I am going to mark on my calendar the date of publication, as soon as I know it, and watch for a market pullback (that is certainly what the market is doing as I write this passage in late September 1998!).

The I Ching

No discussion of oracles would be complete without referring to the granddaddy of all oracles, the I Ching. A Chinese text more than 2,500 years old, it is a classic with many modern interpretations and versions. The version I will use here is very simple, with the hexagrams made into cards and the descriptions of "what to do" very simple and direct. Other versions are listed in Appendix B.

Practical Wisdom

Imagination is more important than knowledge.

—Albert Einstein

Here's the drill:

1. Ask a question. I asked: "What are some wise words for those reading this book who are looking to use their intuition to build wealth in this world?"

2. Shuffle the cards and pick one: I got number 42.

3. Look it up in the book: "Expansion, Wood over Thunder suggests: Thunder at the root of a fruit tree: exceptional growth this summer." Basic Meaning: This is a favorable time for undertaking great tasks, even significant journeys and moves.

4. Reflect: The I Ching seems to support our endeavor here to build wealth using intuition, in fact the image of the "fruit tree" representing wealth and the "Thunder" as intuition, suggests that it is a powerful combination and will propel all of us to exceptional growth!

Oracles are fun and insightful. Only when I've asked really stupid questions have I been disappointed. You can do them with your friends or by yourself. I often use them with corporate groups and encourage teams to use them to expand the scope of a discussion. At the very least, they help focus a particular question, tap another part of your mind, and get you thinking in new ways about the situation at hand.

Intuition Groupthink

Intuition is always enhanced by working with a group. Sharing intuitive experiences builds confidence and double-checks "fantasy thinking." Doing the workouts in this book together makes it easier: one can read the workout while the rest of the group does it, or one person can pre-record the workout and play it for the group. During times of difficult decisions, group intuition can provide added clarity. The long-term support working with a group keeps your progress going.

Here are a few suggestions for getting started:

➤ Just do it. Call three or four of your friends and set a one-time meeting to discuss the possibilities. Do one or two of the workouts and decide how you want to proceed.

➤ Put a notice up at work. Several corporate groups meet before or after work hours. Many people in the work force are just looking to join a group like this.

➤ Look around you. Many groups are already started and you may be able to join. Check out the "In-Reach" program listed among the resources in the Appendix A.

➤ Take a class. There are many classes on intuition available. Even if it's a one-time group, you can meet others in your area who are interested and perhaps start your own group.

Intuition is best developed in an ongoing, supportive atmosphere where three or more people are working together to build and prosper from their intuitive skills. While it may take a little effort to bring a group together, the payoffs will be worth it.

Hiring an Intuition Consultant

The field of intuition consultants is growing every day. There are people in every community who are skilled at providing their intuitive insights to you for a fee. There are certainly times when help is needed and an intuition consultant can offer clarity to a situation. When you're really confused about a situation and feel pressured from different sources to make a decision, an intuition consultant can help. Intuition consultants work in both the corporate and public arena. Here is some help in working with both varieties.

Practical Wisdom

If it has become essential to use lawyers and accountants to provide advice on structuring agreements and on the short- and long-range tax implications of something, why not get advice that expands the intuitive possibilities?

Help! I Need Somebody

At its very best, a session with a personal intuition consultant gets you back in touch with what you intuitively know. Confusion is a result of trying to please too many people with one decision or one action. The effort is enough to create static in your Intuition TV so that no channel is coming in clearly. Here are some practical guidelines for working with intuitive consultants:

➤ Get a referral. Use someone a friend has gone to and can recommend.

➤ Be as clear as you can about what you want to solve.

➤ Go in with an open mind—ready to hear whatever the intuitive has to tell you.

➤ Look for "resonance" with what the intuitive is saying.

➤ Tape record the session so you can listen to it later. Sometimes the best benefit from a session comes when you listen to a session one or two years after it happened.

➤ After the session, review your notes and listen to the tape. Pay close attention to what you feel about what the intuitive said. If something feels untrue, it most likely is. If something opened your eyes to something, or felt like it was completely familiar and something you "knew, but didn't know you knew," take note. That's your intuition talking to you.

➤ After a competent session, you should feel more in touch with your own ability to make good decisions, not dependent on them.

➤ Use an intuition consultant sparingly and as an adjunct to your own intuitive development.

Remember, you are the one responsible for your decisions, not the advisors and consultants you use. You are the one who has to live with the results. Make your own decisions and put your whole self into making them.

Corporate Angels

A friend of mine is the spiritual advisor behind many successful business and non-profit endeavors. She prefers to remain behind the scenes where she feels her work can be accomplished effectively. She was inspired to create a business that would "give light to any and all who need it." She pulled together a team that started the business "Angel Feet," a reflexology business in New York City. She is not an owner of the business, she is its spiritual advisor. In that role she troubleshoots, problem-solves, and helps guide the "force" of the business as it makes its way into the real world.

Practical Wisdom

We often tend to limit our explorations of what's possible by surrounding ourselves with large amounts of information that tell us nothing new. We collect information from measures that tell us how we are going—whether we're up to standard, whether we're meeting our goals. But these measures lock us into learning only about a predetermined world. They keep us distracted from questioning our experience in a way that could create greater possibilities. They don't ask us to question why we're doing what we're doing. They don't ask us to notice what learning is available from all those things we decided not to measure.

—Margaret J. Wheatley and Myron Kellner-Rogers, *A Simpler Way*

Practical Wisdom

In the board meetings of the future, techniques will be used to tune the group to a larger, more creative, and encompassing vision before making decisions.

Practical Wisdom

Everybody gets so much information all day long that they lost their commonsense.

—Gertrude Stein

In less than three years, the business has boomed, providing healing foot massages to between 45 and 75 cement-weary feet every day. It's known around the world and has appeared in diverse media channels including *The New York Times* and Japanese television. My friend has done the same for many non-profit groups and individuals.

Working with a gifted intuitive provides not only information and guidance, but also focused support in the achievement of goals. By clarifying individual and group intention and heightening awareness of everyone's intuition, problems are anticipated, powerful ideas are shared, and teams work together more effectively.

Other businesses are also hiring intuition consultants to help with hiring, planning, new business deals, and a variety of other strategic issues. Some companies are even training their executive and management teams to pay more attention to the intuitive insights. Bringing an intuition consultant into a business setting gives the folks who work there permission to know what they know and to share it with their teammates.

Developing intuitive mastery does not mean that you have to do it all alone. As we have seen, working with a group, with oracles, and with professionals can help pinpoint your own intuitive knowing.

The Least You Need to Know

➤ Get to know where intuition lives in your body and develop a link to it.

➤ A sense of connection to a greater whole helps develop intuitive mastery.

➤ You are a unique point in time, transforming the past into the future—do it with awareness.

➤ Develop your own daily spiritual practice.

➤ Oracles can be helpful tools for developing intuitive skill.

➤ Professional intuition consultants provide guidance and power boosts to your success.

Share Your (L)Earnings

A church in Virginia Beach, Virginia, found itself constantly low on both funds and parishioners. Because one of its consistent teaching points over the years had been the importance of tithing—giving away 10 percent of whatever you had—the church leaders decided to levy a tithe on the parishioners in order both to practice more closely what they were preaching and to reap the benefits that they hoped would occur. Amazing as it may seem, within a year the church had significantly increased its membership and had more than enough money to cover its expenses.

The business world has its own form of tithing. Many businesses have increased their visibility and their reputations by giving away their products. Mrs. Fields is famous for the great cookie giveaway that started her business with a positive bang. Amazon.com gave away stock, as did Travelzoo and Yahoo! .

This chapter is about the power of sharing. You'll learn the ultimate wealth-building strategy of "giving it away." You'll enjoy walking your path of prosperity, and begin to harvest what you have learned. Finally, you'll discover how becoming a mentor and helping other people achieve their goals will make you even more successful.

The Ultimate Investment Strategy: Tithing

In Part 2 you began tithing to yourself. If you have followed through on that, you no doubt have seen the incredible benefits, both financially and spiritually, that have occurred since then. It's now time to pay tithe to your community. You can see the advantage of investing in yourself. It's common sense to support yourself to become even more successful.

Sixth Sense

The word *tithing* comes from the Old English word *teothian,* which means to take one tenth.

Now if that makes sense to you, think of investing in your community as increasing your investment in yourself 10 times. Remember, we're talking intuitive world mathematics here. Let me explain what I mean and then give you a sample plan for tithing.

Tried & True

John D. Rockefeller was a tither, and it has become a family practice. During the Great Depression in the 1930s, he would pass out dimes on the street. He did it knowing that he was following the Law of Universal Abundance, that he would get it back tenfold, and because it was the right thing to do. They all go together.

Cosmic Mutual Funds

You understand the value of investing in company stocks, right? You buy a certain number of shares of a business you believe will do well, the business does well, and your money increases in value. Investing in mutual funds takes that same principle and spreads the investment into many stocks, most of which you do not know. If enough of them do well, your investment will do well. If you don't invest, the companies may still do well, but you won't benefit. The nature of investing is that you have to participate without knowing what the ultimate outcome will be, in order to benefit.

Now imagine investing in the market that feeds all life. There is no more powerful or certain investment: Life continues to create constantly and abundantly. What's more, investing in this universal market is guaranteed to increase your investment at least tenfold. Now, you may or may not get it back in dollars, you may get it back in the form of opportunities. However it comes back to you, it will be concrete and it will help build your wealth.

Tried & True

For the past 15 years, I have been calling for the establishment of an ethical state with a concrete plan for change. . . Today, there is only one entity whose effort to create stability in the world matches its self-interest. That entity is a corporation acting globally. The essence of a successful company is to strive to contribute on three dimensions: to its customers, its employees, and to society. This is the essential element of the "spirit of Canon" and has been since its founding in 1933.

—R. Kaku, Chairman of Canon, speaking to J. Jaworski in *Synchronicity*

If that wasn't enough to send you to your checkbook, there's more. You also get back waves of love and gratitude, just for doing what anyone would do, once the principles are understood. You get to decide the particulars of your investment—what organization or individual gets it. This is no pyramid scheme where the ultimate beneficiaries are hidden. Everything is done in full view, without coercion or sales. How much you invest is up to you, although the recommended amount over the centuries has been a tithe, or 10 percent of what you have.

The Law of Universal Abundance

No matter where you are in your wealth-building plan, start tithing now. It will only support whatever other efforts you're making. To some of you, it may seem like I'm asking you to give away lots of money. In Part 2, I asked you to start seeding your financial future by investing in yourself and now I'm asking you to pay a tithe to the Universal Investment Pool. Of course, if you can look at my request with your intuitive mind, you'll see that I'm really revealing to you the pot of gold at the end of the rainbow.

Buying food is investing in your health, right? You need to buy food, eat it, and then it nourishes you. Is the nourishment you receive from the food worth more or less than what you spent for it? If you get to continue living because you're eating and continue living abundantly because you're eating especially nourishing food, then the investment is minimal compared to the return you're receiving. Every place you invest yourself, your money and your time returns you much more than you paid. It's what I call the Law of Universal Abundance, and it's obvious once you take a close look at it. Here's a workout to help you do just this:

1. Take a piece of paper and turn it sideways.

2. Draw a circle in the middle and write in the circle the name of something you own, love, and spent lots of money on at the time you bought it.

3. Around the circle write down all of the benefits you can think of that you have gained from this purchase. Spend a few minutes doing this to allow new thoughts and ideas to flow to you. Reminisce about the history of this purchase and all the people, places, and things that it, through you, has touched.

4. Draw a larger circle around all of the things you wrote in Step 3. Outside of that circle, write all the benefits of this purchase that will come in the future.

5. Reflect on all that you have written and ask yourself if the price you paid comes even close to the benefits you have gained.

Practical Wisdom

Every single thing we have and use is a gift of Mother Earth. There is nothing that doesn't come from the generosity of the Earth. Metals, plastics, fabrics, food, minerals, water, even air is generated from plants.

—Native American Elder and Healer

You can do this workout with a favorite dress or suit, a car, home, piece of jewelry, fine bottle of wine, day at the spa, or a pet. It doesn't matter. This purchase has returned its value many times over. Even the purchase of one seed provides years of color, joy, and beauty.

Plan Your Intuitive Investment

Tithing is very simple, but it isn't always easy. It requires an open heart, a belief in the principles discussed previously, and personal discipline. Here are the steps you can take to begin:

1. Figure out how much money you make every year and write it down. You can use your net income (after payroll taxes have been taken out), but don't reduce it any more than that. If your income fluctuates because you are paid on commission, average the last two years with what you expect to earn this year.

2. Divide that amount by 10. The final figure is the amount you get to invest in the Universal Investment Pool.

3. Decide on three or four causes, charities, institutions, community projects, or similar organizations. Pick ones that you believe will help move the world in a positive direction if they're successful in accomplishing their mission. Some people find it helpful to pick something local, something for the broader community within which they live, and something that functions globally.

4. Decide the best way for you to give the money: monthly, quarterly, or yearly.

5. Call the organizations you're going to donate to and let them know your donation plan, how much you plan to give, and when you plan to give it. You may

want to let them know that they don't have to send you constant requests for money because you have already decided what you're doing. Let them know which information you'd like to receive, such as annual reports, project updates, meeting times, and so on. Begin to build a relationship with them. If you decide how much you're going to give before you decide who you are going to give it to, just put it aside in an account until you find the right opportunity. For example, it may be to individuals in need.

6. Do it. Write the checks. Send the money knowing that you are now tapping in to the Universal Investment Pool. Once you do, notice how you feel.

Keep your giving limited to three or four organizations or causes for the first year or so. Get used to tithing, make it a part of your life, then you can increase your giving to other groups. Keep in mind that just as investing in the stock market has uncertainty, the uncertainty in investing in this program is that you can't know when you will receive your returns. It might be next week, and it might be 10 years from now. Anyone I know who has done this hasn't waited very long to see results, but there's no guarantee. The Universe has its own clock.

Expand Your Cosmic Portfolio

Once you begin to realize the benefits of investing in this way, you'll want to do more and more. Over time you may want to share and invest more of yourself, your time, your resources, and your wisdom. You may be inspired to develop your own program and to organize others to join you.

The one other investment that I highly recommend is mentoring. There will be times when someone comes into your life who is ready for guidance. It's an opportunity for you to walk beside another human being for awhile, be a role model, and share a little of what you have learned.

Once you have "made it" in your own life, there's a natural longing to help others do the same for themselves. Making it is not limited to financial gain. Some of you will make it past a self-destructive lifestyle, others will make it through a personal loss, others will survive a life-threatening illness. Whatever the victory, it deserves to be shared.

Practical Wisdom

The unspoken yet universally understood law of wholeness states that whoever finds his or her way in this challenging life, goes back and pulls at least one other person through.

Become a Mentor

One of the side effects of making it is that you gain personal power and presence. Achieving your goals and manifesting your intention naturally builds personal magnetism. As you attract more success to you, you'll also attract attention. This is your opportunity to become a positive role model and take your success to an even more effective position. Your ability to allow your influence to be felt through others will lead you to yet another set of challenges and rewards.

Mentoring is a great blessing and a huge responsibility. Most of the time you'll mentor informally. Just by circumstances, someone will be watching you and learning from you—this is a huge responsibility. You'll have a few golden moments where something you say or do might have a significant and positive impact on this person. Sometimes, you may even be privileged enough to receive their thanks and appreciation—this is a blessing. Most often those who are mentored, don't even realize it until much later.

The challenge of this stage is obvious. Just look at a newspaper; everyday we read about leaders who abuse their power and take advantage of those around them by using their influence to gratify their own personal needs. You can gain tremendous power and influence in your life and lose it all if you don't mentor well. Becoming powerful is like becoming a powerful magnet. Yes, you attract lots of goodies and with them comes lots of attention. If you don't manage what you attract, you'll clog your magnetic power with nails instead of precious metals.

Put on a Good Show

As your personal power builds, the TV signal you generate becomes stronger and stronger. It's up to you to keep the programming in line with your life intention. Everyone around you is tuning in to your channel whether you know it or not. Your daily spiritual practice, which you developed in Chapter 22, will go a long way toward keeping your signal clean and sharp.

For those golden moments when you have a direct opportunity to provide guidance and advice, don't put on your preacher's or teacher's hat. There is nothing worse than being told what to do when you have your own ideas and intuition. Stephen Covey, author of *The Seven Habits of Highly Effective People*, summarizes the most effective formula for mentoring I have seen. It focuses attention on the student, rather than mentor, giving the student an opportunity to think through the situation and draw his or her own conclusions. I have added an overt intuitive step to his basic formula.

Caveat Mentor

When you find yourself in the position of mentor to others, let the following series of questions guide what you say:

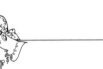

Yellow Light

When someone asks for help, watch out! It's a trap to see if they can get you to take responsibility for what they need to do themselves. Instead of taking their bait, turn it around and ask them what they think and feel about the situation. Always assume that they know what they want and feel, even if they can't clearly articulate it. Your job, as guide or coach, is to help them know what they already know.

➤ How is it going? Get them to describe the problem or situation as clearly as possible. Often, after the situation is described out loud, the solution appears.

➤ What are you learning? Get them to reflect on what this whole situation is doing for them in a positive way, in spite of or because of the pain involved.

➤ What is your intuitive sense? Ask them how they intuitively feel about the situation and the solution. What have they noticed and what do they intuitively know? If there is openness, here is where you can provide more guidance. Walk them through one of the workouts in this book. Help them get more in touch with their intuitive voice.

➤ What do you want to do next? Get them to articulate what the next step is, as they see it. Let them struggle with this, perhaps for a day or two. If you tell them what to do, then they won't be able to own it and be responsible for the action. If it fails, its not really their fault. Let the rubber meet the road.

➤ How can I help? Now you can let them determine how you might help. Allow them to tell you what they need. You may or may not be able to provide it. That will be up to you.

Practical Wisdom

When most people ask for help or advice, they're really looking for validation of their own intuition—whether or not they know what that is.

The whole process may take place over several days or even weeks. It may repeat itself several times. Mentoring in this way supports others to find their own power and use it. You're there as a role model and as a guide. After they articulate their thoughts and feelings, you may want to add something about your own experiences. You can steal the show; just be careful not to steal their thunder.

The Payoff

Investing your wisdom in another person is one of the most lucrative ways to increase your wealth. It increases your stature, your reputation, and your personal power. Whatever you invest in terms of time and energy will be paid back to you at least 10 times over. Besides, it completes a cycle that was started when you received some mentoring that helped you achieve your current position.

Practical Wisdom

You must speak straight so that your words may go as sunlight into our hearts.

—Cochise, Chiricahua Apache, from Cheewa James' *Catch the Whisper of the Wind*

The Flow Must Go On

Flow happens. You can't escape it, but you can fight it if you must. To be in harmony with the world of intuition, your job is to:

➤ Direct—not control

➤ Respond—not react

➤ Anticipate—not panic

➤ Receive—not grab

➤ Enjoy and share—don't hold and hoard

➤ Do what is needed—then move on

You know this; and now you know how to do it. Imagine what the world would look like if you and just 15 percent of others lived in harmony with their intuition. It's in your self-interest to live this way, as it brings prosperity and fulfillment. It also benefits the rest of the world, as living this way brings prosperity and fulfillment to those you influence through your life.

Practical Wisdom

Do your work, then step back.
The only path to serenity...
He who clings to his work
will create nothing that endures.
If you want to accord with the Tao,
just do your job, then let go.

—Lao Tzu, from *The Reinvention of Work* by Matthew Fox

The Prosperity Path

Some people think that there's not enough prosperity to go around; they just aren't paying attention. Others believe they'll never have enough; they aren't enjoying what they have.

To walk the path of prosperity is not easy. As you've learned from this book, it requires a change of outlook and a change of behavior. It demands personal discipline and integrity. You have spent the last few days or weeks reading this book and trying out at least some of the workouts, right? Take a few moments now to assess your own progress and personal next steps.

For this workout, we'll use the mentoring questions discussed previously to guide your self-assessment, after getting in the mood with an intuitive introduction. Get out your journal or pad and pencil and spend some time answering following questions for yourself:

1. Take a few relaxing breaths and close your eyes.

2. Imagine yourself walking along a path. Take a few moments to sense the road under your feet, the weather, the time of year, and the beauty of the moment.

3. Feel the rhythm of walking and look around. What are you seeing? What is the terrain?

4. As you walk along, there will be something that catches your eye. Pick it up and take it with you, if you can. If it's too big, let it impact you from a distance and remember it.

5. Continue walking this path, enjoying the scenery and at some point an animal will become part of this journey. It may be an animal you see to the side and go visit, or it may be an animal that comes to travel with you. However it happens, greet the animal and welcome its presence on your path.

6. Take a few more moments to enjoy your path and then bring yourself back to this moment and open your eyes.

7. Take your pad and pencil and write answers to the following questions, as they relate to what you have learned and experienced from reading this book.

8. How is your path to prosperity going?

9. What are you learning?

10. What is your intuition communicating to you about the process?

11. What do you want to do next?

12. What help do you need?

Take as much time as you need to reflect on these questions and write your answers. When you're ready, read on to discover the significance behind some of the images on your prosperity path.

In devising the preceding steps, I planted some important images in the scene that have specific meaning. Compare the image you created with the meaning discussed and reflect on what your intuition might want you to know.

The thing you either noticed on the path or picked up represents your current overall acceptance of prosperity in your life. Take a few moments to reflect on what this image is saying to you. If it could talk, what would it say?

Practical Wisdom

Security comes from having something in your life that *is* bigger than yourself, something you are reaching for, something that attracts and pulls and calls to you. It makes the petty hurts and insignificant events small by comparison. And yet, many of you seek that bigger thing in each other, rather than in your own growth. To feel secure, you need to feel you are growing, expanding, and enlarging the scope of your world.

—Sanaya Roman, *Living With Joy*

The animal companion represents new behavior that will help you take your next steps towards true prosperity. Take a few moments to reflect on what this image is saying to you. How would this animal act if it were in your shoes? How would acting like this animal help you with something in your life?

Have fun with these images. Let them speak to you over the next few days. After a couple of months, repeat the workout and see what different images appear. Remember, the path of prosperity is meant to be meaningful, shared, and celebrated. If you aren't learning something from whatever is going on in your life now, wake up. If you aren't giving and taking, begin now. And if you aren't celebrating your accomplishments, read on.

The Least You Need to Know

➤ Tithing is the ultimate investment strategy—it's guaranteed to give a substantial return on your investment.

➤ You are constantly receiving tremendous benefit from previously made intuitive investments.

➤ Plan your tithing and execute it with love and discipline.

➤ Become a mentor—it's an investment in your prosperous future.

➤ Walk your own path to prosperity and take a moment to assess your present status.

Chapter 24

Show Me the Money!

In This Chapter

➤ Balance your wallet and your spirit

➤ Let momentum work for you

➤ Work less, make more

➤ Learn how a gratitude journal can help

➤ Use group intuition

The movie "Jerry Maguire" contains a great example of what it takes to be really, truly successful in life. At the outset, Tom Cruise's character is financially successful but personally miserable. After he reconnects to his true values, however, he is fired from his job and has no money, but he's still miserable.

His life comes together when he sticks with his values and goes for the money at the same time. His only client encourages him in both areas, constantly chiding him with the now famous phrase "show me the money!" while also giving him some pointers on integrity in relationships.

This chapter makes it clear how money and values fit together, work together, and need each other. Values and high ideals with no means of support will starve. Financial wealth without personal values and ideals is empty and lacks substance. My final gift to you, dear reader, will be the power to count both your money and your blessings.

Balancing the Spirit and the Wallet

If you stack enough blocks together in an artistic way, you can create a building. It won't look like a building until the top has something on it that completes it. If the finishing touch is not there, it'll just look like a pile of blocks. Take away one or two of the blocks near the bottom and the whole thing will fall down.

The same principle applies to building your wealth. The whole building needs to be finished for it to work. Let the building be a representation of your life, for just a moment. The bottom of the building represents the work, money, and substance of your life. A strong, tall building would represent great wealth and influence—the actual dollars and daily structure. The top of the building represents your focus, purpose, and direction—the completion and finishing touches of your life.

If you just pile up the money without a focus, interest, or direction, it's just a pile of money, or a building half done. Once it's built, if you take away the money at the bottom, the whole thing will fall down, including the beautiful point at the top.

One, without the other, just won't work. We live in a very physical world. You have value and are motivated by your vision, ideals, and creativity. Intuition connects and guides your vision, ideals, and creativity into the physical world. Money is both a result of that successful combination and an integral part of its creation. You can't have a building without the base. You can't live or work in the building until it's complete. Once it's complete and lived in, it needs maintenance. If the functional part of the building breaks down, all the beauty and creativity in the world won't save it.

Here's a workout to help you take an intuitive look at the financial/spiritual balance in your life.

Practical Wisdom

The model that presents the business organization as a cold, impersonal machine denies humanness. People have needs in three areas: body, mind, and spirit. However, most companies, if they acknowledge people have needs at all, act as if there are only two requirements for producing good work: money and job security.

—Richard McKnight, *Spirituality in the Workplace: Transforming Work*

You're going to use the room you're in right now as a synchronistic, symbolic representation of your life. It doesn't matter if the room is not yours or whether it's a room you spend lots or little time in. Use it. Do this exercises step-by-step—no looking ahead until you complete the step:

1. Take a moment to quiet yourself, taking a few deep breaths. Allow your intuitive perception and vision to come to the foreground.

2. Realize that the room you're in is going to reveal something to you about your current wealth-building state.

3. Look around the room and pick three items that attract your attention.

4. Bring these items to where you're sitting and place them in front of you. Create a triangle with them with one item at the top and the other two at the base.

5. Make sure that you have the items placed in a way that feels and looks pleasing to you.

6. Draw this triangle on a piece of paper with the name of each item in its place.

7. You have just created a picture of your Wealth Building. Each of the items will now speak to you about one aspect of your wealth building life.

8. Label the item at the peak as "A," the item on the lower right as "B," and the item on the lower left as "C."

9. The "A" item represents your current ability to allow your vision and your intention to actively participate in the creation of your life. Let the item speak to you symbolically. Look at it and listen to what it might be communicating to you and how you might increase the force of this point in your life.

10. The "B" item represents the current financial stability of your life. Let this item speak to you as you look at it carefully. Notice its relationship to the "A" item. What might this item be communicating to you about improving the force of this point in your life?

11. The "C" item represents your self-esteem, your belief in yourself and your ability to manage the forces currently in your life. Let this item speak to you. What can it tell you about how you feel about what is going on right now in your life and the personal strength and vitality you're expending to keep things going?

12. Look at the relationship of all three items. What does the complete picture say to you.

13. Write all of your thoughts in your journal.

Practical Wisdom

The greatest unexplored territory in the world is the space between our ears. Seriously, I am certain that learning organizations will find ways to nurture and focus the capabilities within us all that today we call "extraordinary."

—Bill O'Brien, CEO,
Hanover Insurance

This workout gives you an intuitive look at your current life. Let the information sink in. Don't see any of the items as bad or good—they are just information. Take it in and move on.

Tried & True

Kazuo Inamori, founder and president of Kyocera, teaches his employees to look inward as they continually strive for "perfection," guided by the corporate motto, "Respect Heaven and Love People." In turn, he believes that his duty as a manager starts with "providing for both the material good and spiritual welfare of my employees."

—Peter Senge, *The Fifth Discipline*

Your Money or Your Life

Jack Benny was famous for telling the story about the time he was held up at gun point and told, "Your money or your life!" After a moment of silent panic from Benny, the thief said, "Well, which is it?" Jack Benny replied, "I'm thinking, I'm thinking!"

When I began to write this book I got two different reactions from my friends. The more spiritually inclined group said things like, "Are you really so crass that you're going teach people to use their intuition to make money? Isn't there something better for them to do with their intuition?" From the other, more materially focused group I heard, "Does that work? It sounds pretty flaky to me."

Yellow Light

Those who ignore dealing directly with money because it's "non-spiritual" will live their lives controlled by the lack of money.

Writing this book has given me the opportunity to formulate what I really think about both worlds and how they fit together. Money provides the means and opens the doors to living the life you want. It also enables dreams, visions, and new ideas to become reality. Without money, or access to money, it won't happen.

So Jack Benny's conundrum—"Your money or your life?"—is a case where neither choice really answers the question. There is no life unless it's actualized in the world—unless it has substance and credibility as symbolized by money; and there is no world if individuals don't use their time on this planet to actualize their dreams and visions. The question is how much of each is needed? What's the right formula? Read on to discover the answer.

Less Really *Is* More

Over 20 years ago, I was starting a marketing company with a friend of mine. The accountant, who was experienced and successful, gave me some advice that I thought was crazy at the time. He said, "Stop trying so hard. The less you do, the more you get; and the more you do, the less you get." At the time I thought, "Well, that's okay for him to say, he's already made it—but what does it have to do with me? If I don't work hard, nothing will happen."

As my intuitive life expanded and my understanding of spiritual principles grew, I realized he was absolutely right. And now I can explain it to you in a little more detail.

Practical Wisdom

Abundance has always meant to me the ability to do what your inner voice is calling you to do regardless of financial status. Money can be used as an excuse not to do something if you have it or if you don't.

Like a Rolling Stone

Imagine a large concrete ball rolling down a mountain. It has momentum and doesn't take much effort to keep it going. Imagine now that you wanted to turn the concrete ball and make it to go in another direction. That would require effort. Once the ball was going where you wanted it to go, its own momentum would take over again, as long as it was headed downhill.

Tried & True

The conflict between intuition and linear, non-systemic thinking suggests to some that rationality itself is opposed to intuition. This view is demonstrably false, however, if we consider the synergy of reason and intuition that characterizes virtually all great thinkers. Einstein said, "I never discovered anything with my rational mind." He once described how he discovered the principle of relativity by imagining himself traveling on a light beam. Yet at the same time, he converted his brilliant intuitions into succinct, rationally testable propositions.

Our ability to get the ball rolling in our lives works in a similar way. You have *momentum* just by being you and living your life. You are on a certain track, rolling down a certain hill. You may or may not like the hill you're rolling down. And although changing the direction of your life takes effort, once you put yourself on the path you want, the rest, as they say, is downhill.

Your momentum comes from your clarity of purpose (intention) and your personal power (integrity). The stronger those parts of you are, the easier it is to manifest what you want, because the momentum is already moving.

The important effort in life is getting your direction and intention in order. Once that's in place, getting things to happen is much easier. The bad news is that even while you're getting your direction and intention in order, you'll still need to pay the rent. The good news is that as soon as you take a step toward bringing your life into some kind of alignment with your intention, intuition pumps up the volume and guides your way.

Laugh, and the Universe Laughs with You

In Chapter 11 you learned about the Universal Law of Adaptability. Now you can really put it to work. That law, combined with the strength of your personal presence, is where the power that creates your life comes from. The essence of it is this: You take a step and the Universe creates the ground for you to walk on.

For example, after being a financial planner for a few years, my husband discovered the type of clients he worked best with. Once he articulated that to himself and made it his intention to have more of those types of clients in his practice, he had more than 10 within two months. This is a specific example that you can learn from. You probably have your own stories that parallel this. My intent in sharing this one is to remind you of this system of creation, so you can use it more effectively:

➤ The cycle began with my husband feeling drained by some of his clients. The practice was too spread out and his effectiveness seemed weakened. The feeling of being drained was his intuition ringing the bell to pay attention. "Hey," it was saying, "there's a better way to accomplish the original intent of the practice."

➤ Frustration mounted to such an extent that we sat down to talk about what was happening. It became clear that something needed to change. Soon, a profile of clients most and least appropriate for this practice was articulated.

➤ My husband took the big step of transferring some clients to another planner, or even releasing them completely. This was the step into the unknown, and for a time sentiments like "We'll have to make do with what is given" and "Who am I to take my fate in my own hands?" and "What if I'm blowing my practice?" dominated his thoughts. At the same time, though, he experienced a huge feeling of relief and release of frustration—intuitive confirmation that he was taking appropriate measures toward realizing his optimum practice.

➤ Within two months at least 10 new clients who fit the desired profile had shown up, with no real extra effort on my husband's part. This was the Universe placing earth beneath the step that was taken.

This is an example of living intuitively. Listen to the message first. Take the appropriate action, without knowing how it will turn out or what exact opportunities there will be, then receive the gift with gratefulness. All I can say is that both my husband and I have successfully lived our lives this way for many years. Our whole story would be another book. One of the discoveries we have made along the way is that recounting blessings actually multiplies blessings.

Practical Wisdom

Just for fun, take an intuition workout from this book and use it for a different situation. Use your creativity to redesign it to fit the new need.

Bank on Gratitude

You were trained to say "thank you" when someone did something for you or gave you a present. Your mom knew it was important, but I wonder if she realized its true significance. For many, saying "thank you" has become an empty ritual. It rolls off the tongue like "Hi, how are you?" without another thought to what is being said or to its impact.

Check It Out

Imagine for a brief moment that you're working in a grocery store at the checkout counter. A customer comes through your line and, as usual, puts the food on the conveyer belt, pays, and gets out of there as fast as possible, avoiding eye contact. You do your job, scarcely noticing the customer.

Then a customer comes along who, while you're doing your job, begins to tell you how grateful he is that you are there. You've made his life easier and more enjoyable by doing your job effectively and efficiently. Your pointing out that he could save money by getting the store circular and using one of the coupons was really extra helpful and above and beyond your duties. You'll most likely remember this customer and give him extra smiles and attention the next time he comes in the store.

Practical Wisdom

The sense of responsibility that arises from work and our response to it is deeper than duty or guilt. This deeper sense of responsibility is a response of gratitude born from awe and wonder. The wonder of our work, of our being able to contribute to the work of the universe, fills us with gratitude and can arouse gratitude in others.

—Matthew Fox, *The Reinvention of Work*

The same principle applies to receiving universal blessings and abundance. The more grateful and aware you are of what you have and what you are given, the more is given to you. You won't be punished if you don't say "thank you," but you won't get special treatment either. You'll just be another customer coming through the line.

This gift that I am giving to you right now is completely painless and requires very little effort on your part. If you do it consistently, you'll see the results. Please try it for one month before dismissing it as silly. Oprah, on her television show, shared her "gratitude journal" and I don't need to tell you about her abundant life. For me, it was after one week of keeping a gratitude journal that my life turned a big corner and it became clear that worrying about money was never again going to be an issue.

Practical Wisdom

The awe inspiring thing is that you never know where your influence begins or ends. Something you said or did 10 years ago may still be affecting someone today. And something said or done to you 10 years ago, may be still inspiring you.

Your Gratitude Journal

Remember the journal I suggested you start in Chapter 18? Here is something you can add to it. Before you go to sleep each night, take a few moments to write down 10 things you noticed that day for which you're especially grateful. Your entry will look like this:

Date: _____

Today I am very grateful for the following things:

1. _____
2. _____
3. _____
4. _____
5. _____
6. _____
7. _____
8. _____
9. _____
10. _____

Your list can include people, places, things, events, animals, or dreams. It can even include unpleasant things that you have learned something from or hope to learn something from. That's it. It takes about 10 minutes.

Feeling Lucky, Punk?

There are over 50 intuition workouts in this book; if you do just one consistently it'll change your life. Will you do it? Those who have stepped over the line into living and thinking abundantly wonder why more people don't do it. There's no limit on opportunity and there's no limit on the amount of people who can live fulfilled lives.

People who learn to live intuitively and work with the system end up at the right place at the right time more often than not. To others they appear lucky, but luck isn't random. It's the result of the conscious application of intuition and an understanding of the Law of Universal Abundance.

I just asked one of my favorite oracles, The Sphericles, what it would take to encourage you to take that first, scary step onto your abundant road (see Chapter 22 for a discussion of more oracles). The answer I received was Sphericle Number 12—the exact same one I received in Chapter 22, where it's written in full. Please reread it. It's called "Imagination," and encourages you to go for it—to set aside your limiting mind and rethink your life.

Try the following workout to stimulate unlimited thinking right now:

1. Have ready your pen and your journal or a few pieces of paper.

2. Take a few relaxing breaths and connect with your intuitive, imaginative mind.

3. Read the following phrase and then begin writing, completing the phrase with whatever comes to you: "If I were lucky…"

> **Practical Wisdom**
>
> Could be a blessing, could be a curse: only Allah knows.
>
> —Sufi saying

4. When you feel like you've gone as far as you can, take a deep breath, read the sentence again, and begin writing once more. Do this for about 15 minutes.

5. Reflect on what you wrote as well as how you feel. How does feeling lucky change your outlook? Your view of current problems and decisions?

6. Look at what you wrote about what would happen in your life with more luck. Can you allow that to happen now?

Let's Dance

This book is a treasure chest of tools. None of them requires more than 30 minutes and most can be done much more quickly. No fancy tools or equipment are necessary. You can do them just about anywhere and many are designed to be done while commuting.

Practical Wisdom

Imagine what the world might be if more people used their intuition. Just think: you could help create a world that makes it safe to trust and use intuitive wisdom.

Statistics tell us that many of you will pick up this book, but most of you won't follow through with the material. Intuition does not rely on statistics. Intuition relies on imagination. Imagine for a moment that just a few more people in your life began to live more personally fulfilled and abundant lives. How would that influence you? How would it influence them if you lived a more fulfilled and abundant life? It reminds me of a junior high school dance where most of us wanted to dance desperately, but no one wanted to be the first out on the dance floor. Most of the time we stood around staring at each other. Every once in a while someone had the courage to ask someone to dance and the place started rocking. Those were the best dances. All it took was one person to start it off.

Get the Group Intuit

You learned earlier in this chapter that you can step into the unknown with just an intuition in your heart, and the Universe will reach up to meet you with opportunities and direction. You learned in Chapter 8 how to harness the intuition of your business team to move collectively toward new solutions?

The image I hold is one where groups of people come together to discuss important issues—whether in corporate, political, community, or family settings—and access their intuitive wisdom together, blending their insights with analytic skills, to create new solutions, innovations, and renewed visions.

Practical Wisdom

The really valuable thing *is* intuition.

—Albert Einstein

My husband and I make joint decisions regularly using intuitive skill, and the few times we've been able to get our children to sit with us to decide on issues important to the whole family, the results have been quite successful. Issues that began with lots of disagreement and different points of view were resolved with relative ease. From the intuitive level, we all could see and accept the appropriate way to go, without the ego conflicts.

If you're involved with a team or group that you think would like to try this, here are some steps to get it going:

1. Share one or two of the workouts in this book with your group to use individually.

2. Discuss your results. Once the group is comfortable sharing their own intuitive insights, they are ready to work as a group.

3. Articulate the group question or intention.

4. Choose one intuition workout from this book. Guide the group through the workout.

5. Share your results.

Use each workout as a platform for a new discussion on the question at hand. Don't expect everyone to immediately agree, let each insight help build a new picture, new solutions, and new perspectives.

May the Road Rise To Greet You

Okay, enough lecturing. I'll leave you not with a final nugget of wisdom, nor with shouts of encouragement, but with an intuitive blessing:

> "May we meet on the road to prosperity and have an opportunity to share stories and challenges. May your path be filled with opportunities, and your vision clear enough to choose wisely among them. And may your intuition be your constant companion, guiding you every step of the way."

The Least You Need to Know

➤ Wealth and intuitive awareness go together.

➤ Doing less will bring you more; doing more will bring you less.

➤ If you take the first step, your intuition will support you.

➤ Gratitude should be a regular part of your wealth-building routine.

➤ Try using intuitive tools with a group of people focused on solving the same problem.

Further Reading

Blakeslee, S. *Complex and Hidden Brain in the Gut Makes Stomaches and Butterflies.* The New York Times, January 23, 1996.

Blakeslee, S. *In Work On Intuition, Gut Feelings Are Tracked to Source: The Brain.* The New York Times, March 4, 1997.

Dean, D. and J. Mihalasky. *Executive ESP.* Prentice-Hall, 1974.

Hotz, L. R. *Scientists Try To Pinpoint the Biochemistry of Faith.* Books section 1C–3C, p. 1, July 5, 1998.

Pert, Candice B. *Molecules of Motion.* New York: Scribner, 1997.

Radin, Dean. *The Conscious Universe: The Scientific Truth of Psychic Phenomena.* San Francisco: Harper, 1997.

Weston, Agor. *Intuitive Management: Integrating Left and Right Brain Management Skills.* Prentice-Hall, 1984.

Internet Resources

Intuition Network: www.intuition.org

Intuition Support Groups: Inreaching@aol.com

Intuition Magazine
PO Box 460773
San Francisco, CA 94146
(415) 538-8171 (phone)
(415) 538-8175 (fax)
E-mail: intuitmage@aol.com

Nancy Rosanoff: intuitionatwork.com

Bibliography

Adrienne, Carol. (1998). *The Purpose of Your Life.* New York: Eagle Brooks.

Agor, H. Weston. (1989). *Intuition in Organization.* California: Sage.

Arrien, Angeles. (1993). *The Four Fold Way.* California: Harper.

Aubrey, R. and Cohen, M. P. (1995). *Working Wisdom.* California: Jossey-Bass.

Autry A. James. (1991). *Love and Profit.* New York: Avon Books.

Barks, Coleman. (1995). *The Essential Rumi.* California: Harper.

Barrett, Richard. (1995). *Spiritual Unfoldment.* Virginia: Unfoldment.

Brandenburger, A. and Nalebuff, J. B. (1996). *Co-opetition.* New York: Doubleday.

Bundles, P. A'Lelia. (1991). *Madam C. J. Walker.* New York: Chelsea House Publishers.

Buzan, T. and Israel, R. (1997). *Brain Sell.* New York: McGraw-Hill.

Cameron, Julia. (1992). *The Artist's Way.* New York: Putnam Books.

Campbell, M. Susan. (1995). *From Chaos to Confidence.* New York: Simon & Schuster.

Chopra, Deepak. (1993). *Creating Affluence.* California: New World Library.

_____. (1994). *The Seven Spiritual Laws of Success.* California: Amber-Allen Publishing.

Chuckrow, Robert. (1998). *The Tai Chi Book.* YMAA Publishing Center; 4354 West Street; Boston, MA 02131.

Coelho, Paulo. (1993). *The Alchemist.* New York: Harper.

Contino, M. Richard. (1996). *Trust Your Gut.* New York: American Management Association.

De Becker, Gavin. (1997). *The Gift of Fear.* New York: Dell.

Emery, Marcia. (1994). *Intuition Workbook.* New Jersey: Prentice Hall.

Enkelis, L. and Olsen, K. (1995). *On Our Own Terms.* California.

Fahden, Allen. (1993). *Innovation on Demand.* Minnesota: The Illiterati.

Fisher, Mark. (1993). *The Instant Millionaire.* Great Britain: Hammond.

Fox, Matthew. (1994). *The Reinvention of Work.* New York: Harper Collins.

Franquemont, Sharon. (1997). *Do It Yourself Intuition.* California: Intuition Enterprises.

_____. (1999). *You Already Know What To Do.* Los Angeles: Tarcher Press.

Goleman, Daniel. (1995). *Emotional Intelligence.* New York: Bantam Books.

Greenleaf, K. Robert. (1977). *Servant Leadership.* New Jersey: Paulist Press.

Gresser, Julian. (1995). *Piloting Through Chaos.* California: Five Rings Press.

Heider, John. (1985). *The Tao of Leadership.* Georgia: Humanics New Age.

James, Cheewa. (1993). *Catch The Whisper of the Wind.* California: Horizon 2000.

Jampolsky, G. Gerald. (1979). *Love Is Letting Go of Fear.* California: Celestial Arts.

Jaworski, Joseph. (1996). *Synchronicity.* California: Berrett-Koehler.

Johnson, Spencer. (1992). *Yes or No.* New York: Harper Collins.

Katz, L. William. (1995). *Black Women of the Old West.* New York: Atheneum.

Kaye, Les. (1996). *Zen at Work.* New York: Crown Trade Paperbacks.

Kroeber, Theodora. (1964). *Ishi Last of His Tribe.* New York: Bantam Books.

Land. G, Jarman B. (1992). *Break Point and Beyond.* New York: Bantam Books.

Levy, Joel and Michelle. (1998). *Living in Balance.* Berkeley, CA: Conari Press.

Lieber, Ron. (1998). *Upstart Start-Ups.* New York: Broadway Books.

McGee-Cooper, Ann. (1992). *You Don't Have To Go Home from Work Exhausted.* New York: Bantam Books.

_____. (1994). *Time Management for Unmanageable People.* New York: Bantam Books.

Munn, W. Michael. (1998). *Beyond Business As Usual.* Massachusetts: Butterworth-Heinemann.

Myss, Carolyn. (1998). *Why People Don't Heal.* New York: Harmony Books.

Norris, Chuck. (1996). *The Secret Power Within.* Little, Brown & Company.

O'Neil, J. William. (1995). *How To Make Money in Stocks*. New York: McGraw-Hill, Inc.

Owen, Harrison. (1997). *Expanding Our Now*. California: Berrett-Koehler Publishers, Inc.

Popcorn, F. and Marigold, L. (1997). *Clicking*. New York: Harper Business.

Quinley, Cariel. (1993). *Crop Circle Cards*. California: Cosmic Connections Center.

Rax, M. and Myers, R. (1986). *Creativity in Business*. New York: Bantam Doubleday Dell.

Ray, Michael and Rochelle Myers. (1989). *Creativity in Business*. New York: Doubleday Books.

Redfield, James. (1993). *The Celestine Prophecy*. New York: Warner Books.

Roman, Sanaya. (1986). *Living With Joy*. California: HJ Kramer.

Rowan, Roy. (1986). *The Intuitive Manager*. Little, Brown and Company.

Schneider, David. (1993). *Street Zen*. Massachusetts: Shambhalla.

Schultz, Ron. (1994). *Unconventional Wisdom*. New York Harper Business.

Schwager, D. Jack. (1992). *The New Market Wizards*. New York: Harper Business.

Senge, M. Peter. (1990). *The Fifth Discipline*. New York: Currency Doubleday.

Sher, Barbara. (1979). *How To Get What You Really Want*. Ballantine Books.

Stacey, D. Ralph. (1992). *Managing The Unknowable*. California: Jossey-Bass Publications.

Stanley, J. T. and Danko, D. W. (1996). *The Millionaire Next Door*. Georgia: Longstreet Press.

Van Oech, Roger. (1983). *A Whack on the Side of the Head*, Menlo Park, Calif: Creative Think.

Vaughan, Alan. (1998). *Doorways to Higher Consciousness*. Virginia: Celest Press.

Wakefield, Dan. (1998). *Returning a Spiritual Journey*. New York: Penguin Books.

_____. (1995). *Expect a Miracle*. New York: Harper Collins.

Weintraub, Sandra. (1998). *The Hidden Intelligence*. Butterworth Heineman.

Wheatley, J. M. and Rogers-Kellner, M. (1996). *A Simpler Way*. California: Berrett-Koehler Publishers, Inc.

Whyte, David. (1994). *The Heart Aroused*. New York: Doubleday.

Winokur, Jon. (1996). *The Rich Are Different*. New York: Pantheon Books.

Zohar, Danah. (1997). *Rewiring the Corporate Brain*. California: Berrett-Koehler Publishers, Inc.

Extra Credit

Surely your intuition told you there were a few things left to cover in the book! Here are some exercises and some ideas to ponder as you proceed intuitively through life.

Personal Intuition Development Plan

Continue to build your intuitive skill and apply the intuition exercises in the book effectively by using this handy chart. Here is how you do it.

Skill	Questions to Ask	Practice	Exercise
Awareness	Am I awake?	Being present	Object
	What's going on?	Noticing	Yes or No
	Is there another way?	Journal writing	Note cards
Clarity	What do I want?	Non-judgment	Try it on
	What do I fear?	Integrity—especially during challenging times	What I'd never do Set goals—reality check
Intention	Where am I going?	Non-attachment	Look for open door
	What are my goals?	Establish clear intentions	Applause meter Flow check
Attunement	Am I present to this moment?	Be present	Timing tree
	What is needed right now?	Be patient	Power moments
	Where is the opportunity?	Use the power of not knowing	Sphericle or other oracle

The Skill column lists four major intuitive skills that can be developed and improved over time. They are skills that can never be completely mastered, we all just continue to get better at them.

Ask yourself the questions in the second column to stimulate that particular skill.

The Practice column provides suggestions for daily practices that will enhance the skill, and the Exercise column lists three intuition workouts learned in the book which will improve each skill.

Here is more information on each of the intuitive skills:

➤ *Awareness* is the skill of noticing a broad spectrum of information, non-analytic data, inconsistencies, anomalies and other details. The more you notice, the more you know.

➤ *Clarity* is the ability to see through the "hidden-agendas" of yourself and others. There is often emotional baggage, past history and hidden desires which fog and distort the situation and how it is being handled. The clearer you are about your own hidden-agendas, the clearer you can be about others.

➤ *Intention* is the ability to put your whole self behind what you want. A strong intention helps create the possibilities for it to happen.

➤ *Attunement* is the skill of connecting to the larger whole—the "web" which connects all life. When attuned, necessary information and events flow, timing is perfect, moments are powerful.

Eight Biggest Mistakes in Decision-Making

1. Over-analyzing.
2. Talking to the wrong people.
3. Hesitating.
4. Jumping the gun.
5. Not looking beyond the obvious.
6. Talking yourself out of what you feel.
7. Going with experts rather than gut.
8. Not having a goal—not relating a decision to the larger vision.

Nine Secrets to Fulfilling Your Heart's Desire Through Tapping Your Intuitive Power

1. You know more than you think you know.
2. Intuitive information is all around you.
3. You have all the answers you need—when you need them.

4. It's scary to know as much as we know—and this fear can block our ability to know.

5. You can get better at hearing and trusting your intuitions.

6. If it is intuitively right for you, it is right for everyone involved.

7. Great ideas come from nothing.

8. Successful people can see what is not there, yet.

9. When you take a step toward following your intuition, unexpected support and guidance will appear.

Index

J

K

X-Y-Z

When You're Smart Enough to Know That You Don't Know It All!

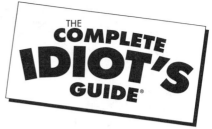

THE COMPLETE IDIOT'S GUIDE®

For all the ups and downs you're sure to encounter in life,
The Complete Idiot's Guides give you
down-to-earth answers and practical solutions.

Personal Business

The Complete Idiot's Guide to Assertiveness
ISBN: 0-02-861964-1
$16.95

The Complete Idiot's Guide to Business Management
ISBN: 0-02-861744-4
$16.95

The Complete Idiot's Guide to New Product Development
ISBN: 0-02-861952-8
$16.95

The Complete Idiot's Guide to Dynamic Selling
ISBN: 0-02-861952-8
$16.95

The Complete Idiot's Guide to Getting Along with Difficult People
ISBN: 0-02-861597-2
$16.95

The Complete Idiot's Guide to Great Customer Service
ISBN: 0-02-861953-6
$16.95

The Complete Idiot's Guide to Leadership
ISBN: 0-02-861946-3
$16.95

The Complete Idiot's Guide to Marketing Basics
ISBN: 0-02-861490-9
$16.95

The Complete Idiot's Guide to Office Politics
ISBN: 0-02-862397-5
$16.95

The Complete Idiot's Guide to Project Management
ISBN: 0-02-861745-2
$16.95

The Complete Idiot's Guide to Starting a Home Based Business
ISBN: 0-02-861539-5
$16.95

The Complete Idiot's Guide to Successful Business Presentations
ISBN: 0-02-861748-7
$16.95

The Complete Idiot's Guide to Freelancing
ISBN: 0-02-862119-0
$16.95

The Complete Idiot's Guide to Changing Careers
ISBN: 0-02-861977-3
$17.95

The Complete Idiot's Guide to Terrific Business Writing
ISBN: 0-02-861097-0
$16.95

The Complete Idiot's Guide to Getting the Job You Want
ISBN: 1-56761-608-9
$24.95

The Complete Idiot's Guide to Managing Your Time
ISBN: 0-02-862943-4
$18.95

The Complete Idiot's Guide to Speaking in Public With Confidence
ISBN: 0-02-861038-5
$16.95

The Complete Idiot's Guide to Winning Through Negotiation
ISBN: 0-02-861037-7
$16.95

The Complete Idiot's Guide to Managing People
ISBN: 0-02-861036-9
$18.95

The Complete Idiot's Guide to a Great Retirement
ISBN: 0-02-861036-9
$16.95

The Complete Idiot's Guide to Starting Your Own Business
ISBN: 0-02-861979-X
$18.95

The Complete Idiot's Guide to Protecting Yourself from Everyday Legal Hassles
ISBN: 1-56761-602-X
$16.99

The Complete Idiot's Guide to Surviving Divorce
ISBN: 0-02-861101-3
$16.95

The Complete Idiot's Guide to
Organizing Your Life
ISBN: 0-02-861090-3
$16.95

The Complete Idiot's Guide to
Reaching Your Goals
ISBN: 0-02-862114-X
$16.95

The Complete Idiot's Guide to
the Perfect Cover Letter
ISBN: 0-02-861960-9
$14.95

The Complete Idiot's Guide to
the Perfect Interview
ISBN: 0-02-861945-5
$14.95

The Complete Idiot's Guide to
the Perfect Resume
ISBN: 0-02-861093-8
$16.95

Personal Finance

The Complete Idiot's Guide to
Buying Insurance and Annu-
ities
ISBN: 0-02-861113-6
$16.95

The Complete Idiot's Guide to
Managing Your Money
ISBN: 1-56761-530-9
$16.95

The Complete Idiot's Guide to
Making Money with Mutual
Funds
ISBN: 1-56761-637-2
$16.95

The Complete Idiot's Guide to
Buying and Selling a Home
ISBN: 0-02-861959-5
$16.95

The Complete Idiot's Guide to
Getting Rich
ISBN: 0-02-862952-3
$18.95

The Complete Idiot's Guide to
Finance and Accounting
ISBN: 0-02-861752-5
$16.95

The Complete Idiot's Guide to
Investing Like a Pro
ISBN:0-02-862044-5
$16.95

The Complete Idiot's Guide to
Making Money After You
Retire
ISBN:0-02-862410-6
$16.95

The Complete Idiot's Guide to
Making Money on Wall Street
ISBN:0-02-861958-7
$16.95

The Complete Idiot's Guide to
Personal Finance in Your 20s
and 30s
ISBN:0-02-862415-7
$16.95

The Complete Idiot's Guide to
Wills and Estates
ISBN: 0-02-861747-9
$16.95

The Complete Idiot's Guide to
401(k) Plans
ISBN: 0-02-861948-X
$16.95

Lifestyle

The Complete Idiot's Guide to
Etiquette
ISBN0-02-861094-6
$16.95

The Complete Idiot's Guide to
Dating
ISBN: 0-02-861052-0
$14.95

The Complete Idiot's Guide to
Trouble-Free Car Care
ISBN: 0-02-861041-5
$16.95

The Complete Idiot's Guide to
the Perfect Wedding
ISBN: 0-02-861963-3
$16.95

The Complete Idiot's Guide to
the Perfect Vacation
ISBN: 1-56761-531-7
$14.99

The Complete Idiot's Guide to
Trouble-Free Home Repair
ISBN: 0-02-861042-3
$16.95

The Complete Idiot's Guide to
Getting Into College
ISBN: 1-56761-508-2
$14.95

The Complete Idiot's Guide to
a Healthy Relationship
ISBN: 0-02-861087-3
$17.95

The Complete Idiot's Guide to
Dealing with In-Laws
ISBN: 0-02-862107-7
$16.95

The Complete Idiot's Guide to
Choosing, Training, and
Raising a Dog
ISBN: 0-02-861098-9
$16.95

The Complete Idiot's Guide to
Fun and Tricks with Your Dog
ISBN: 0-87605-083-6
$14.95

The Complete Idiot's Guide to
Living with a Cat
ISBN: 0-02-861278-7
$16.95

The Complete Idiot's Guide to
Turtles and Tortoises
ISBN: 0-87605-143-3
$16.95

Leisure/Hobbies

The Complete Idiot's Guide to
Baking
ISBN: 0-02-861954-4
$16.95

The Complete Idiot's Guide to
Beer
ISBN: 0-02-861717-7
$16.95

The Complete Idiot's Guide to
Cooking Basics
ISBN: 0-02-861974-9
$18.95

The Complete Idiot's Guide to
Entertaining
ISBN: 0-02-861095-4
$16.95

The Complete Idiot's Guide to Mixing Drinks
ISBN: 0-02-861941-2
$16.95

The Complete Idiot's Guide to Wine
ISBN: 0-02-861273-6
$16.95

The Complete Idiot's Guide to Antiques and Collectibles
ISBN: 0-02-861595-6
$16.95

The Complete Idiot's Guide to Boating and Sailing
ISBN: 0-02-862124-7
$18.95

The Complete Idiot's Guide to Bridge
ISBN: 0-02-861735-5
$16.95

The Complete Idiot's Guide to Chess
ISBN: 0-02-861736-3
$16.95

The Complete Idiot's Guide to Cigars
ISBN: 0-02-861975-7
$17.95

The Complete Idiot's Guide to Crafts with Kids
ISBN: 0-02-862406-8
$16.95

The Complete Idiot's Guide to Fishing Basics
ISBN: 0-02-861598-0
$16.95

The Complete Idiot's Guide to Gambling Like a Pro
ISBN: 0-02-861102-0
$16.95

The Complete Idiot's Guide to Hiking and Camping
ISBN: 0-02-861100-4
$16.95

The Complete Idiot's Guide to Knitting and Crocheting
ISBN: 0-02-862123-9
$16.95

The Complete Idiot's Guide to Photography
ISBN: 0-02-861092-X
$16.95

The Complete Idiot's Guide to Quilting
ISBN: 0-02-862411-4
$16.95

The Complete Idiot's Guide to Yoga
ISBN: 0-02-861949-8
$16.95

The Complete Idiot's Guide to the Beatles
ISBN: 0-02-862130-1
$18.95

The Complete Idiot's Guide to Elvis
ISBN: 0-02-861873-4
$18.95

The Complete Idiot's Guide to Understanding Football Like a Pro
ISBN:0-02-861743-6
$16.95

The Complete Idiot's Guide to Golf
ISBN: 0-02-861760-6
$16.95

The Complete Idiot's Guide to Motorcycles
ISBN: 0-02-862416-5
$17.95

The Complete Idiot's Guide to Pro Wrestling
ISBN: 0-02-862395-9
$17.95

The Complete Idiot's Guide to Extra-Terrestrial Intelligence
ISBN: 0-02-862387-8
$16.95

Health and Fitness

The Complete Idiot's Guide to Managed Health Care
ISBN: 0-02-862165-4
$17.95

The Complete Idiot's Guide to Getting and Keeping Your Perfect Body
ISBN: 0-02-861276-0
$16.95

The Complete Idiot's Guide to First Aid Basics
ISBN: 0-02-861099-7
$16.95

The Complete Idiot's Guide to Vitamins
ISBN: 0-02-862116-6
$16.95

The Complete Idiot's Guide to Losing Weight
ISBN: 0-02-862113-1
$17.95

The Complete Idiot's Guide to Tennis
ISBN: 0-02-861746-0
$18.95

The Complete Idiot's Guide to Tae Kwon Do
ISBN: 0-02-862389-4
$17.95

The Complete Idiot's Guide to Breaking Bad Habits
ISBN: 0-02-862110-7
$16.95

The Complete Idiot's Guide to Healthy Stretching
ISBN: 0-02-862127-1
$16.95

The Complete Idiot's Guide to Beautiful Skin
ISBN: 0-02-862408-4
$16.95

The Complete Idiot's Guide to Eating Smart
ISBN: 0-02-861276-0
$16.95

The Complete Idiot's Guide to First Aid
ISBN: 0-02-861099-7
$16.95

The Complete Idiot's Guide to Getting a Good Night's Sleep
ISBN: 0-02-862394-0
$16.95

The Complete Idiot's Guide to
a Happy, Healthy Heart
ISBN: 0-02-862393-2
$16.95

The Complete Idiot's Guide to
Stress
ISBN: 0-02-861086-5
$16.95

The Complete Idiot's Guide to
Jogging and Running
ISBN: 0-02-862386-X
$17.95

The Complete Idiot's Guide to
Adoption
ISBN: 0-02-862108-5
$18.95

The Complete Idiot's Guide to
Bringing Up Baby
ISBN: 0-02-861957-9
$16.95

The Complete Idiot's Guide to
Grandparenting
ISBN: 0-02-861976-5
$16.95

The Complete Idiot's Guide to
Parenting a Preschooler and
Toddler
ISBN: 0-02-861733-9
$16.95

The Complete Idiot's Guide to
Raising a Teenager
ISBN: 0-02-861277-9
$16.95

The Complete Idiot's Guide to
Single Parenting
ISBN: 0-02-862409-2
$16.95

The Complete Idiot's Guide to
Stepparenting
ISBN: 0-02-862407-6
$16.95

Education

The Complete Idiot's Guide to
American History
ISBN: 0-02-861275-2
$16.95

The Complete Idiot's Guide to
British Royalty
ISBN: 0-02-862346-0
$18.95

The Complete Idiot's Guide to
Civil War
ISBN: 0-02-862122-0
$16.95

The Complete Idiot's Guide to
Classical Mythology
ISBN: 0-02-862385-1
$16.95

The Complete Idiot's Guide to
Creative Writing
ISBN: 0-02-861734-7
$16.95

The Complete Idiot's Guide to
Dinosaurs
ISBN: 0-02-862390-8
$17.95

The Complete Idiot's Guide to
Genealogy
ISBN: 0-02-861947-1
$16.95

The Complete Idiot's Guide to
Geography
ISBN: 0-02-861955-2
$16.95

The Complete Idiot's Guide to
Getting Published
ISBN: 0-02-862392-4
$16.95

The Complete Idiot's Guide to
Grammar & Style
ISBN: 0-02-861956-0
$16.95

The Complete Idiot's Guide to
an MBA
ISBN: 0-02-862164-4
$17.95

The Complete Idiot's Guide to
Philosophy
ISBN:0-02-861981-1
$16.95

The Complete Idiot's Guide to
Classical Music
ISBN: 0-02-8611634-0
$16.95

The Complete Idiot's Guide to
Learning Spanish On Your
Own
ISBN: 0-02-861040-7
$16.95

The Complete Idiot's Guide to
Learning French on Your Own
ISBN: 0-02-861043-1
$16.95

The Complete Idiot's Guide to
Learning German on Your
Own
ISBN: 0-02-861962-5
$16.95

The Complete Idiot's Guide to
Learning Italian on Your Own
ISBN: 0-02-862125-5
$16.95

The Complete Idiot's Guide to
Learning Sign Language
ISBN: 0-02-862388-6
$16.95

The Complete Idiot's Guide to
Astrology
ISBN: 0-02-861951-X
$16.95

The Complete Idiot's Guide to
the World's Religions
ISBN: 0-02-861730-4
$16.95

**Look for the Complete Idiot's Guides at your local bookseller,
or call 1-800-428-5331 for more information.**

You can also check us out on the Web at
http://www.mgr.com

alpha
books